CONTENTS

PROTECTING CONSUMERS AGAINST SLAMMING

HEARING

BEFORE THE

SUBCOMMITTEE ON TELECOMMUNICATIONS, TRADE, AND CONSUMER PROTECTION

OF THE

COMMITTEE ON COMMERCE
HOUSE OF REPRESENTATIVES

ONE HUNDRED FIFTH CONGRESS

SECOND SESSION

ON

H.R. 3050 and H.R. 3888

JUNE 23, 1998

Serial No. 105–101

Printed for the use of the Committee on Commerce

U.S. GOVERNMENT PRINTING OFFICE

49–326CC WASHINGTON : 1998

For sale by the U.S. Government Printing Office
Superintendent of Documents, Congressional Sales Office, Washington, DC 20402
ISBN 0-16-057444-7

COMMITTEE ON COMMERCE

TOM BLILEY, Virginia, *Chairman*

W.J. "BILLY" TAUZIN, Louisiana
MICHAEL G. OXLEY, Ohio
MICHAEL BILIRAKIS, Florida
DAN SCHAEFER, Colorado
JOE BARTON, Texas
J. DENNIS HASTERT, Illinois
FRED UPTON, Michigan
CLIFF STEARNS, Florida
BILL PAXON, New York
PAUL E. GILLMOR, Ohio
Vice Chairman
SCOTT L. KLUG, Wisconsin
JAMES C. GREENWOOD, Pennsylvania
MICHAEL D. CRAPO, Idaho
CHRISTOPHER COX, California
NATHAN DEAL, Georgia
STEVE LARGENT, Oklahoma
RICHARD BURR, North Carolina
BRIAN P. BILBRAY, California
ED WHITFIELD, Kentucky
GREG GANSKE, Iowa
CHARLIE NORWOOD, Georgia
RICK WHITE, Washington
TOM COBURN, Oklahoma
RICK LAZIO, New York
BARBARA CUBIN, Wyoming
JAMES E. ROGAN, California
JOHN SHIMKUS, Illinois

JOHN D. DINGELL, Michigan
HENRY A. WAXMAN, California
EDWARD J. MARKEY, Massachusetts
RALPH M. HALL, Texas
RICK BOUCHER, Virginia
THOMAS J. MANTON, New York
EDOLPHUS TOWNS, New York
FRANK PALLONE, Jr., New Jersey
SHERROD BROWN, Ohio
BART GORDON, Tennessee
ELIZABETH FURSE, Oregon
PETER DEUTSCH, Florida
BOBBY L. RUSH, Illinois
ANNA G. ESHOO, California
RON KLINK, Pennsylvania
BART STUPAK, Michigan
ELIOT L. ENGEL, New York
THOMAS C. SAWYER, Ohio
ALBERT R. WYNN, Maryland
GENE GREEN, Texas
KAREN McCARTHY, Missouri
TED STRICKLAND, Ohio
DIANA DeGETTE, Colorado

JAMES E. DERDERIAN, *Chief of Staff*
CHARLES L. INGEBRETSON, *General Counsel*
REID P.F. STUNTZ, *Minority Staff Director and Chief Counsel*

SUBCOMMITTEE ON TELECOMMUNICATIONS, TRADE, AND CONSUMER PROTECTION

W.J. "BILLY" TAUZIN, Louisiana, *Chairman*

MICHAEL G. OXLEY, Ohio,
Vice Chairman
DAN SCHAEFER, Colorado
JOE BARTON, Texas
J. DENNIS HASTERT, Illinois
FRED UPTON, Michigan
CLIFF STEARNS, Florida
PAUL E. GILLMOR, Ohio
SCOTT L. KLUG, Wisconsin
CHRISTOPHER COX, California
NATHAN DEAL, Georgia
STEVE LARGENT, Oklahoma
RICK WHITE, Washington
JAMES E. ROGAN, California
JOHN SHIMKUS, Illinois
TOM BLILEY, Virginia,
(Ex Officio)

EDWARD J. MARKEY, Massachusetts
RICK BOUCHER, Virginia
BART GORDON, Tennessee
ELIOT L. ENGEL, New York
THOMAS C. SAWYER, Ohio
THOMAS J. MANTON, New York
BOBBY L. RUSH, Illinois
ANNA G. ESHOO, California
RON KLINK, Pennsylvania
ALBERT R. WYNN, Maryland
GENE GREEN, Texas
KAREN McCARTHY, Missouri
JOHN D. DINGELL, Michigan,
(Ex Officio)

PROTECTING CONSUMERS AGAINST SLAMMING

TUESDAY, JUNE 23, 1998

HOUSE OF REPRESENTATIVES,
COMMITTEE ON COMMERCE,
SUBCOMMITTEE ON TELECOMMUNICATIONS,
TRADE, AND CONSUMER PROTECTION,
Washington, DC.

The subcommittee met, pursuant to notice, at 10:15 a.m., in room 2123, Rayburn House Office Building, Hon. W.J. "Billy" Tauzin (chairman) presiding.

Members present: Representatives Tauzin, Upton, Gillmor, Deal, Largent, White, Rogan, Shimkus, Markey, Gordon, Engel, Sawyer, Eshoo, Wynn, Green, McCarthy, and Dingell (ex Officio).

Staff present: Justin Lilley, majority counsel; Mike O'Rielly, legislative analyst; Cliff Riccio, clerk; and Andy Levin, minority counsel.

Mr. TAUZIN. The committee will please come to order. Today the subcommittee meets to take testimony on two related bills introduced to prevent the common practice of slamming, H.R. 3888, a bill I introduced, and H.R. 3050, a bill by my distinguished friend, the ranking member of the full committee, Mr. Dingell.

These two bills are legislative attempts to help consumers and help promote fair competition in the telecommunications marketplace.

H.R. 3888 represents a slimmed-down version of legislation introduced and already passed overwhelmingly in the Senate. It represents a commitment to reduce or eliminate the practice of slamming, the illegal changing of a customer's telecommunications carrier of choice. H.R. 3050 represents the hard work of Mr. Dingell to address in similar fashion this harmful practice.

Let me put this practice in perspective. You have a contractual agreement with the telecommunications carrier to provide certain services, such as long distance or local telephone service. Then, unbeknownst to you or your carrier of choice, for that matter, another carrier steals you away. Even more unforgiving in this practice is the fact that most people don't carefully examine their phone bills. You probably should, but many don't. Accordingly, many times consumers don't realize they have been slammed until 3 or 4 months have passed. During this time, they have been paying higher phone rates without their knowledge.

On top of this, oftentimes their previous carrier, the one that they wanted to stay with and maintain, drops them from all benefits or incentive packages that they had offered. Thus, consumers that have been slammed often lose promotional ties such as free air miles, discounted rates or discounted purchases that were tied to the contract with their former carrier. This is a double whammy, all done without their knowledge or approval.

When a company steals another carrier's customer because they want to take advantage of the competitive marketplace, but they don't want to compete to win that consumer, that is fraud, pure and simple. In 1997, the FCC received 20,000 complaints about slamming.

Sometimes slamming occurs by accident without any harmful intent by the infringing company. I suggest to not know what is occurring within your company is at least severe, perhaps even gross negligence.

Carriers have an obligation to maintain high standards of selling practices. We intend to fix this problem in Congress, whether by passing legislation or pushing the FCC to prevent slamming from occurring. H.R. 3888 and H.R. 3050 would provide a remedy to this consumer tragedy.

And I might point out that my own mother was slammed, and when I mentioned to Chairman Bliley that we were going to move a bill like this, I found out that the chairman of our full committee had been slammed about a week after he had been named as chairman of the full committee. In both cases, the problem was fixed by a call to the offending company, and in neither case, I suspect, was a report made to the FCC, so the 20,000 reports that we have came from some other poor souls who were slammed and whose complaints eventually reached the FCC. One wonders how many like the chairman and my mother were slammed and had no evidence of that practice reported to the FCC.

Spamming—I should point out that the spamming policy contained in H.R. 3888 is somewhat different from the one contained in H.R. 2368, the Data Privacy Act, a bill which we introduced earlier in Congress. These policies don't necessarily contradict each other, but they do reflect different perspectives on the same topic.

We are not giving up on the free market voluntary guidelines approach in the earlier bill. We are moving, however, these provisions advanced by the Senate and hope literally to shed some light on the whole issue of spamming while we take up that bill in July. Without a doubt, this is a positive first step to a much larger debate, and I look forward to that debate.

I want to mention that we have done research at a member level on the issue of cramming, which is another practice that is troublesome, meddlesome and requires a great deal of attention by this committee. We will give it the attention that it requires, as well, sometime during the remaining days of this Congress.

The chairman now yields to my good friend from Massachusetts, Mr. Markey, for an opening statement.

Mr. MARKEY. Thank you, Mr. Chairman.

Do you know what would be a good thing to do would be to create a multi-industry policy, self-regulatory of course, consistent with the mood of the times, but one in which they understand that they should never spam or cram or jam or anything like that to anybody's mother on this committee. That is like terrible policy for any industry at any time to do anything to any of our mothers.

And at the same time never ever quadruple the cable rates of anybody's father on our committee. That is a terrible thing to do. It brings to the attention of members of the committee in a vivid way issues that might otherwise be outside of the general attention of the members of the committee. That is a general, helpful rule of thumb for all industry representatives out there.

I know that many of you have more than one client. Just a general—you should send out memos to people. Who are the members of this committee, and where do their mothers and fathers live because we will be hearing about it real soon.

Mr. TAUZIN. Would the gentleman yield?

Mr. MARKEY. Yes.

Mr. TAUZIN. I suggest that he come up with some word that rhymes with "slam" and "jam" and "cram" to cover this business of raising cable rates 4 or 5 times on somebody's poor father.

Mr. MARKEY. My father has a word for it, and it starts with "D." So it is not just good policy. I am trying to help you out, although many of you want your clients to get in trouble and then they will need you to come before us. I understand your conflict.

These are particularly thorny issues to address because there are multiple players involved in resolving these problems in the telecommunications industry and in the Federal Government, and at the State level as well. It is hard to find someone these days who has not had firsthand experience with one or all of these issues.

When someone is slammed, their telephone carrier is changed without proper authorization, and it usually leads to higher bills for slammed customers.

When someone is subject to cramming, their telephone bill gets filled up with all sorts of new and unauthorized charges.

And with the rise of the Internet and growth of unsolicited electronic messages, spamming is becoming the daily nuisance experience for countless people on-line and a burden on Internet service providers, who often have their systems swamped with spamming traffic.

Unfortunately, all three of these issues appear to be a growing problem. The issue of slamming was addressed in the Telecommunications Act of 1996 where unauthorized switches in carrier selection were prohibited and a liability provision for unauthorized charges included in section 258 of the Communications Act. The FCC is currently in the process of developing rules to implement that provision and protect the public. I want to encourage the commission's efforts to crack down on this problem and look forward to the commission completing any rule revisions in the near future.

Mr. Dingell has introduced slamming legislation of which I am a cosponsor, and Mr. Tauzin also has pending slamming legislation; and I believe both bills provide a number of excellent ideas to amplify the protections encompassed in section 258, as well as modify the conditions and procedures affecting carrier selection rules and consumer protection.

Moreover, cramming is increasing as a problem, and I believe that this issue also ought to be addressed in any comprehensive legislative solution that this subcommittee develops.

Mr. Gordon and Mr. Dingell have introduced legislation recently addressing the cramming issue, and I look forward to working with them as the process continues after this hearing.

And finally, the issue of spamming is quickly becoming the bane of many on-line surfers who log onto their computers only to find their mailbox stuffed with unsolicited electronic messages. Beyond the nuisance factor that massive spamming creates, it also engenders problems associated with the unsolicited sending of indecent material and on-line fraud perpetrated by a cadre of high-tech hucksters who attempt to dupe people on-line into parting with their money.

In addition, the millions of unsolicited e-mail messages clog up the networks of any on-line providers, and this does a terrible disservice to other subscribers to such service and to on-line commerce generally.

I have prepared draft legislation that I plan to introduce later this week to help address this spamming issue by building upon work that this subcommittee performed a few years ago in addressing unsolicited telephone marketing which is codified in section 227 of the Communications Act.

In that earlier legislation, we granted authority to the commission and authorized, at the commission's discretion, the creation of a "do not call" data base for people who no longer wanted to receive unsolicited telemarketing at home. The commission elected not to utilize this authority in its 1993 rulemaking.

I believe it may be worth exploring the creation of a "do not contact" data base for people who want to be put on a no-solicitation list in cyberspace and to stop the flood of junk e-mail. This could be done at the Federal or State levels, and technology has advanced to a point where this might be a cost-effective and efficient remedy.

The legislation I will introduce will also include provisions building upon section 258 of the Act to help address slamming and cramming issues.

Again, I want to thank you, Chairman Tauzin, for calling this hearing. These are very important consumer protection issues that must be thoroughly addressed by the subcommittee, and I want to work closely with my good friend the chairman, Mr. Tauzin, as well as Mr. Dingell and Mr. Gordon and Mr. Bliley, my other colleagues on the committee, and our very distinguished witnesses here this morning, who are giving us important testimony.

And with that, Mr. Chairman, I yield back the balance of my time.

Mr. TAUZIN. I thank my friend. Let me suggest something to the subcommittee and perhaps you want to agree with me on this. It is not often that we have three of our colleagues at one time to visit us and give testimony to us.

I would suggest, perhaps by unanimous consent, we agree to go back to opening statements after we have heard their testimony so that we might pay them the courtesy I know that they would give us if we were attending their own committee hearings.

The Chair will then suspend the opening statements by the committee, and the Chair will turn to our colleagues, all interested in the several issues that we began to discuss this morning.

First of all, Bob Goodlatte, the Representative of the Sixth Congressional District of the State of Virginia; Chris Smith of the Fourth Congressional District of New Jersey; and Charles Bass of the Second Congressional District of New Hampshire. We deeply appreciate your coming to shed light on this. Bob, we will start with you.

STATEMENT OF HON. BOB GOODLATTE, A REPRESENTATIVE IN CONGRESS FROM THE STATE OF VIRGINIA

Mr. GOODLATTE. Thank you. I have a statement that I will submit for the record.

Mr. TAUZIN. By unanimous consent, all written statements will be made a part of the record. We like to keep it conversational here.

Mr. GOODLATTE. I want to thank you for holding these hearings and for moving forward quickly to consider H.R. 3888, the Anti-slamming Amendments Act which you introduced, along with myself and our good friend Congressman Bass from New Hampshire.

Let me start by taking a little bit of exception with the observations of the gentleman from Massachusetts. One of the problems that we have in Congress, we have members who are not into all of this communications stuff and issues like encryption and slamming and spamming and a whole host of other things, but there is no more effective form of communications than to get a call from your mother about something that will raise the awareness of members about these issues.

So I want to encourage the industry to do the opposite, and if there is any interest in continuing these things—and I think for the vast majority of folks in the telecommunications industry, they want, like we want, to eliminate this stuff. But if there is anybody out there who thinks that we can defend these things, please call my mother and she will call me, and other Members of Congress getting the same thing will become increasingly aware of this in a way that sometimes they are not really paying attention until somebody focuses their attention on it.

Most Members of Congress are getting more and more communications from their constituents about being slammed and spammed, so I think the time is right to move legislation like this forward.

Mr. MARKEY. I have a name for it, too. When they go after grandmothers, we will call it gram-slamming. There should be an industry protection against that.

Mr. GOODLATTE. Well, I think that is perfect and when the chairman, Chairman Bliley was slammed, that was a grand slam, right?

Mr. Chairman, as you know, the Senate recently passed similar legislation with one addition that I want to call to your attention and I support. The Senate-passed bill would establish new criminal penalties for intentional slamming. Currently it is not a crime, yet some unscrupulous telephone companies use blatant, deceptive practices to steal consumers' telephone service. Some unscrupulous long distance resellers have stolen millions of dollars from consumers, billing companies and long distance carriers on slamming. Theft on this scale should be a criminal offense.

FCC Chairman William Kennard, GAO's Assistant Comptroller General for Special Investigations, L.J. Bowron, and FCC Commissioner Susan Ness agree that criminalization of intentional slamming would aid law enforcement efforts against this practice.

The addition of language to the Senate-passed bill would only criminalize intentional and deliberate slamming which must be proven beyond a reasonable doubt in Federal court. Slamming caused by mistake or negligence would not be a criminal offense, but instead considered under civil penalty provisions.

The bill also addresses the growing problem of spamming, which is the mass distribution of unsolicited e-mail messages to private computers. This annoying practice, which has become more widely used as the use of e-mail grows, is not only disruptive but highly intrusive. This bill will make it illegal to transmit an unsolicited commercial e-mail message to a person's computer.

The characters who commit the crimes of slamming and spamming are striking at one of our most basic human freedoms, communication. Our ability to communicate with others free from interruption and through our choice of services must be protected. This bill gives law enforcement the ammunition that they need to defend consumers against telephone slammers and e-mail spammers and will help bring an end to this pervasive practice.

I want to thank you for holding this hearing and inviting me to participate. Thank you, Mr. Chairman.

Mr. TAUZIN. Thank you, Bob.

Now we will hear from Chris Smith.

STATEMENT OF HON. CHRISTOPHER H. SMITH, A REPRESENTATIVE IN CONGRESS FROM THE STATE OF NEW JERSEY

Mr. SMITH. Thank you, Mr. Chairman. It is estimated that over 40 million people are now using the Internet, including my family. And in its short life span, the Internet and e-mail clearly have become an integral part of American life. I believe that, above all, consumers should not be forced to pay for unsolicited ads. Congress has an obligation to protect the Internet user from unwanted e-mail that often promotes illegitimate business practices, uninvited pornography or other unwelcome solicitation. The legislation that I have introduced, H.R. 1748, empowers the consumer. It lets the consumer take action against the spammer, and it allows consumers who choose to be reached by direct marketers via the e-mail, to say "yes" by "opting in."

This legislation, which I hope will be favorably considered by the committee, is patterned after the legislation we passed in the early 1990's dealing with the junk e-mail that was coming in from the fax machines.

Mr. Chairman, that legislation has been upheld by the courts. It has been challenged and upheld in one particular case, Destination Ventures v. FCC, and they found that there is "substantial government interest in protecting consumers from having to bear the cost of third-party advertising," and that is what this is all about.

If you or I turn on our e-mail and we have loads of junk e-mail that is unsolicited, we are paying for it. Whether we are—we pay a 1-cent fee or are paying by the hour to our Internet service provider, those costs are not free. And to say that you advertise and I pay for it—we need to reverse that.

If I choose to "opt in," which our legislation would allow, then I receive everything under the sun. But if I choose to "opt out," which our legislation would empower the consumer to do, then you are in a situation where nothing comes to my computer unless I want it; and I think this is basic fairness.

I have some examples in the written testimony, some horror stories, if you will, and I think we are going to hear more of those as time goes on, and the time has come. The legislation has been endorsed by the Coalition Against Unsolicited Commercial E-mail. They testified before the Subcommittee on Communications over in the Senate on June 17 and made a clear case that we comport with the first amendment. We have already been upheld in terms of a parallel with the fax machines, but this legislation, I think, should be passed, and the sooner the better.

The legislation that has been passed on the Senate side has it entirely the opposite. You have got to opt out so the burden is put on the consumer to contact these spammers and say, "I don't want any more of your junk." That has it reversed as to the way that it should be. I do hope that this legislation will be favorably considered.

[The prepared statement of Hon. Christopher H. Smith follows:]

PREPARED STATEMENT OF HON. CHRISTOPHER H. SMITH, A REPRESENTATIVE IN CONGRESS FROM THE STATE OF NEW JERSEY

It is estimated over 40 million people are now using the Internet and that number is growing every day. In its short life span, the Internet and e-mail have become an integral part of American life.

Now that the Internet and its many communication capabilities are here to stay, consumers should not have to relinquish their control over it. Consumers must be allowed to decide who they want to correspond with and what messages they want to receive.

Consumers should not have to pay for any and all messages someone wants to sell them nor should their Internet service provider. If an Internet user is not paying for additional time on-line to retrieve unwanted mail, then they are being charged a higher flat rate by the Internet Service Provider (ISP) for filter services or larger bandwidths to combat "junk e-mail." Unwanted e-mail, so called "spam," is costly to both the provider and consumer.

Congress has an obligation to protect the Internet user from unwanted e-mail that often promotes illegitimate business practices, uninvited pornography, and other unwelcome solicitations. My legislation H.R. 1748, the "Netizens Protection Act" empowers the consumer. It lets the consumer take action against the spammer. And, on the other hand, it allows consumers, who choose to be reached by direct marketers via e-mail, to say "yes" by "opting-in."

Unfortunately, the well-intentioned language on spam contained in H.R. 3888 and in S. 1618, the Anti-Slamming bill recently approved in the Senate, will not solve the spamming problem. Some netizens have even argued that it will actually encourage spammers to send out more junk e-mail because the spammer will now be able to claim that "all legal standards have been met." My bill protects consumers from spam by stopping it before it starts. H.R. 1748 prohibits the sending of junk e-mail, unless a business or personal relationship exists between the sender and e-mail recipient.

The Netizens Protection Act is really nothing new. It is based on the Telephone Consumer Protection Act of 1991 which banned junk faxes. This act rightly reasoned that the marketer or advertiser, as with direct mail and other marketing, should bear the cost of an advertisement or promotion, not the fax machine owner, not the owner of a computer.

The legislation banning junk e-mail is a natural extension of the existing law that has successfully banned junk faxes—a law that has been held up in court. The Ninth Circuit Court, in *Destination Ventures v. FCC*, found that there is "substantial" government interest in protecting consumers from having to bear the costs of third-party advertising. Additionally, the court held that advertisers have no right to turn consumers into a "captive audience" that is incapable of declining to receive a message.

I believe in the First Amendment, and for that matter, the traditional right that allows anyone to advertise their products as much and as widely as they can afford to advertise them. However, I do not believe the American consumer should have to pay for anyone's newspaper, television, radio, direct mail, fax advertising, or e-mail advertising.

Marketing by e-mail in cyberspace, does not have the traditional costs associated with other forms of advertising, including direct mail to which it has been compared. Direct Mail advertising includes a predetermined cost for each recipient of the advertising. That cost includes, paper, printing, handling, and, of course, postage. Spammers, however, can send out millions of messages with a few clicks of their mouse. Unlike the direct mailer, the spammer's costs are minimal and not in direct proportion to the number of people receiving the advertising. Direct mailers have to "target" their reach very carefully because they lose when a recipient does not respond. Therefore, there is a natural limit on the number of recipients the direct mail marketer can reach. There is no comparable natural limit for spammers. One software package called *Cyber-Bomber* claims to allow spammers to send 50,000 e-mails an hour.

Junk e-mail costs the owner of a home computer time and money while the economics of e-mail almost frees the sender of any costs. This puts the e-mail consumer, who must spend time searching through numerous junk e-mail messages to find the legitimate ones, at a disadvantage. Filters and other methods now used to slow down the amount of junk e-mail have proven to be costly for consumers and ISP's, and they have been only modestly successful.

The most recent issue of *Newsweek* magazine (June 22, 1998) relates one company's problems after a disgruntled former employee sent out a phony ad for the company to about 50,000 Internet users. Over 9,000 people complained to the company about the phony ad—so many people the company had to hire an extra employee just to answer the complaints.

Fortunately, my legislation would not interfere with or affect direct e-mail advertising or marketing, except those unwanted e-mail solicitations like the phony ad placed by the disgruntled employee. If any previous relationship existed between the e-mailer and the e-mail recipient my legislation would not affect the e-mail transaction. For example, if someone: made a small purchase at a local electronics store, a business relationship would exist.

My bill also would not affect electronic billboard and banner advertising on the Internet, and in no way would it interfere with the path of communication between businesses and their customers or friends and acquaintances. All avenues of legitimate direct marketing would remain. My legislation would only remove unwanted mail from a consumer's Internet mailbox. It simply would allow consumers to take action against spammers if they wanted to stop receiving unsolicited e-mail.

Mr. TAUZIN. Thank you very much, Chris.

The Chair would like to note the presence in the hearing room of the wife of Mr. Markey.

Susan, we welcome you and we appreciate your being here. I suspect that Mr. Markey is going to be on much better behavior for the rest of the hearing. Thank you for coming.

Also if the beeper goes off, it is because Justin's wife is any time now ready to deliver their first child, so he may run out of here in a hurry. It is nothing that any of you said.

We now welcome Mr. Bass for your testimony.

STATEMENT OF HON. CHARLES F. BASS, A REPRESENTATIVE IN CONGRESS FROM THE STATE OF NEW HAMPSHIRE

Mr. BASS. Thank you, Mr. Chairman. I will not repeat anything that my two distinguished colleagues have mentioned or discussed with reference to this legislation. I would make one comment.

I hear the newest mechanism for dealing with unsolicited telemarketing is to tell the caller that you are busy at the moment, could you please get his home phone number so you can call him back that evening, and usually that terminates the conversation pretty quickly.

This is a rather fascinating subject, the subject of cramming. I am also familiar with slamming and spamming, but the cramming issue, from one who ran a company that was driven by sales, it is rather extraordinary to me the thought process and the pragmatism that goes into a decision that would lead a company to, in essence, embark on an unsolicited marketing campaign understanding that the risks associated and the costs associated with such an action must be less than what one gains through embarking on this program, knowing that you will probably pick up a number or many thousands of new customers and they wouldn't have either the initiative or knowledge or understanding to change back.

It is rather extraordinary to me, because I have always operated in my own life under the concept of wanting to have a willing buyer and willing seller, not a totally ignorant buyer with a seller basically operating as a con artist.

I am very glad that you have chosen to take up this important piece of legislation. Over the last couple of years the number of complaints that I have received in my district offices and by mail from constituents who have been slammed is really quite extraordinary, and I have in my record a fellow in Lancaster, New Hampshire, who before he was able to terminate his service ended up owing some telephone company over $500 that he hadn't really preauthorized.

So I think this is an extraordinarily important and useful piece of legislation. It is a very high priority for consumer protection; and in a world where telecommunications marketing as well as telecommunication itself is changing so rapidly, becoming increasingly complex by the day, it is not only important that we pass this piece of legislation with the Senate amendments, but also that we remain vigilant here in Congress to make sure that our oversight of this whole process of telecommunications remains as vigilant as possible to prevent the kinds of financial, as well as emotional, if you will, crises that can occur not only through spamming, but also in slamming.

So I commend you, Mr. Chairman and Mr. Markey, for having brought this legislation to the floor.

[The prepared statement of Hon. Charles F. Bass follows:]

PREPARED STATEMENT OF CHARLES F. BASS, A REPRESENTATIVE IN CONGRESS FROM THE STATE OF NEW HAMPSHIRE

Mr. Chairman, I would like to thank you for providing me with the opportunity to testify before the Subcommittee today. First of all, I would like to commend you and Ranking Member Dingell for holding this hearing today and for your interest in anti-slamming legislation. As both of you know, Mr. Goodlatte and I introduced H.R. 3749 in April of this year, which we were able to work with Chairman Tauzin to have incorporated into one of the bills which is the subject of today's hearing, H.R. 3888.

H.R. 3749 and H.R. 3888 will help increase consumer protections against having their long distance telephone service switched without their knowledge or consent, otherwise known as slamming.

My interest in anti-slamming legislation was sparked by the many complaints I have received from constituents that have been slammed. The problem seems to be wide ranging and non-discriminating.

I would like to share with the Subcommittee one egregious example of slamming from my home state. Dr. Hal Goolman, a Podiatrist from Lancaster, New Hampshire, was slammed. Like most victims of slamming, Dr. Goolman had no idea that his long distance telephone service had been switched until he received his bill. Dr. Goolman's business long distance service had been switched from his traditional service with AT&T to a company of which he had never heard.

In his case, the change in service was easy to detect, considering that his monthly bill had increased by over 500 percent. What was usually a $25-$30 bill had increased to over $200 a month. When Dr. Goolman called his new long distance carrier to ask who had given them permission to change his long distance service, they indicated that they had his receptionist on tape agreeing to the change. Dr. Goolman protested that his receptionist had no authority to change the service and asked to hear the tape, at which point the long distance carrier refused to his request.

Dr. Goolman expected that the FCC would be able to help him correct this problem. However, numerous attempts to get through to the FCC hotline were unsuccessful. Only after four months and dozens upon dozens of phone calls was Dr. Goolman finally able to restore his original long distance service.

Dr. Goolman's story is particularly relevant in view of the consumer protection provisions contained in the legislation being discussed today. It is helpful to look at how Dr. Goolman's story would have been different had H.R. 3749 or H.R. 3888 been the law of the land.

1) The long distance carrier would have been required to get verification of a change in telephone service in oral, written, or electronic form and to send this information to Dr. Goolman upon request.

2) Because permission to change the service could have only been given by the person authorized to do so, his receptionist would not have been a scapegoat for some underhanded telemarketing scheme.

3) The long distance service provider would have been required to acknowledge the type of service to be changed.

4) The long distance service carrier would have been required to notify Dr. Goolman of the change in his service 15 days after the change was made. Therefore, he would not have been surprised when he received his bill.

5) And, finally, the FCC would have the ability to award damages to Dr. Goolman for charges by the long distance carrier.

One of the most disturbing aspects of Dr. Goolman's story was his inability to contact the FCC. Although the FCC recorded over 25,000 slamming complaints last year alone, I am left to ponder how many tens of thousands of American were slammed but did not or could not report their case to the FCC.

Mr. Chairman, I think the need for anti-slamming legislation can be summed up best by the Chairman of the FCC, William Kennard, in a speech he gave before the United States Telephone Association, "With hundreds of long distance carriers battling for the consumers' business, the rigors of competition will cause some to look for a way to cheat. And indeed, slamming has become our number one consumer protection issue."

Again, I would like to thank the Chairman and the Subcommittee for the opportunity to testify today.

Mr. TAUZIN. The Chair will recognize himself quickly, and then I will recognize any other member who wishes to dialog with our friends.

I have to assume, because we are in this transition from monopoly marketplaces to competitive marketplaces, that we have some of this confusion, that customers are used to being served by a single telephone company, and they never thought that there would be many telephone companies and they would have to bother with deciding. I suspect that some companies must gain new customers who don't complain.

Mr. BASS. Clearly.

Mr. TAUZIN. Have you experienced something different?

Mr. BASS. Clearly we are in a state of transition which began with all of the marketing efforts that were put on by the major long distance carriers; and now with telecommunications deregulation, we are going to have competition for local services and across with cable and so forth, and I think there is a point at which the consumer needs to catch up with the technology and with the options available; and the level of education isn't as high as it will be in 5 or 10 years.

Telecommunications is a fascinating service because it isn't easy to tell what your service is, whereas if you have a fuel oil dealer or a lawyer or a doctor, you have a name. But telephone bills are complicated and difficult to understand, and they are many pages long, and I think—and the issue of cramming is just as significant where it is hard to tell that your service is being increased. I think we are way overdue in terms of responding, and I feel that this issue is definitely one that you should address.

Mr. TAUZIN. Thank you, gentlemen. One final thought and then I will yield to other members who have not made opening statements yet. I want to make sure that everyone understood the difference between your approach, Chris, and the approach taken in the legislation before the committee today.

What is the difference?

Mr. SMITH. The major difference is who makes the decision to opt in or opt out. The Senate-passed legislation says to the consumer, you have to tell your Internet service provider, I don't want this.

The other way, you have to opt in. Our legislation says if I want to receive junk e-mail, I opt into the program and then they are not unsolicited. They strike "un" in their solicited part. That is the difference.

We are only talking about advertisements. We are not talking about conversations between individuals who have a friendship, or bulletin boards where there is a preexisting friendship. We are not talking about that.

Mr. TAUZIN. The Chair recognizes the other members in the order of their appearance who may wish to make an opening statement.

The lady from California, Ms. Eshoo.

Ms. ESHOO. Thank you, Mr. Chairman, I would like to thank our colleagues for being here today and giving us their thoughts through their testimony.

I am curious to ask if any of you have contacted—as a result of the slamming that has taken place and the experience of your constituents, have you contacted any of the long distance carriers, and if so, what was their response to you?

Mr. GOODLATTE. We have had instances where constituents have contacted my office.

Ms. ESHOO. What about you?

Mr. GOODLATTE. We have contacted the carriers on their behalf. And as you might suspect, those legitimate companies are quick to say that that is not something that they voluntarily participate in, and they correct the problem for the constituent promptly.

Ms. ESHOO. So they say that they didn't do it, but they are able to correct it?

Mr. GOODLATTE. Right. We are talking about more fly by-night operations that in some instances act as a go-between and sell this service and then notify the carrier of the change.

Ms. ESHOO. In pursuing this on behalf of constituents, did you find that any of the long distance carriers contract for these services?

Mr. GOODLATTE. I have not discovered that to be the case from my individual inquiries, but I would hope that we would hear about that from the other witnesses today.

Ms. ESHOO. Mr. Bass or Mr. Smith, do you wish to comment?

Mr. BASS. I would agree with Mr. Goodlatte. The problems that occur are either unintentional, a constituent complains and the carrier didn't realize, it was a mistake or miscommunication. There are a lot of complications here.

But there seems to be too many complaints. I understand that there were over 20,000 complaints that the FCC was unable to address, and I would suspect that the major carriers don't need to resort to this kind of a sales technique and probably wouldn't want to take the risk; and it is more likely the brokers, who are just brokering large accounts from one level to the next and can get away with something like that.

Ms. ESHOO. So your experience is that it is not something that the major carriers engage in, but rather they are smaller outfits that either do it directly or that they contract for this?

Mr. BASS. In order to answer that question accurately, I would probably have to go back through the specific complaints and try to categorize them for you, which I would be glad to do.

Ms. ESHOO. Thank you for being here today and bringing your ideas forward on how best to approach this.

Is there unanimous consent that we submit opening statements?

Mr. TAUZIN. Without objection.

[Additional statements submitted for the record follow:]

PREPARED STATEMENT OF HON. FRED UPTON, A REPRESENTATIVE IN CONGRESS FROM THE STATE OF MICHIGAN

Thank you for calling today's hearing on the issue of telephone "slamming". Since the beginning of this year, not a week goes by without me hearing from a constituent in Michigan who has been "slammed".

This Subcommittee has taken a leading role in oversight of this issue and attempting to develop legislation to address it. In particular, Chairman Tauzin's bill (H.R. 3888) is a step in the right direction and I'm pleased to be an original cosponsor. It's clear that Congress must act; in fact, the Chairman of the Federal Communications Commission has stated that "slamming has become our number one consumer protection issue."

My home state of Michigan, according to one report, ranks 8th overall in the number of state and federal slamming complaints. In 1997, the Michigan Public Service Commission received about 800 calls regarding slamming which seems like a small amount. But we must keep in mind that only a fraction of those who are slammed actually contact the agency to complain. And the problem is only going to get worse unless Congress toughens the penalties.

This is one specific issue in H.R. 3888 that I hope we can explore today. A provision in the bill focuses on switchless resellers of telecommunication services and requiring them to post a "surety bond". It appears that this language may have a harmful effect on resellers and contains tough penalties which their competitors would not have to face. I hope we can work with all affected parties to craft a provision that does not impose undue burdens on any particular service or company.

I look forward to hearing the testimony of our witnesses.

Thank you.

PREPARED STATEMENT OF HON. PAUL E. GILLMOR, A REPRESENTATIVE IN CONGRESS FROM THE STATE OF OHIO

Mr. Chairman, I thank you for holding this hearing on slamming, the unauthorized switching of consumer telephone carriers. I know that this is an issue which is of concern to many residents of Ohio's Fifth Congressional District.

I also understand that we are examining the problem of "spamming," which is sending massive quantities of unsolicited electronic mail, or e-mail. This is something which my constituents tell me is a great inconvenience and annoyance to computer users and I would particularly welcome any insight that our witnesses could provide on this subject. It is certainly an issue which arouses strong feelings on the part of computer users, and if the Congress is going to act, then we should be as educated as possible.

Mr. Chairman, I yield back the balance of my time.

PREPARED STATEMENT OF HON. TOM BLILEY, CHAIRMAN, COMMITTEE ON COMMERCE

Thank you, Mr. Chairman.

We are here, in part, because of the fruits of our success and efforts. In the 1980s, we pushed to open the long distance telecommunications marketplace to competition. In the Telecommunications Act of 1996, we pushed to open our local telephone markets to competition.

History has proven that with competition comes lower prices, more choice, better services. Unfortunately, competition also stirs the juices of scoundrels and fraud-artists and it sometimes pushes companies to try to cut corners. In a one company world, it is easier to ensure; that the company does not take advantage of consumers. In a multiple provider world, it is harder.

Slamming has become a large problem. The FCC reports that slamming is the number one consumer complaint filed and bilks consumers out of their hard-earned money. Many of the telecommunications debates that come before us deal with company vs. company. Slamming is different; it deals with the end-user: our constituents.

The answer to the problem, however, is not to take a step back. It is possible to let competition flourish while still protecting consumers from anti-competitive behavior. That is why the Telecom Act outlaws the changing of a customer's carrier of choice in violation of the FCC rules. Unfortunately, the Commission hasn't completed its work on these rules.

And, I must ask the question where is the Commission? What are they waiting for? When will they stop telling us there is a problem and take appropriate action to prevent it, as required by existing law?

The subcommittee has before it two bills introduced by Chairman Tauzin and Full Committee Ranking Member Dingell that attempt to put some teeth to the Commission rules to prevent slamming. I understand that Mr. Markey is also working on a bill to deal with this issue.

While I am not sure if additional law is needed in this area, I am always happy to listen to the debate. I noticed that over 150 Members of the House have cosponsored some type of anti-slamming legislation.

I would be remiss if I didn't thank the hard work of Senators McCain and Burns in the other body on this matter. After careful consideration, the Senate passed anti-slamming legislation by an overwhelming majority only a short time ago.

This issue reminds me somewhat of work this Committee did in passing international satellite reform legislation. This Committee took action because we didn't like the privatization plans presented by the Administration and INTELSAT and Inmarsat. We didn't like the Administration's timetable and we didn't like the Administration's delay. I am confident that we can correct the Administration's satellite reform direction by passing my legislation into law this Congress.

I am usually troubled when I look out and see a bunch of Members before the Committee testifying—if so many Members are interested it gives you a little hesitation on what they are selling. But there doesn't seem to be a worry today, so I welcome our distinguished witnesses, and I yield back my time.

PREPARED STATEMENT OF HON. ELIOT L. ENGEL, A REPRESENTATIVE IN CONGRESS FROM THE STATE OF NEW YORK

Mr. Chairman, I am pleased that we are taking time to hold this important hearing today. We have heard many reports in the press about slamming we have also heard from our constituents who have been slammed. Most of those who are victims of this practice are not aware that their long distance service has been changed until after the fact and often after they owe money to the slamming carrier.

This is a situation that must be addressed and I am pleased that we are considering two worthwhile bills that would curtail slamming. I support competition in the long-distance market but we must guard against sham artists who switch innocent customers unknowingly in order to trump up their sales. Customers who have been slammed must spend time and money in order to restore their basic telephone services. These sham practices must be stopped.

To this end, I am a cosponsor of H.R. 3050 because I believe this measure would be the most effective way to fight slamming. However, I believe both bills before us today have merit and would address slamming in different ways. I believe this hearing is a good forum to consider the differences in the legislation and to discuss any consequences that could result should the legislation be enacted. I look forward to hearing from the witnesses and to learn how we can most effectively curtail slamming.

PREPARED STATEMENT OF HON. THOMAS C. SAWYER, A REPRESENTATIVE IN CONGRESS FROM THE STATE OF OHIO

I think it is fair to say that we've all heard of at least one person who has had her telephone service provider changed without authorization—commonly referred to as being slammed. When consumers select a long distance provider they do so with the understanding that that particular company will provide the service on the terms they agreed to. However, for many consumers when they receive their bill they discover that the terms and even the carrier are not what they chose. Unfortunately, this is occurring more and more frequently.

According to a GAO study conducted earlier this year, between 1993 and 1997 the number of slamming complaints received by the FCC went from just under 2,000 per year to 20,000 per year. Some have estimated that approximately 2 million subscribers are slammed each year. These numbers will probably continue to rise in this new, era of telecommunication deregulation unless something is done to prevent slamming from occurring. The effects of such actions have broad implications not just for consumers, but for the entire telephone industry. I'm sure everyone knows of the "Fletcher" case. In a short span of three years, Mr. Fletcher reportedly slammed nearly one-half of a million customers as he promoted his company as being a long distance reseller. Those who changed their services to his company were billed in excess of $20 million. This type of activity cannot and should not be allowed to continue. More importantly, it must be prevented before it happens again.

Mr. Chairman, today we are holding a legislative hearing on two bills, H.R. 3888 the Anti-Slamming Amendments Act, and H.R. 3050, the Slamming Prevention and Consumer Protection Act. I am a cosponsor of the latter bill. While both pieces of legislation are aimed at preventing slamming, their approaches are different.

For years, the FCC has been given the authority to adopt anti-slamming measures. While it has issued fines in a number of cases over the years, the FCC has come under fire because it has not done more to deter companies from slamming others in the future. However, because of its long history in limiting unfair and deceptive businesses practices H.R. 3050 would require the Federal Trade Commission to adopt rules and procedures to prevent slamming.

H.R. 3050 also contains an immediate consumer protection device that allows a private right of action. A subscriber may bring a lawsuit in state court against a company within one year of noticing an unauthorized change in service. Separate from any other penalties imposed against the phone company, the customer is eligible to receive a refund on long distance service for up to three months. H.R. 3888 does not have a similar provision. However, a consumer can elect to pay the original long distance provider for any charges that are supposed to be paid to the slammer.

There are several other provisions that H.R. 3888 contains which are not included in the Slamming Prevention and Consumer Protection Act. One such provision addresses the large number of unsolicited e-mails a person may receive. This is referred to as "spamming." As more people get connected to the Internet, there is a greater potential for more people to get spammed. Certainly this should be looked into further and possibly be included in H.R. 3050.

Mr. Chairman, I hope that whatever action this subcommittee and the full committee takes, we can pass a solid bill with strong bipartisan support. We owe it to our constitutes to make sure effective anti-slamming measures are in place to deter such actions. I look forward to hearing from our witnesses.

PREPARED STATEMENT OF HON. GENE GREEN, A REPRESENTATIVE IN CONGRESS FROM THE STATE OF TEXAS

Thank you Mr. Chairman for having this very important hearing on slamming. Also, I am a cosponsor of H.R. 3050, The Slamming Prevention and Consumer Protection Act, one of the anti-slamming bills that we will be discussing today.

Slamming is a phenomenon we have seen explode since the break up of the AT&T monopoly. It a practice that intrudes in our daily lives and hurts the consumer.

In this committee we all strive to introduce competition into telecommunications markets. This competition is to spur innovation and reduce the cost to consumers. Unfortunately, competition also has it's drawbacks. One such drawback is slamming.

Slamming exploits the consumer. It exploits them by deceiving a consumer who unknowingly and often unwittingly has their long distance service switched to a competing carrier. This switch is an uninvited change that goes unchecked until the bill arrives and a person's long distance rates are sky high.

All of us on this committee have received the constituent call or letter asking for help with slamming. Slamming is an intrusive and deceptive practice that need to be addressed.

We need to put into place effective anti-slamming measures. We need to make sure that a company that offers long distance service provides accurate information to the FCC and it is not a sham business. We need to make sure that when a complaint is filed it is addressed in a timely fashion. Also, we need to make sure that if a company does practice slamming the penalty they face is stiff and appropriate. Most importantly we need to make sure that any anti-slamming measure protects the consumer.

Today we have that chance to come up with some measures that will hopefully address the problem of slamming.

Mr. TAUZIN. The gentleman from Illinois.

Mr. SHIMKUS. Thank you, Mr. Chairman. I would like to refer back to this GAO report of April 1998. It is just amazing, the lack of involvement from the FCC in trying to rein in some of this. My question is on the legislation and the surety bond issue. When you have small, startup companies who may find it very difficult to post a surety bond versus the fly by-night operations, which is the intent of the surety bond, to add credibility to companies. I would like the panel to add any comments on that.

My dilemma is balancing the two, and how do we get the bad guys while not discouraging the small startups?

Mr. BASS. I will just give you a quick answer.

Surety bonds are just exactly what they are called. If you can qualify for a surety bond, you don't have to be a huge company in order to do that. Lots of very small businesses can get surety bonds. I don't know about the telecommunications industry per se, but I can tell you in a lot of other industries, some of which I have been involved with, surety bonds can be acquired. They add to the cost of service, but they are definitely a consumer protection, and I am not sure that it necessarily would discriminate. Some future witnesses may dispute what I am saying, but I am not sure that it would discriminate against a small provider versus a larger one.

Mr. SHIMKUS. I would just respond that this debate is also occurring in the home health issue, and with our reforms of last year on the surety bond issue for the small home health agencies. In my district, which is rural, they claim it is a great burden to them, so that is why I ask the question.

Mr. BASS. I suspect that there is a difference in malpractice and medicine and telephone service in terms of premium, what the cost might be.

Mr. TAUZIN. Would the gentleman yield?

Mr. SHIMKUS. Yes.

Mr. TAUZIN. The Chair did invite the resellers to come today to give us their advice on what would be appropriate on surety bonds, or not, to ensure the responsibility of the players here, particularly when the legislation provides civil relief to consumers who have been slammed perhaps inappropriately although not criminally.

So the invitation is still open to hear whether or not there is a better way of guaranteeing responsibility in the area without necessarily discriminating against small companies. The gentleman has raised a legitimate point.

Thank you.

Mr. SHIMKUS. The surety bond is $50,000, the same as home health.

The second issue is, we heard from Mr. Klug who said that some companies are not even offering surety bonds in this area. So it is an issue that we do have, and that is why we have these hearings, to try to address these concerns.

Does anyone else want to respond? If not, I will yield back to the chairman.

Mr. TAUZIN. The Chair thanks the gentleman, and the Chair recognizes the gentleman from Tennessee, Mr. Gordon.

Mr. GORDON. Thank you, Mr. Chairman, for holding this hearing and also for working with me as we try to develop the next sort of step in this cramming issue. I am a cosponsor of Mr. Dingell's, as well as Chairman Tauzin's, slamming legislation, and I think this hearing is going to go a long way toward helping us fine-tune this, and I think we will be able to come up with a good solution here.

Mr. Markey and Mr. Tauzin and the panel have done a good job of explaining and defining the issue, so I am not going to repeat that.

One point, there was some tongue-in-cheek discussion about mothers being slammed, and certainly we are all sensitive to that, but the fact of the matter is that we all read our mail. This is a personal issue. Whether it is our mother or next-door neighbor, all of us have heard from folks at home; and that is why something needs to be done and, I think, will be done.

To Mr. Bass, you made a very gracious and courteous comment about cramming from business people that was very pragmatic. I would say that they were fraudulent would be more accurate. You were being courteous, but the difference—certainly you would not think about doing that, because you have a long-term business, you want to be in for the long term.

What we are finding is that most of these practices come from folks that set up a sham corporation. They do it with little overhead, and there is so much money to be made that they just make what they can and then they move on to the next scam.

And in this, as Mr. Goodlatte knows better than most, in this electronic age, there is a new scam right around the corner that we don't know about yet. That is one of the difficulties with legislation, you set up a bar, and these are the greatest entrepreneurs in the world, and they will slip around and do something just a little different.

I do want to thank the FCC and I know that the chairman was here some days ago. I brought up the issue of cramming, and

Chairman Kennard has called together a group to start looking at that. We have some more meetings, and I think we are going to be able to report back very soon with, hopefully, a consensus as to the best way to handle this.

I thank you for coming today, and I look forward to hearing this next panel; and particularly, Mr. Tauzin, I thank you for your courtesies and for bringing this important bill before us.

Mr. TAUZIN. Would the gentleman yield?

Mr. GORDON. Yes.

Mr. TAUZIN. I would also like the friends, witnesses and all to know that Mr. Gordon has spent a great deal of time on this issue of cramming and has gone to the extraordinary length of educating the chairman on some of the intricacies on this question. I thank him for that and pledge my continued efforts to him and Mr. Markey and Mr. Dingell in, hopefully, arriving at some sort of solution to what is becoming a larger and larger problem apparently out there.

Mr. GORDON. I would make one last comment—and thank you for that—and say that the National Consumer League says now that cramming is the No. 1 complaint that they receive. And I will be glad to yield to my friend.

Mr. MARKEY. I would like you and the audience to know that Mr. Gordon's concern about this issue is so great, as well as his concern about mothers in America, that he is going to the extraordinary length of getting married this weekend so he can have a mother-in-law as well.

I just want to congratulate you.

Mr. GORDON. Thank you. You were a good role model and the lady in the audience, we won't identify and embarrass her right now. It took 10 years for me to get over you taking her off the market and trying to find someone of that caliber. So thank you.

Mr. TAUZIN. We want to extend our best wishes to both of you, but particularly to the young lady who is obviously—you have lied to a great deal. We want to wish you well.

Any other members wishing at this time for time?

The gentlelady Ms. McCarthy.

Ms. MCCARTHY. Thank you very much, Mr. Chairman. Thanks to you and ranking member Mr. Dingell for the legislation and, I understand, Mr. Smith also for addressing this issue.

I am not clear and would love one of the witnesses to respond a little further as to who ideally should referee this problem. The bill has tried to address it through the Federal Communications Commission, as I understand the briefing that we got from FCC, to adopt specified additional verification procedures or the adoption of additional or modification procedures. The proposal speaks to that, but is the FCC really the best referee in all of this, because it seems that is what this is calling for. You are absolutely correct in identifying the bad players as not your major companies, but the fly by-night, snake oil artists who are in it for the quick money and then are out.

It would seem to me that as we craft legislation, we need to determine who is the referee to make sure that those are the folks that we get at and that we don't exacerbate the problem by putting in place additional rules and regs that just hinder the whole process, including the good guys.

Mr. GOODLATTE. If I might respond, the problem that the GAO report revealed was that the FCC has very little at all that it can do about it right now. They are a focal point of the receipt of these 20,000 complaints. If 20,000 people bothered to complain and the chairman of the full committee who got his problem corrected did not submit a complaint and he is as aware as anyone is of the nature of the process to file, you know there have to be hundreds of thousands, if not millions, who have been slammed like this, and so I think a central place where it can be dealt with is good.

But I also noted that the Senate legislation had criminal penalties for some of these really bad actors, the ones who are engaged in a mass-produced fraudulent activity; and there I think it would be appropriate to have criminal sanctions that would allow U.S. attorneys to prosecute them in Federal court.

Ms. MCCARTHY. I appreciate that, but it is hard to find these people. They come and they go. They change names and locations, they call themselves this and that, and they are the problem. You are absolutely right. I want to be sure criminal penalties then are geared toward that effort and not your legitimate companies who come before us and tell us, yes, we make mistakes on occasion and we try very hard to correct those. To fine them $10,000 when we are after these other types isn't perhaps fair either.

I think that is where we need to further define the efforts at capturing those who are in this effort just for the purpose of making money, not for the purpose of legitimately serving the customer.

Mr. GOODLATTE. I would agree with that, but I do think that some basic mechanisms to protect the consumer from the accidental slam by requiring that there be some form of authorization given before one's long distance service can be transferred from one company to another, that sort of thing seems to be appropriate for a government agency like the FCC.

Ms. MCCARTHY. You are right, there has to be some place where this conversation that was had between company and customer is verified. That is what is missing.

Mr. GOODLATTE. In my opinion, you shouldn't have to go to court to handle every problem that a consumer encounters, but you should be able to take those major offenders to court under criminal sanctions when they are clearly involved in mass producing these unsolicited, unrequested slams for multimillion dollar profits.

And you are absolutely right, it is difficult to detect these people. We have a bill that just passed the House which I am sure that you voted for, because it had only one dissenting vote, that I introduced dealing with telemarketing fraud in general, that just passed last week; and we want to increase the penalties on this because when you do catch them, we want to make sure that a good, strong example is made.

A lot of them use international borders to evade detection. Canadian provinces are 4 of the top 11 sites of these boiler room operations that make calls into the United States to defraud consumers of all types of different activities over the telephone. Slamming is just one that requires our particular attention.

You are right, it is a problem and let's throw the book at those folks that really are the big offenders.

Ms. McCarthy. Thank you.

Thank you, Mr. Chairman.

Mr. Tauzin. Does any other member wish to dialog with our guests?

Let me thank you, Bob, Charles and Chris. This committee intends to move forward so we will get some action. Thank you.

The Chair will now recognize members who would like to make an opening statement on the subject under the waiver that we agreed upon. Does any member wish to make an opening statement?

The Chair sees none, and we will welcome our second panel, which will consist of Mr. Lawrence Strickling, Deputy Bureau Chief of the Common Carrier Bureau of the FCC; Mr. Ernie Kelly of the Telecommunications Resellers Association—and would you please come forward and take chairs—Mr. Otto Schultz of the American Association of Retired Persons; Ms. Riley Murphy, Executive Vice President of the e.spire Communications, Inc.; Robert McDowell, Deputy General Counsel of American Carriers Telecommunications; Jerry Cerasale of Direct Marketing Association; Ms. Deirdre Mulligan, Center for Democracy and Technology; Susan Grant, the Vice President from National Consumers League; and Barbara Dooley, the Commercial Internet Exchange of Herndon, Virginia.

We welcome you all.

Let me sort of describe the rules. The committee tries not to have multiple panels, so we try to bring all of our guests together. The purpose is so we can get an exchange and dialog among you. Some of you may say something that provokes another witness to respond.

In order to get to that point, it is important that we not spend all of our time reading material that is presented to us in the form of written statements. So let me urge you, please, don't read your written statement this morning. If you can, summarize the key points of the document you have already presented to us. We have your written statement, and I assure you that the members and the staffs deeply appreciate the work that you have put into them. You may use your 5 minutes to summarize and hit the key points, so we can get into a dialog and exchange among you as rapidly as we can.

We will start with Mr. Strickling of the Federal Communications Commission, Common Carrier Bureau, Mr. Strickling for your 5 minutes.

You will note that I have that light system working here. No hammer is going to come down on you when the red light comes on, but it is a good indication that it is time to wrap it up.

Mr. Strickling.

STATEMENT OF LAWRENCE E. STRICKLING, DEPUTY BUREAU CHIEF, COMMON CARRIER BUREAU, FEDERAL COMMUNICATIONS COMMISSION

Mr. Strickling. Chairman Tauzin and members of the subcommittee, I want to thank you for the opportunity to testify today on the problem of slamming. I think as the opening statements and the testimony of the previous panel demonstrates, slamming is one of the most serious consumer protection issues that we face today in the telephone industry.

I am not going to take up your time convincing the subcommittee of the seriousness of the problem. What I would like to do is tell you what the FCC and the Common Carrier Bureau is doing about the problem. When I joined the Bureau 2 months ago to work with the Enforcement Division, Chairman Kennard gave us three challenges.

First, pursue slammers as quickly and aggressively as possible.

Second, take the profit out of slamming.

And third, educate consumers about the problem so they are armed to make intelligent choices and protect themselves against slamming.

In the past 2 months, we have made substantial progress in meeting the chairman's challenges. In April, the Commission took the strongest enforcement action it has ever taken against a slammer, assessing the Fletcher companies nearly $6 million and revoking their operating authority. But in that case concerns were expressed that the Commission had not taken action against Fletcher soon enough to protect consumers. What was needed was a mechanism by which the Bureau can identify slammers as soon as they have entered the market and take swift and sure enforcement actions against them.

The development of the National Call Center in Gettysburg, Pennsylvania, has provided us with a golden opportunity to create that mechanism. The Center which just created its second anniversary is run by the Commission's Compliance and Information Bureau and processes hundreds of thousands of calls from consumers each year. The Center tracks caller complaints by carrier and provides us with a nearly real-time look at who in the marketplace is engaging in these practices that generate a lot of consumer complaints.

Accordingly, working closely with the Compliance Bureau, we are reviewing this raw complaint data each week to identify the carrier with the most egregious complaints for more detailed investigation. Teams of investigators from the two bureaus are contacting consumers to gather the evidence that we will be using to seek substantial fines from these companies. We currently have several companies under active investigation that have been identified from this call center data, and we expect to bring strong enforcement actions against these companies in the next several weeks.

With this new approach, we will be attacking today's slammers, not last year's complaints, and we will be seeking fines of at least $1 million against these companies to make it clear to them that they cannot treat our enforcement actions as just another cost of doing business.

In addition, over the summer, we hope to make modifications in the Gettysburg operations to allow our representatives there to take down all of the information from consumers necessary to initiate their own informal complaints with the Commission. Today, when callers call Gettysburg, they are provided with information as to how to file a written complaint with us in Washington. We would like to make it easier for consumers so that they can simply supply over the phone the information necessary to bring a complaint.

The Bureau is also going to improve the Commission's Web site to make it easier for consumers to find information on slamming and other consumer protection issues and to provide a form or template on the Internet that consumers can fill out on their computer and transmit to us directly to complain against a carrier. The Bureau understands that to eliminate consumer fraud in this ever-changing marketplace, we must respond to slammers in a faster and more responsive manner, and I firmly believe that we are taking the steps necessary to meet the chairman's challenges.

Now, while we believe that these new mechanisms will have a significant impact on slamming, the Bureau does welcome the additional enforcement tools that are being proposed in the draft legislation that is the subject of today's hearing.

I would now like to briefly suggest for the subcommittee's consideration several points that we feel should guide the subcommittee as it considers additional legislation in this area.

First and most important, it is critical that the profit be taken out of slamming. While million dollar fines go a long way in that regard, it is important that the Congress create a more general mechanism that prevents the money from ever getting to the slammers or requires the slammers to disgorge the money as quickly and thoroughly as possible. Both the chairman's bill and the bill offered by Congressman Dingell provide different processes to achieve this goal, and we look forward to working with you and the staffs as we work to craft the most appropriate mechanism.

Second, we support the provisions of the draft legislation that ensure that States can take stronger measures if they want to protect their consumers. We feel the more cops on the beat, the better. We are confident we can work closely with the States to ensure that no slammer is able to elude the law.

Third, as the telecommunications industry continues to be more competitive, we will need the ability to identify who is in the market and to find those companies when enforcement action is called for. While the chairman has expressed concerns in the past about using the tariffing process as a vehicle for this, we do support the registration and bonding requirements of the chairman's bill. Our challenge will be to implement those provisions in a manner which protects consumers but does not erect a barrier to the entry of new companies which fully intend to comply with the law.

Fourth, the question of who should referee, as we are dealing with the carriers, the FCC is the appropriate referee. And this legislation would also extend jurisdiction to us to deal with the clearinghouses that are also part of the process in the slamming and cramming area. We feel that we will be able to respond promptly and strongly to these sorts of complaints in the future and take the action to protect consumers.

In closing, we will work with you and the staff of the subcommittee in any way we can to assist in this legislative effort and we stand ready to implement any new legislation as swiftly as we can. Thank you for this opportunity to testify and I look forward to your questions.

[The prepared statement of Lawrence E. Strickland follows:]

PREPARED STATEMENT OF LAWRENCE E. STRICKLING, DEPUTY BUREAU CHIEF, COMMON CARRIER BUREAU, FEDERAL COMMUNICATIONS COMMISSION

Chairman Tauzin, Congressman Markey, and members of the subcommittee, thank you for the invitation to testify today on the topic of telephone "slamming," the practice of changing a consumer's preferred carrier without that consumer's knowledge or express consent. Slamming deprives individual and business consumers of one of the fundamental principles underlying the Telecommunications Act of 1996—the right to use their carrier of choice. Slamming is more than just an unfair or questionable legal practice—it is illegal and, if done intentionally, it constitutes a clear case of consumer fraud. Even before the Act specifically made slamming illegal, Commission rules prohibited the practice of switching consumers' preferred long-distance carrier without authorization. Nonetheless, the number of slamming complaints received by the Commission from consumers continues to increase. Accordingly, we have re-examined our approach to eliminating the problem of slamming with a recognition that the Commission will need to be as aggressive as possible in order to take the profit out of this consumer fraud.

This morning I would like to briefly discuss some of these new enforcement approaches being instituted within the Commission to identify slammers much more quickly and to take swift and severe action against them in a manner that we believe will send a message to the industry that these types of consumer fraud will not be tolerated.

The Extent of Slamming

As I have already noted, the number of slamming-related complaints received by the Commission continues to grow at a rapid pace, and constitutes the single largest source of our consumer complaints. In 1997, the Common Carrier Bureau's Enforcement Division handled approximately 45,000 telephone-related complaints. Of those, over 20,000—or nearly half—involved allegations of slamming. Of course, we find that many consumers only complain to the Commission after exhausting other avenues of relief; and some never complain because they simply do not realize that they have been slammed—a fact, by the way, upon which the bad actors in this field actually rely. Thus, it is fair to say that the complaints received by the Commission provide only a limited indication of the extent of the slamming problem.

Consumers are angry, and rightfully so. In their complaints, they commonly use words such as "abused," "cheated," "pirated," and "violated" to describe the emotional impact of having been slammed. These consumers do not believe that they should have to pay for services provided by a company that they did not choose, and which they feel has somehow violated their privacy. They are further angered by the time and effort required of them to switch back to their preferred carrier, and want to receive prompt and caring assistance from the various carriers—including the local exchange carrier, the interexchange carrier and in many cases, a reseller—in undoing the slam. Ultimately, the practice brings the industry into disrepute and leaves consumers frustrated with a system that should instead be providing them with the full and undisputed benefits of competition.

To be fair, it must be pointed out that some cases of slamming are simply the result of legitimate errors, such as the transposition of telephone number digits. However, I believe that the vast majority of slamming incidents are due to inadequate safeguards and verification procedures being implemented by the carriers, or, in far too many instances, outright fraud. Many slamming cases involve forged signatures; deceptive sweepstakes; television advertisements for 800 numbers that fail to adequately disclose that calling the number will lead to a carrier switch; and slick telemarketing that result in carrier switches without the consumer ever realizing what has happened.

The Commission's Rules

Even before the 1996 Act specifically made the practice illegal, the Commission adopted rules to ensure consumers' rights to use their preferred carrier. In crafting these goals, the Commission sought to balance the twin goals of consumer protection and unfettered competition. Clear, forceful rules are the first prong of our anti-slamming efforts. But we must be careful not to adopt rules that create unnecessary barriers to entry in the industry.

The rules leave no doubt as to a carrier's obligation before switching a customer's service and a consumer's rights if an unauthorized switch does occur:

* A carrier must obtain the consumer's express written or verbal authorization before it may lawfully submit a change order.

* If the authorization is written, the document—a Letter of Authorization (LOA)—must conform to our rules that detail the information to be provided in clear, unambiguous language. Among other things, these rules prohibit promotional language from appearing on the document, and require that the LOA be use only to switch service. In other words, we prohibit combining LOAs with contest entry forms, which some carriers previously used in a deceptive manner.

* If a consumer's authorization is verbally provided to a telemarketer, then the carrier may not submit a change order until it has separately verified the authorization by one of four methods spelled out in the Commission's rules.

* Finally, if a consumer is switched without authorization, the local telephone company must credit any fees imposed for the switch, and the slamming carrier must re-rate any calls that the consumer made so that the consumer is charged no more than he or she would have been by their preferred carrier.

The 1996 Act also added Section 258, which makes it unlawful for any telecommunications carrier to "submit or execute" a change in a subscriber's carrier selection, except in accordance with the Commission's verification procedures. The statute also provides that any carrier that violates the Commission's verification procedures, and collects charges for telecommunications services, shall be liable to the subscriber's properly authorized carrier for all charges collected. That is, the slamming carrier is required to pay all revenues it has received from the consumer and turn them over to the authorized carrier.

Enforcement

Needless to say, strong rules are meaningless without strong and timely enforcement of those rules. It is in this area that Chairman Kennard has asked the Common Carrier Bureau to place particular emphasis. I would add that this directive, and the steps we are taking in furtherance thereof, are not limited to slamming, but are equally applicable to other consumer protection issues facing the Commission, such as cramming.

First, it has become clear that we can modify our enforcement actions to take swifter and more severe action against the wrongdoers. No longer will the slammers and crammers of the world be allowed to treat our fines as simply a cost of doing business in this extremely lucrative fraud on consumers. Accordingly, we are in the process of changing the approach in this area by significantly increasing both the number and monetary amount of the forfeitures we issue for violations of our consumer protection rules.

For example, in April the Commission issued an order revoking the operating authority of a group of long-distance companies run by Daniel Fletcher for engaging in slamming and numerous other violations of the Communications Act. The Commission also assessed forfeitures against these companies totalling nearly $5.7 million. Fletcher and his partners are now out of business and may not provide common carrier service again. Over the next few months, the Common Carrier Bureau intends to submit to the Commission proposed orders of forfeiture against several additional companies for violating the Commission's slamming rules—each for a minimum of $1 million. Combined with the statutory mandate that disgorges slammers of any charges collected from consumers that did not authorize a carrier change, we believe this type of aggressive enforcement action goes a long way toward taking the profit out of slamming.

Second, the Commission's history with slamming has underscored the need for more proactive enforcement activities. Historically, we have relied upon the filing of complaints by consumers as the basis for targeting the Commission's limited enforcement resources. As I noted previously, however, the filing of complaints with the Commission is often the last resort by consumers who have been unable to get relief from other sources. As in the Fletcher matter, by the time we see a trend in filed complaints, the bad actors have often profited handsomely and have moved on to new scams. Thus, working closely with the Compliance and Information Bureau, we are implementing procedures which will provide us with the earliest warning of the latest scams and bad actors, and streamlining other procedures in order to take swift enforcement action against these carriers. Among other initiatives, we are looking to information generated by the Commission's call center, which consumers typically contact for information before deciding to file a written complaint. Indeed, we hope to streamline our current processes ultimately to eliminate the current duplicative requirement that consumers file written complaints, and instead provide for complaints to be taken directly by the call center operators. This system will also significantly shorten the time it takes to resolve these complaints.

In sum, we recognize that to eliminate consumer fraud in this ever-changing fast-paced market, the Commission must respond to those violations that do occur in a faster, more aggressive, and more responsive manner than we have in the past. I firmly believe that we are taking the steps necessary to meet this challenge.

Proposed Legislation

I also applaud your efforts, Mr. Chairman, to provide us with additional legal resources to attack the problem of slamming. We support the goals of your bill, H.R. 3888, the Anti-slamming Amendments Act, and I believe the legislation will provide the Commission with additional authority to effectively address this and other consumer protection frauds, particularly cramming.

The bill allows the Commission to take a more comprehensive approach to deterring slamming. For example, the bill gives both the Commission and the states more enforcement and regulatory authority to stop slamming. We believe that giving state Attorneys General the authority to bring civil actions in federal court will greatly aid the Commission in a nation-wide enforcement effort. Furthermore, H.R. 3888 permits states to impose more restrictive procedures than those of the Commission. We believe that it is important to authorize the states to provide greater consumer protection for their residents based on their knowledge of local experiences, provided that such measures do not thwart or impede Congress' vision of a competitive telecommunications marketplace.

We also strongly support the efforts of H.R. 3888 to provide consumers with clear and unambiguous information to be able to detect unauthorized changes on their telephone bills. The bill gives the Commission specific authority to impose certain requirements for billing formats, in order to make it easier for consumers to decipher their phone bills to determine whether they have been slammed, or crammed. Under the provisions of the bill, carriers must notify subscribers within 15 days after the carrier change is processed, as well as notify consumers of their rights under the law and how to file a complaint with the Commission. The bill also provides timeframes for carriers to attempt to resolve complaints by consumers, which prevents carriers from dragging out a complaint at the expense of the consumer. Finally, we support the measures in the bill that would provide us with more information about the carriers that are providing services to consumers.

We also support many of the provisions of H.R. 3050, introduced by Congressman Dingell. As noted above, Chairman Kennard supports the provision that would exempt a slammed subscriber from paying for charges for a certain period after being slammed. We particularly approve of the provision that creates a private right of action in state court for a slammed subscriber and permits a state court to award treble damages for willful slamming. We also agree that negative option carrier changes should be prohibited. I note that Congressman Dingell's bill gives the Federal Trade Commission responsibility over some aspects of slamming. We believe that the Federal Communications Commission can and should be the primary agency with jurisdiction for all of the issues related to slamming.

Mr. Chairman, thank you once again for the opportunity to speak to this issue this morning. And, moreover, for the work of yourself and your colleagues towards protecting consumers from this ever-growing fraud. I look forward to working with the subcommittee to resolve this problem.

Mr. TAUZIN. Thank you very much.

The chairman now recognizes Mr. Ernie Kelly, the Executive Director of the Telecommunications Resellers Association.

STATEMENT OF ERNEST B. KELLY, III, EXECUTIVE DIRECTOR, TELECOMMUNICATIONS RESELLERS ASSOCIATION

Mr. KELLY. Thank you, Mr. Chairman. TRA, the Telecommunications Resellers Association, on behalf of more than 615 members, appreciates this opportunity to address the matter of slamming.

Founded in 1993, TRA is a national trade association representing companies who resell a variety of value-added, interexchange, local, wireless and enhanced telecommunications services. Members are typically smaller companies, more than a third of our members have revenues less than $10 million annually. TRA members primarily focus on the commercial market, although a number of our members also serve the residential market. On average, our members have been in business 3 to 7 years.

TRA members certainly share the growing concerns over the escalation of slamming incidents throughout the U.S. Slamming hurts the innocent parties involved, including legitimate carriers who, like the public, become unwitting victims of intentional slamming.

Those few entities who intentionally engage in slamming are criminals whose sole intent is to gain from deceiving and defrauding the public and should be subject to swift, decisive and hard enforcement actions.

We recognize that not all players play by the rules. Consequently we do support congressional action to deter slamming abuses and overall we support legislation.

Now to a specific concern which is the purpose of my testimony.

Title II of H.R. 3888 singles out switchless resellers of telecommunications services for special, punitive action. This section requires that switchless resellers, alone, amongst all competitors in this market, would have to post a surety bond in order to stay in business. Further, the bill prohibits any billing company from doing business with a switchless reseller unless it ascertains it has furnished the bonds.

In our opinion it is discriminatory toward small business entrants in this market; and is, therefore, anticompetitive. In trying to catch a few criminals, Title II of this bill sets out a solution that will penalize and handicap a large number of small businesses operating ethically in the marketplace today while discouraging others from even entering.

Switchless resellers are by nature small companies, many of which have entered the market in the last few years when the government finally opened telecom to competition and, by virtue of its resale rules and regulations, created first-time opportunities for small companies to have an equal chance to compete. This provision will have a negative effect on the ability of lesser capitalized companies to conduct business, because it will impose additional costs on them that their larger, better financed competitors will not have to face.

TRA estimates the amendment will adversely affect between 500 and 1,000 existing companies and will inhibit startup companies from entering the market.

Further, suppliers to these companies also will be negatively impacted by this requirement. Dozens upon dozens of billing companies, most of which are small businesses themselves have ongoing contracts to provide billing services to switchless resellers. This requirement not only puts these companies in the awkward position of policing their own customers, but also losing those customers who are unwilling or unable to post the bonds.

Finally, it hurts wholesale carriers, large and small, that depend on switchless resellers with traffic. The point is, switchless resellers are often the biggest victims of slamming. As their customers are stolen away, these small companies can little afford to lose customers through slamming. In fact, under the bill, legitimate switchless resellers would actually be penalized a couple of times by slamming—first, with the loss of their customers; and second, by having to pay a surety bond to repent for the actions of a few illegal operators.

It is imperative to the long-term survival of the competitive telecommunications market to preserve the ability of smaller players to compete. Therefore, I strongly urge the subcommittee to eliminate the surety bond requirement in H.R. 3888. The bill already effectively deters slamming with a number of provisions. It should not also deter competition.

TRA pledges its continued support to work with you to find a way to do that. Thank you.

[The prepared statement of Ernest B. Kelly III follows:]

PREPARED STATEMENT OF ERNEST B. KELLY, III, PRESIDENT, TELECOMMUNICATIONS RESELLERS ASSOCIATION

The Telecommunications Resellers Association (TRA), on behalf of its more than 615 members nationwide, appreciates this opportunity to address the matter of unauthorized customer service account transfers (also known as "slamming") and suggest how the telecommunications industry, regulators, and the public may eliminate this serious and harmful practice through uniform competitively-neutral verification procedures, swift enforcement action, and consumer education.

Introduction

Founded in 1993, TRA is a national industry association representing companies who offer a variety of value-added, interexchange, local, wireless, and enhanced telecommunications services. Members are typically smaller companies. More than half of TRA's member companies earn annual revenues of less than $25M and more than a third of TRA's members earn less than $10M annually. TRA members primarily focus on the commercial market, although a number of TRA members serve the residential market as well. The rapid growth and emergence of Association members as viable service providers is testament to the desirability of the competitive services TRA members offer the public. TRA members represent the very competitive entities that Congress envisioned would deliver the benefits of telecommunications competition to the public when it passed the Telecommunications Act of 1996.

TRA members certainly share the growing concerns over the escalation of "slamming" incidents throughout the U.S. Slamming harms the innocent parties involved including legitimate carriers who, like the public, become unwitting victims of intentional slamming. Legitimate service providers too must bear the significant cost and inconvenience of intentional slamming at the hands of unscrupulous providers who disregard their obligations to the public. Unscrupulous providers taint the reputation of an otherwise responsible industry. Those few entities who intentionally engage in slamming are indeed criminals whose sole intent is to gain from deceiving and defrauding the public, and should be subject to swift, decisive, and harsh enforcement action accordingly.

Yet, it is important to recognize that claims of unauthorized account transfers also result from unintentional error from which no service provider is immune. The sheer volume of annual account transfers for example, estimated between 20M and 25M in 1997 alone, creates the potential for unintentional error.[1] In some instances, customers themselves experience "buyer's remorse" and claim that they have been slammed. In others, a spouse or resident authorizes a change in carriers without the knowledge or consent of others. Although erroneous slamming has been viewed under the same light as intentional slamming, a distinction between both types of slamming should be made. In any event, TRA finds any form of slamming unacceptable. All service providers have a responsibility to ensure that their procedures for obtaining new subscribers limit the potential for error. When honest errors do occur, however, service providers should be accorded due process to demonstrate their compliance with applicable regulations and to correct errors immediately and with a minimum impact to the end user.

The potential for abuse of the service subscription process also resides in the ability of individuals or incumbent carriers to "game" the process for their own dishonest or anti-competitive gain. Examples abound of individual end users claiming to have been slammed in an effort to receive "free" service. TRA has also witnessed examples of incumbent local exchange carriers who have capitalized on the public's

[1] While the significant increase in slamming is alarming, the level of slamming in relation to the number of subscriber initiated requests for changes in primary carrier remains small—less than one percent for 1996—based on figures from the Federal Communications Commission's Common Carrier Scorecard Report (December 1997).

fear of slamming by deceptively promoting a lock or "freeze" on their customers' accounts, effectively preventing customers from changing service providers, even if they so desired. Such practices are equally harmful to the public and advance of competition, and should be prohibited.

As will be discussed more fully below, the key to eradication of intentional unauthorized account transfers remains in effective competitively-neutral verification procedures, swift enforcement action, and consumer education. These functions, more than any other, will serve to prevent intentional slamming and redress its victims.

The Surety Bond Requirement in H.R. 3888 Unjustly Punishes Switchless Resellers Who are Themselves Victims of Slamming

Title II of H.R. 3888, the Anti-Slamming Amendment Act, singles out switchless resellers of telecommunications services for special, punitive action. In our opinion, it is discriminatory towards small business entrants in this market and is therefore anti-competitive. This section requires that switchless resellers, alone amongst all competitors in this market, would have to post a surety bond in order to stay in business. Further, the bill prohibits any billing company from doing business with a switchless reseller unless it ascertains that such reseller has furnished the bond.

While the bill contains many appropriate safeguards against the scourge of slamming, the surety bond requirement unfairly singles out switchless resellers for special, punitive action that is not imposed upon the larger facilities-based companies with which they compete. Furthermore, in trying to catch a few criminal operations, Title II of this bill sets out a solution that will penalize and handicap a large number of small businesses operating ethically in the marketplace today and discourages others from even entering.

TRA's primary concern is that the surety bond requirement is discriminatory as it would affect only the small business segment of this competitive market. Switchless resellers are by nature small companies, many of which have entered the market in the last few years when the government finally opened long distance to competition and, by virtue of its resale rules and regulations, created first-time opportunities for small companies to have an equal chance to compete. Their contribution to the competitiveness of this market has been extraordinary. This amendment will have a chilling effect on the ability of lesser capitalized companies to conduct business because it will impose additional costs on them that their competitors will not have to face.

TRA estimates that the amendment will adversely affect between 500 and 1,000 existing companies and inhibit start-up ventures from entering the market. Further, suppliers to these companies also will be negatively impacted by this onerous requirement. Dozens of billing companies, most of which are small businesses themselves, have ongoing contracts to provide billing services to switchless resellers. This requirement not only puts these companies in the awkward position of policing their customers, but also of losing those customers that are unable or unwilling to post the bond. Finally, it hurts wholesale carriers—large and small—that depend on switchless resellers to fill their networks with traffic.

What is most distressing about this language is that it was adapted, with little or no debate on the Senate floor, from a GAO report on slamming that makes sweeping generalizations and draws non-empirical conclusions. Prepared for the Senate Permanent Subcommittee on Investigation of the Committee on Governmental Affairs by the General Accounting Office, the April 21, 1998, report concludes from interviews with regulators that a majority of slamming activity is committed by switchless resellers. "Switchless resellers—having the least to lose and the most to gain—most frequently engage in intentional slamming, according to the FCC, state regulatory agencies and the telecommunications industry," the report said. As an example, the report cites the now infamous Fletcher Companies, a group of long distance telephone companies owned/operated by Daniel Fletcher, which had their operating authority removed and were fined more than $5.6 million for slamming violations by the FCC in April. Fletcher is now the subject of a manhunt launched by the Federal Bureau of Investigation.

Few, if any, switchless resellers fit the profile of those companies formed by Fletcher, whose extraordinary and willful slamming activities the GAO chose to use as their case study. Furthermore, criminals like Daniel Fletcher are unlikely to be discouraged by the Senate bill's requirements. The practical effect of the provision, then, will be to penalize hundreds of legitimate small businesses nationwide in an effort to deter a much smaller number of criminals.

Among its over 600 members, TRA counts 185 switchless resellers, very few of which have a substantial number of slamming complaints levied against them. TRA has both switchless and switch-based members. On the FCC's 1997 list of companies with more than 100 slamming complaints, a majority of the 37 companies are not TRA members or switchless resellers. Of those who were, a higher percentage of them were switch-based as opposed to switchless. In fact, among those companies with the highest number of complaints are market leaders AT&T, MCI and Sprint. These companies are not willful slammers any more than the hundreds of small businesses that have been competing against them for years are.

The point is, switchless resellers are often the biggest victims of slamming, as their customers are stolen away by the Daniel Fletchers of this world. These small companies can least afford to lose customers through slamming. In fact, under this bill, legitimate switchless resellers could actually be penalized twice by slamming—first through the loss of customers and secondly by having to pay a surety bond to repent for the actions of a few illegal operators.

TRA's Code of Ethics and Member Education Serve to Discourage Intentional Slamming by TRA Members

At the time TRA was founded, the Association's members and leadership recognized the importance of establishing a Code of Ethics to guide TRA member business conduct. The new Association believed that its membership should be comprised exclusively of ethical entities committed to serving the public responsibly. This belief led to adoption of TRA's Code of Ethics, which all new members receive when joining the Association. TRA's Code of Ethics is recognized as the original such code in the telecommunications industry.

Under TRA's Code of Ethics, members are expected to serve the public honestly and responsibly. Intentional slamming is identified as a violation of the Code's responsible business practice obligations. Members who do not comply with the Code of Ethics are subject to censure procedures. Regrettably, instances of slamming have occurred among Association members, although these instances have been negligible in proportion to TRA's total membership. In the number of cases where slamming by TRA members was determined to have been intentional, membership privileges were denied or membership terminated.

TRA's Code of Ethics by itself is not enough to ensure that Association members do not intentionally transfer customer accounts without authority. TRA frequently informs members of regulatory enforcement action through its monthly member publication, and more importantly, conducts periodic seminars which address slamming and preventative measures to curb unintentional slamming during its semi-annual conferences. TRA has also developed a white paper on slamming which is made available to the membership.

Through TRA's consumer outreach program, TRA strives to inform the public about slamming and how to guard against it. Slamming information appears in TRA's Internet web site. Consumer brochures are routinely distributed to the media, consumer groups, and the public. The Association's emphasis on public and member education and enforcement of the Code of Ethics have paid dividends in eliminating unethical service providers from the ranks of TRA members.

Each Service Provider Must Assume Responsibility for its Own Actions

Each service provider, whether it manages and controls a network or resells the services of an underlying carrier, assumes responsibility for the manner in which it serves subscribers. From a regulatory perspective, most states do not differentiate between facilities-based carriers and resellers. Both types of service providers are subject to the same regulatory requirements. End users also do not distinguish between the type of service provider. When subscribing to a reseller, the end user holds the reseller fully responsible for the provision of service, not its underlying carrier—who is typically unknown to the subscriber.

Facilities-based carriers are network service vendors to resellers. Although facilities-based carriers remain responsible for the quality of the service they provider to resellers, they can not be held responsible for the operations of a reseller any more than a radio manufacturer could be held responsible for a paint defect in the new automobile which carries the company's radio. The underlying carrier can not, nor should it be required to, assume responsibility for policing its resale customers, outside of enforcing its own contracts. This is not to suggest that underlying carriers may not exert discretion in which resellers they wish to serve. It is in a facilities-based carrier's best interest to serve reputable resellers. Yet, once a resale agreement is in effect, responsibility for service to end users and regulatory compliance rests squarely with the reseller.[2]

---

[2] "Resellers" and, "Agents" are not synonymous. Where agents act exclusively as service provider representatives, resellers are service providers in their own right, responsible for their own

Effective Verification Procedures, Swift Enforcement Action, and Consumer Education are the Keys to Eliminating Intentional Slamming

Establishment of uniform, competitively-neutral verification procedures, swift regulatory enforcement action, and consumer education, will curb the proliferation of intentional slamming all too prevalent in today's competitive telecommunications markets.

Uniform Competitively-Neutral Verification Procedures. Reliance on written letters of agency, electronic and third party verification procedures to confirm end-user account transfers pursuant to 47 C.F.R. §§64.1100 and 1150, has proven effective in documenting the basis for customer account transfers. No single verification process has been demonstrated to be decisively more effective than others, and none should be favored or mandated accordingly. The variety of verification methods has enabled service providers to institute a verification process best suited to their individual operations. These verification methods should be retained at both the federal and state levels.

Account transfer verification requirements should remain uniform throughout the country. While each state should retain the ability to establish state-specific requirements as necessary, state and federal requirements should be harmonized to prevent a patchwork quilt of regulatory approaches. A harmonized approach will avoid establishment of 51 unique, and potentially conflicting, regulatory approaches to protect against slamming. Congress, federal and state regulators, and the industry should work together to develop a flexible regulatory framework which can be overlaid on individual federal and state slamming rules.

Institution of primary (interexchange) carrier account "freezes" or "PIC freezes," which allow end users to block account transfers, has also demonstrated their effectiveness in curbing slamming. Yet PIC freezes should not be used as anti-competitive devices to lock in existing customers, primarily by incumbent local exchange carriers. End users should be in full control of exercising PIC freeze options and should not be coerced into PIC freezes. Nor should resellers be required to obtain costly carrier identification codes they do not require, simply to enable reseller PIC freezes to be available to the public. Imposition of such a requirement would unfairly single out resellers and impose unsustainable costs that would prevent most resellers from remaining in business with little countervailing benefit to the public.

Swift Enforcement Action. The removal of any financial incentive for engaging in the unauthorized transfer of customer accounts coupled with swift enforcement action is crucial to the eradication of slamming. Federal Communications Commission and state commission imposition of material fines on companies engaged in slamming and requirements to make victims financial whole have stemmed the tide of slamming abuse. These enforcement actions have sent the strong message that regulators embrace a zero tolerance slamming policy.

However, a distinction should be made between instances of intentional and unintentional slamming when considering the appropriateness of fines and penalties. When slamming is unintentional, service providers should nevertheless be held accountable for restoring the end user to its preferred carrier expeditiously, and assume all associated expenses. Service providers should not, however, be unilaterally required to refund all amounts billed for service, so long as the amount billed remains at or below the effective rate paid by the end-user to its preferred carrier. Otherwise, service providers may themselves become victims of repeated scams by unscrupulous individuals who claim to have been slammed in an effort to unfairly enrich themselves at the expense of legitimate service providers. These serious scams have been documented repeatedly and remain on the rise in the telecommunications industry.

Some have proposed a "three strikes you're out" approach whereby service providers found to have engaged in repeated intentional slamming would be prohibited from providing services to the public through revocation of operating authority. TRA generally supports the proposal to the extent that such an approach is taken in instances of repeated intentional slamming or failure to take corrective action. Revocation of operating authority is appropriate when an accused provider fails to demonstrate that it has taken decisive steps to eliminate slamming or has not controlled the actions of its representatives and agents, but only after according due process to service providers.

An expeditious process for enforcement action will enhance efforts to end slamming. In some instances, the enforcement process may exceed nine months before fines and other penalties are imposed. This process is entirely too long. Those enti-

---

operations and actions to the public. All service providers must assume responsibility for the actions of the agents who represent them.

49-326 98 - 2

ties determined to be engaging in willful slamming should be given no more than 10 business days to provide evidence that the entity properly complied with verification requirements. A provider's failure to provide such evidence should serve as *prima facie* evidence that the provider was not in compliance and engaged in intentional slamming. Commission enforcement action should follow immediately. Delays in enforcement action will accomplish little in stopping unscrupulous providers from striking again.

Consumer Education. The old adage "forewarned is forearmed" rings true in relation to slamming. Knowledgeable consumers are less likely be victims of slamming. By arming the public with information concerning the carrier selection process, consistent with the information required to appear on letters of agency pursuant to 47 C.F.R. §64.1150, the public will be less vulnerable to deceptive claims and advertising. Regulators and the industry share the responsibility of informing the public of how to protect themselves from the potential of slamming. To that end, TRA supports regulatory and industry efforts to fully disclose service information to the public.

Conclusion

Intentional slamming can be eradicated through uniform competitively-neutral verification procedures, swift enforcement action, and public education. While the potential for unintentional slamming will always remain, adoption of these actions will serve the public well in curbing the tide of intentional slamming.

It is imperative to the long-term survival of the competitive telecommunications market to preserve the ability of smaller players to compete. The House needs to eliminate the surety bond requirement in the bill and in any conference on the bill that might take place. The bill already effectively deters slamming; it should not also deter competition from small players. TRA pledges its continued support to work with legislators, regulators, its members, and the industry, to ensure that the public remains protected against the actions of unscrupulous individuals.

Mr. TAUZIN. Thank you, Mr. Kelly.

Now Mr. Otto Schultz with the Association of Retired Persons, with whom I just became eligible for more discounts.

STATEMENT OF OTTO SCHULTZ, BOARD OF DIRECTORS, AMERICAN ASSOCIATION OF RETIRED PERSONS

Mr. SCHULTZ. Mr. Chairman and members of the committee, on behalf of AARP, I thank Chairman Tauzin and the other members of the committee for inviting us to participate in today's hearing regarding the impact of unauthorized switching of long distance telephone service providers or "slamming" on older Americans.

The Association would like to voice its support for the strong deterrents to the practice of slamming and for the remedies available to consumers detailed in H.R. 3888, the Anti-slamming Amendments Act. As you may be aware, we endorsed S. 1618, the version of this bill sponsored by Senator McCain last month, and we applaud the House for moving so quickly to entertain the passage of similar legislation.

AARP commends the chairman for introducing H.R. 3888. We believe that the provisions in your bill to amend the Communications Act of 1934 to curtail slamming are good for consumers. Slamming often happens in the context of high pressure and deceptive marketing telephone contacts or as part of contests in which participants are not fully informed that they have authorized a change in their carrier. Unfortunately, these tactics have proven successful in defrauding older Americans.

Ultimately, many of these firms charge rates far higher than the major carriers and consumers see their monthly bills skyrocket. AARP believes that many of the provisions in H.R. 3888 will go a long way toward deterring and even eliminating these fraudulent practices by individuals and companies.

H.R. 3888 includes a number of elements necessary to close off the loopholes in the existing law that make telephone subscribers vulnerable to fraudulent and deceptive practices. I will mention six of the key provisions, and speak in detail on one:

First, the verification of authorization procedures; the second is the prohibition of negative option marketing; third, notice to subscribers; four, damages awarded by the Commission; five, civil penalties and anti-cramming language, which I would like to speak to in a little more in detail.

AARP is extremely pleased by the inclusion of section 231 in the bill entitled "Obligations of the Telephone Billing Agents." This section addresses some of the concerns that we have with cramming. Cramming is the practice of adding subscription services to a consumer's bill without proper authorization to do so. In fact, the National Fraud Information Center, NFIC, recently reported that their 1–800 hotline now receives more cramming complaints than slamming complaints.

We strongly support the requirements that each consumer bill will disclose the name and number of the telecommunications provider, the services for which the subscriber is being charged and the charges associated with these services. Section 231 also prohibits the knowing inclusion of unauthorized telecommunications services. This language represents a giant step toward effectively dealing with this onerous practice. AARP would like to offer a couple of suggestions, however, that would provide even stronger protection for consumers.

We suggest the addition of language similar to that in section 101, which requires the provider to notify the subscriber in writing within 15 days of activation in specific and unambiguous language that the subscriber is now receiving that service. Also, we strongly recommend that the change in service or services be highlighted and described in detail on a separate page for at least the initial billing statement following a change in service or services.

For the reasons stated previously, AARP supports the passage of H.R. 3888. We would be remiss, however, if we did not point out some of the concerns that remain to be addressed. We believe that some of the elements contained in H.R. 3050 introduced by Representative Dingell would make the chairman's bill an even stronger guardian of consumer rights.

While AARP agrees with the provisions in H.R. 3888 that give the FCC more authority, we are concerned about the amount of time it currently takes the Commission to resolve complaints. We are hopeful that upon passage of this legislation, the FCC will adhere to the letter of the law and improve its complaint resolution process.

Because of our concern, however, we are intrigued by the inclusion in provisions of Mr. Dingell's bill that authorize the Federal Trade Communication, the FTC, to prescribe rules to prohibit unfair and deceptive advertisements and solicitations while giving the agency enforcement authority over the same. This allocation of new authority may help accelerate the ultimate end to the practice of slamming.

Another element of H.R. 3050 that we would urge the chairman to consider incorporating into his bill is the refund entitlement provision. This provision entitles consumers to a full refund for charges incurred as a result of slamming or at least releases a consumer from liability to a slammer for unauthorized charges up to 90 days. Adoption of this provision, in combination with the other elements of H.R. 3888, would send a strong message to all interexchange carriers and would begin to restore consumer confidence in the telecommunications industry.

Mr. Chairman, in conclusion, AARP welcomes your efforts to enact legislation designed to reduce and, hopefully, eliminate the instances of slamming. H.R. 3888 is a well-crafted effort to accomplish that goal, and we offer our support here today.

We also want to compliment Representative Dingell for introducing H.R. 3050, the attributes of which I have already discussed. AARP asks that the committee recognize the positive elements of both pieces of legislation and take this opportunity to craft a stronger H.R. 3888.

On behalf of AARP, thank you again for providing us with this forum to discuss the practice of slamming and to comment on the legislation proposals before you. AARP stands ready to work with you in seeking final passage of this important legislation.

[The prepared statement of Otto Schultz follows:]

PREPARED STATEMENT OF OTTO SCHULTZ, MEMBER, BOARD OF DIRECTORS, AARP

Mr. Chairman and Members of the Committee: My name is Otto Schultz and I am a member of the Board of Directors of AARP. On behalf of AARP, I thank Chairman Tauzin and the other members of the Committee for inviting us to participate in today's hearing regarding the impact of unauthorized switching of long distance telephone service providers, or "slamming", on older Americans. The Association would like to voice its support for the strong deterrents to the practice of slamming and for the remedies available to consumers detailed in H.R. 3888, the "Anti-Slamming Amendments Act." As you may be aware, we endorsed S. 1618, the version of this bill sponsored by Senator McCain, last month and we applaud the House for moving so quickly to entertain the passage of similar legislation.

AARP commends the Chairman for introducing H.R. 3888. According to the Federal Communications Commission (FCC), the practice of "slamming" is the largest source of consumer complaints in telecommunications. We believe that the provisions in your bill to amend the Communications Act of 1934 to curtail "slamming" are good for consumers.

The advent of competition in interexchange services in the 1980's brought many benefits to consumers in terms of pricing and choice. Unfortunately, it also ushered in the harmful marketing practice of "slamming." Slamming often happens in the context of high pressure and deceptive marketing telephone contacts or as part of "contests" in which participants are not fully informed that they have authorized a change in their carrier. Unfortunately, these tactics have proven successful in defrauding older Americans. Ultimately, many of these firms charge rates far higher than the major carriers, and consumers see their monthly bills skyrocket.

AARP believes that many of the provisions in H.R. 3888 will go a long way toward deterring and even eliminating these fraudulent practices by individuals and companies.

In 1997, 44,000 consumers contacted the Federal Communications Commission to complain that they had been slammed. This figure, however, pales in comparison to the over ° million residential ratepayers that AT&T reports were slammed in that same year among its own customers. Add to this the potentially large number of consumers with other primary long distance service providers who have been slammed and it becomes clear why resolution of this problem is of paramount importance to consumers.

H.R. 3888

H.R. 3888 includes a number of elements necessary to close off loopholes in the existing law that make telephone subscribers vulnerable to fraudulent or deceptive practices. I will highlight six of the key provisions.

1) Verification of Authorization Procedures—AARP endorses the verification system proposed in the Chairman's bill. At a minimum, the legislation requires a series of affirmations from the subscriber prior to verifying the switch of long distance service providers. The new carrier must ensure that the subscriber:

- acknowledges the type of service to be changed;
- affirms not only the subscriber's intent to switch but his or her authority to do so; and
- seeks agreement that the selection will mean a change in provider.

Putting these elements into practice will provide all consumers with a series of safeguards that will allow them ample opportunity to understand what the telephone exchange service provider is asking them to do. This is a significant improvement over the current system where the provider can obtain authorization by receiving a "yes" answer to a single question.

2) Prohibition on Negative Option Marketing—The preclusion of negative option marketing is a necessary step toward the elimination of slamming. Ending this onerous practice of switching subscribers due solely to the consumers failure to tell the carrier that they are not interested in changing providers is long overdue.

3) Notice to Subscriber—This important provision requires a detailed, written notice of change from the new long distance service provider to the subscriber. AARP supports the explicit legislative language which directs the telecommunications carrier to notify the consumer in writing within 15 days after the change of carrier and provides the subscriber with the opportunity to verify the date on which the change was agreed to as well as the individual who authorized the change.

4) Damages Awarded by the Commission—AARP is pleased with the provision that gives the FCC authority to award damages equal to the greater of $500 or the amount of actual damages to the aggrieved consumer. This provision is further enhanced by the clause that provides the FCC with discretion in resolving a complaint to triple the damage award.

5) Civil Penalties—The Chairman is to be applauded for including language that punishes violating carriers with severe fines for first and second offenses. AARP believes that the imposition of fines of not less than $40,000 for the first offense and not less than $150,000 for each subsequent offense, will be a substantial deterrent to violating carriers. And;

6) Anti-Cramming Language—AARP is extremely pleased by the inclusion of Section 231 in the bill. Titled "Obligations of the Telephone Billing Agents," this section addresses some of the concerns we have with "cramming." "Cramming" is the practice of adding subscription services to a consumer's bill without proper authorization to do so. In fact, the National Fraud Information Center (NFIC) recently reported that their 1-800 Hotline now receives more "cramming" complaints than "slamming" complaints. We strongly support the requirement that each consumer's bill will disclose; the name and number of the telecommunications provider, the services for which the subscriber is being charged and the charges associated with those services. Section 231 also prohibits the knowing inclusion of unauthorized telecommunications services. This language represents a giant step toward effectively dealing with this onerous practice.

AARP would like to offer a couple of suggestions, however, that would provide even stronger protection for consumers. We suggest the addition of language similar to that in Section 101 that requires the provider to notify the subscriber in writing within 15 days of activation, in specific and unambiguous language, that the subscriber is now receiving that service. Also, we strongly recommend that the change in service or services be highlighted and described in detail on a separate page for at least the initial billing statement following a change in service or services.

H.R. 3050

For the reasons stated previously, AARP supports the passage of H.R. 3888. We would be remiss, however, if we did not point out some of the concerns that remain to be addressed. We believe that some of the elements contained in H.R. 3050, introduced by Rep. Dingell, would make the Chairman's bill an even stronger guardian of consumer's rights.

While AARP agrees with the provisions in H.R. 3888 that give the FCC more authority, we are concerned about the amount of time it currently takes the Commission to resolve complaints. We are hopeful that upon passage of this legislation, the FCC will adhere to the letter of the law and improve its complaint resolution process. Because of our concern, however, we are intrigued by the provisions in Mr. Dingell's bill that authorize the Federal Trade Commission (FTC) to prescribe rules to prohibit unfair and deceptive advertisements and solicitations while giving the agency enforcement authority over the same. This allocation of new authority may help accelerate the ultimate end to the practice of "slamming."

Another element of H.R. 3050 that we would urge the Chairman to consider incorporating into his bill is the "Refund Entitlement" provision. This provision entitles consumers to a full refund for charges incurred as a result of slamming or at the very least releases a consumer from liability to a slammer for unauthorized charges for up to 90 days. Adoption of this provision in combination with the other elements of H.R. 3888 would send a strong message to all interexchange carriers and would begin to restore consumer confidence in the telecommunications industry.

Before closing, I would like to comment on one other issue that should be addressed by this Committee either now or in the very near future. That is the need to include the commercial mobile service, or wireless, providers under this legislative umbrella. As competition develops throughout the telecommunications industry and as the proportion of calls made on wireless phones increases, it is inevitable that, without similar regulation, "slamming" will become a problem in that sector of the industry as well.

Conclusion

Mr. Chairman, in conclusion, AARP welcomes your efforts to enact legislation designed to reduce and hopefully eliminate the instances of "slamming." H.R. 3888 is a well-crafted effort to accomplish that goal and we offer our support here today. We also want to compliment Rep. Dingell for introducing H.R. 3050, the attributes of which I have already discussed. AARP asks that the Committee recognize the positive elements of both pieces of legislation and take this opportunity to craft a stronger H.R. 3888. On behalf of AARP, thank you again for providing us with this forum to discuss the practice of "slamming" and to comment on the legislative proposals before you. AARP stands ready to work with you in seeking final passage of this important legislation.

In compliance with House Rule XI, clause 2(g) regarding information of public witnesses, attached is AARP's statement disclosing federal grants and contracts by source and amount received in the current and preceding two years.

Mr. TAUZIN. Thank you very much, Mr. Schultz. I do appreciate the support of you personally in this and the association.

Now we welcome Ms. Murphy, Executive VP of e.spire Communications, Annapolis, Maryland.

So, Ms. Murphy, if you will summarize your statement.

STATEMENT OF RILEY M. MURPHY, EXECUTIVE VICE PRESIDENT, E.SPIRE COMMUNICATIONS INC.

Ms. MURPHY. Thank you, Mr. Chairman and members of the committee, for this opportunity to address this very important legislation. I am appearing here today on behalf of CompTel, which is a trade association representing long-distance and local exchange carriers. My company, e.spire, is one of the fastest growing integrated providers of both——

Mr. TAUZIN. It is a new name, isn't it?

Ms. MURPHY. Yes. We changed our name in April. We are formerly American Communications Services, ACSI.

But, at any rate, we were recognized by Network World magazine as the fastest growing network company in 1997, so I am addressing you here today as a backbone network provider, and my comments are directed specifically toward the spamming provisions of this legislation.

Unfortunately, we have a great deal of experience with spamming. As a backbone provider, we provide connectivity to Internet service providers, who then have customers, some of whom may be spammers. So we are a couple of steps removed from the actual spammers.

We learned about spam the hard way. We originally provided access to our network to all comers, as we are required to do as a common carrier, including ISPs who serve spammers. We believed that, as a common carrier and not a content provider, as long as the use was legal, it wasn't our concern who used our network or for what purpose. As spammers used and abused our network, we were inundated with literally thousands of complaints from spamming victims. These were innocent end-user customers who were flooded with unsolicited e-mails. They were irate. Not only were they subjected to unwanted and often offensive e-mails, but these e-mails cost them and their ISPs a great deal of resources and time spent in reviewing, downloading and storing these voluminous messages.

Unlike junk mail where the sender pays the postage, with spam, the recipient pays for the cost of the transmission. It is like having a telemarketer reach you on your cellular phone. What is worse, the magnitude of spam and the subsequent complaints actually caused jams on our network which are already congested. In fact, as much as 30 percent of Internet traffic is spam.

To deal with the complaints we received, e.spire had to expend thousands of hours tracking down the sources. We also had to hire additional employees and consultants at a cost of about $10,000 a month. It wasn't easy, because many spammers don't want to be found. They provide fake routing information so that the backbone network provider's address is sometimes the only valid information the victims can find. This is why complaints come to companies like ours.

In the face of these complaints, we learned quickly that we needed an acceptable use policy, sometimes referred to as an AUP, which we incorporated into our contracts and quickly instituted one of the toughest standards in the business. I would like to say it was the end of our problems, but it wasn't.

In retaliation, spammers soon attacked us with the Internet equivalent of bombs. Their weapon of annihilation was spam. They actually overloaded our internal network at our company with e-mails and ultimately shut it down.

We believe we now have the problem under control. At the height of the crisis, we received hundreds of complaints per day. Today, since adoption of our AUP, we have fewer than five complaints. Although our acceptable use policy has triggered some backlash from spammers, it has increased the robustness of our network and the satisfaction of our customers.

We believe that the market has begun to provide a solution for spamming. In this light, I would like to comment more specifically on the provisions of the legislation.

H.R. 3888, as it stands, could lead to backsliding in our efforts to stop spam. We believe that the bill, if passed without the modifications we recommend, could be used by spammers to argue that spamming is legal as long as it is done pursuant to Federal guidelines. Thus, the bill reduces the control that ISPs and Internet network access providers like e.spire exercise over our networks.

It is critical that we retain control over our own networks. If unabated, huge amounts of spam can slow down or shut down backbone networks. Importantly, the bill gives each spammer at least one bite, that is B-I-T-E, one bite at the apple and possibly more if the victim simply deletes the message without opening it, as many users do, or lacks the time to open a barrage of e-mails. Moreover, H.R. 3888 improves on victims of spam the cost of performing to remove the process for each unsolicited e-mail and sending it back, which could be expensive for users who pay for Internet access by the minute.

To deal with this and other problems, we suggest a number of changes to the bill. First, it should be made absolutely clear through explicit language that ISPs and backbone providers have the right to control, through the use of private contracts, the use of their networks. This includes a right to refuse to carry junk e-mail and to disconnect spammers. At a minimum, the legislation must make clear that the backbone network providers like e.spire can control our own networks and, of course, our own policies.

Second, in light of legislative measures adopted in some States to deal about spamming, it is essential that the Federal law make it clear that it does not prevent State law in this regard.

Finally, we would suggest that spammers be limited to sending e-mails only to those with whom they have a prior relationship, so that innocent recipients are not burdened with having to respond to every unsolicited e-mail with a stop order.

Again, I appreciate the opportunity to testify today and welcome any questions. Thank you.

[The prepared statement of Riley M. Murphy follows:]

PREPARED STATEMENT OF RILEY M. MURPHY, EXECUTIVE VICE PRESIDENT FOR LEGAL AND REGULATORY AFFAIRS AND GENERAL COUNSEL FOR E.SPIRE COMMUNICATIONS, INC.

Good morning. Thank you for the opportunity to appear before you today to talk about the important slamming and spamming legislation that this subcommittee is considering. I am Riley Murphy, Executive Vice President for Legal and Regulatory Affairs, and also General Counsel, for e.spire Communications, Inc.

Formerly known as "ACSI," e.spire was formed in 1993, and seeks to be a leading facilities-based integrated communications provider ("ICP") to businesses primarily in major markets in the southern half of the United States. By the end of 1997, the Company had become one of the first competitive local exchange carriers ("CLECs") to combine the provision of dedicated, local and long distance voice services with frame relay, asynchronous transfer mode ("ATM") and Internet services. Having established this suite of telecommunications services which emphasizes data capabilities in addition to traditional CLEC offerings, the Company has evolved into an ICP. e.spire seeks to provide customers with superior service and competitive prices while offering a single source for integrated communications services designed to meet its business customers' needs. The Company's facilities-based network infrastructure is designed to provide services to customers on an end-to-end basis, and, as of March 31, 1998, was comprised of 1,314 route miles of fiber in its 32 local networks in 19 states, 44 Newbridge ATM switches, 17 Lucent 5ESS switches and approximately 22,000 backbone longhaul miles in its coast-to-coast broadband data network.

I am also here on behalf of the Competitive Telecommunications Association, better known as CompTel. CompTel has been active since 1981, advocating policies that promote the development of full and fair competition in telecommunications services. Today, CompTel's members include all types of competitive telecommunications providers, such as small and mid-sized long distance carriers (also called interexchange carriers or IXCs), competitive local exchange carriers (CLECs), wireless carriers and Internet service providers.

Let me start by saying that e.spire supports much of what H.R. 3888, the Anti-Slamming Amendments Act, seeks to accomplish in protecting consumers. Although I am prepared to discuss all aspects of H.R. 3888 and H.R. 3050, the Slamming Prevention and Consumer Protection Act of 1997, and have a few suggested changes which CompTel would like to see adopted, I would like to devote most of my testimony today to the issue of junk e-mail, better known as "spam."

In order to understand our approach to curbing spamming, it is important to understand how our service works. ISPs lease space in telecommunications network equipment—called pipe—from e.spire in order to provide access to the Internet to their end user customers. When offering wholesale Internet access, e.spire acts as a data communications provider. In other words, we move other people's data, just like a pipe moves water. We do not examine the content of this data, which is just bits of information, 1's and 0's. But when this data is spam, it can have very serious consequences. Spam fills our pipe, slows the flow of information, floods end users who mistakenly blame us, and creates a variety of very serious problems that can wipe out a network, as I will describe today.

H.R. 3888 includes provisions adopted by the Senate which were authored by Senators Murkowski and Torricelli that seek to address the very real problem of unsolicited junk e-mail. e.spire, however, has not endorsed the slamming solution proposed by H.R. 3888 because it has the potential to permit spammers the leeway to flood our network—and ultimately the end user—with unwanted and very costly junk e-mail. e.spire learned the hard way why this is such a grave problem.

I. SPAMMING

e.spire initially had no formal policy against spam, although we did contractually prohibit usage of our services that had the effect of damaging the network. Since it was not prohibited by law, and e.spire is not a regulator of content, we did not impose restrictions on the use of our network to distribute spam. In addition, as I have mentioned, as a data communications provider, e.spire acts as a common carrier, exercising no control over content.

Given our policy, perhaps it was inevitable that spam-hosting ISPs would begin to take advantage of our Internet access service. The consequences were catastrophic. In a short time, e.spire was deluged by complaints from spamming victims. We got hundreds, even thousands of e-mail complaints each day. The complaints came to us instead of the spammer because when the consumers tried to trace the route of the spam, they often could find no other addressing information except that the spam had been transmitted across our backbone. Even though e.spire was not a party to the spam in any way, the fact that it was transmitted across our backbone made it appear as though we were somehow involved. In order to respond to the wave of complaints, e.spire ordered all available data operations personnel to begin investigating spamming complaints full time. The investigations involved tracing spam to ISPs. We spent thousands of hours reviewing the complaints in an effort to preserve our good name and our network.

Here's what e.spire learned during this extensive review. First, spam is like direct mail advertising, except that the charges are reversed. For direct mail, the marketer pays the postage. But for spam, the recipient and recipient's ISP pay the "postage" costs in the form of Internet access charges that are paid for the downloading time and data storage charges incurred by the ISP. Ray Everett-Church, from the Coalition Against Unsolicited Commercial E-Mail (CAUCE), testified at a Senate hearing last week that in 1997 his business e-mail account received more than six thousand pieces of junk mail, totaling 41 megabytes of data. That's about 16 junk e-mails a day. He pays for his Internet access in increments like millions of Americans and he estimated that those unwanted e-mails cost his business hundreds of dollars. Spam is even more costly for rural Internet users, or those who travel often. Those users must pay toll charges, multiplying the cost of receiving spam. Junk e-mail is, in effect, like getting telemarketing calls on a cellular phone—you can get stuck with the charges just to tell the marketer that you don't want anything.

The cost of spam is also enormous for retail ISPs who pay millions of dollars a year and hire teams of workers just to help combat it. e.spire provides such retail ISP services through its Cybergate subsidiary. The problem is worse for small ISPs who could be put out of business by these costs. Spam not only costs consumers and ISPs money, it also harms the viability of the Internet. Spammers send thousands and thousands of e-mail messages at a time and this slows down Internet backbone speeds. Right now, I know it is a national priority to find a way to speed up the Internet. According to Senate testimony, cutting down on spam could reduce the amount of traffic on the Internet by up to one-third.

Further, ISPs pay for their backbone according to projected usage, so if their backbone capacity is swallowed up by spam, they must buy more to ensure that their legitimate customers have the capacity they need. Blasts of e-mail can overload an ISP, shutting it down altogether. Earlier this year, PacBell's Internet service was hit so hard with spam that, two days after the attack, some customers were still struggling to gain access to the service.

In stark contrast to the costs heaped on ISPs, backbone providers and consumers, the spammer gets a free ride. According to Senate testimony, a spammer can buy the hardware and software needed to generate a million spam messages a day for a hundred dollars. Databases of e-mail addresses are available for 10 dollars per million targets. You can see how, for a small investment, a spammer could overwhelm a network with unwanted messages.

Spam also harms thousands in the Internet community who participate in Usenet groups and are victims of "harvesting," a process by which spammers illicitly acquire e-mailing lists. This rampant practice undermines the security of those who seek to engage in common interest discourse through the use of Usenet groups. Unfortunately, those individuals that are most active in Usenet groups tend to be victimized by spam most often.

Spammers can also harm Usenet groups by sending unwanted e-mails directly to all Usenet members. These users occasionally fight back. Some have imposed "Usenet death penalties" and directed their ire at the backbone providers such as e.spire. One such self-appointed anti-spam patrol threatened Netcom with a Usenet death penalty. The death penalty would have prevented Netcom's half-a-million subscribers from posting messages to Usenet newsgroups. If successfully imposed, such a death threat could kill a company. For example, had Netcom been unable to provide connectivity to Usenet groups, its value as a network would have been seriously compromised. Netcom, at great cost, averted the disaster by implementing a stringent anti-spamming policy.

e.spire adopted its anti-spamming policy for much the same reason. We now have one of the industry's most stringent acceptable use policies, or AUPs. I have attached the original AUP that e.spire adopted as Attachment A hereto. All users of e.spire data and Internet access services are now prohibited by contract from using those services for the purpose of spamming. We investigate all spam complaints and our enforcement policy is "two strikes and you're out." Naturally, we have encountered substantial resistance to the policy and we pay a high price for it in terms of lost revenues from ISPs that we are forced to cut off. We have also suffered from what are fondly called "e-mail bomb attacks" by unhappy spammers. In one case, after we enforced our acceptable use policy by cutting off a spammer, the spammer retaliated by sending thousands of e-mails to e.spire's officers, ultimately crashing e.spire's internal servers. It took days to restore our internal e-mail network to its previous condition.

Although our acceptable use policy has triggered some backlash, overall it has increased the health of our network and the satisfaction of our customers. We believe that, in this case, the market has begun to provide a solution for spamming. Spammers have been forced off e.spire's and other networks. Eventually spammers will have no place left from which to blast their mail, and will have to turn to other enterprises.

Efforts to Address Spamming

We don't reject the possibility that in addition to private policies that curb slamming, legislation may also play a role. We believe, however, that the proposal embodied in H.R. 3888 may lead to undesirable unintended consequences, unless modified to allow providers to protect their networks and to clarify that state law is not preempted.

Successful, if nascent, efforts to contractually prohibit spamming could be undermined by the provisions of the bill. We believe that the bill, if passed, could be used by spammers to argue that spamming is legal as long as it is done pursuant to federal guidelines. Thus, the bill reduces the control that ISPs and Internet access providers exercise over their networks. It is critical that we retain control over our own networks. If unabated, huge amounts of spam can slow down—or shut down—our network.

While the provision in the bill that requires spammers to provide a "remove" response is designed to reduce the gross amount of spam that is flung at the network, it may not have that effect. Instead, as the network grows, increasing numbers of spammers will seek to use e-mail to distribute their unwanted messages. Right now, Internet traffic doubles every 100 days. Although H.R. 3888 provides that, once spammed, a consumer can stop the spam from that source, it is likely another spammer will come along the next day to take its place. Importantly, the bill gives each spammer at least one bite at the apple and possibly more if the victim simply deletes the message without opening it, as many users do, or lacks the time to open a barrage of e-mails. Moreover, H.R. 3888 imposes on victims of spam the cost of performing the "remove" process for each unsolicited e-mail and sending it back, which could be expensive for users who pay for Internet access by the minute.

To deal with this and other problems, we would suggest a number of changes to the bill. First, it should be made absolutely clear that ISPs and backbone providers have the right to control, through the use of private contracts, the use of our networks. This includes a right to refuse to carry junk e-mail.

Second, in light of legislative measures adopted in some states, and being considered by others to deal with spamming, it is essential that the federal law be clarified to ensure that it does not preempt anti-spamming state laws in this regard.

Finally, we would like to suggest that the Subcommittee closely examine whether spammers should be limited to sending e-mails only to those with whom they have a previous relationship, so that unwitting recipients are not burdened with having to notice every unsolicited e-mail with a stop order.

II. SLAMMING

As I mentioned earlier, in addition to our Internet services, e.spire also provides local and long distance telephone service, and is a member of CompTel, an association that has done significant work to shape policies against slamming and cramming. In an industry effort to combat slamming, this spring CompTel unveiled a set of proposals designed to maximize choice and protect telephone consumers from slamming and cramming. Specifically, CompTel advocates that all carriers accept the responsibility to prevent slamming and cramming, and to fully educate their customers, employees, and agents about these practices.

Moreover, CompTel has proposed a "*zero tolerance*" policy toward intentional slamming and cramming—whereby carriers would agree to: (1) investigate fully all allegations of slamming and cramming; (2) take appropriate action to remunerate consumers who have been victimized by any slamming or cramming; and (3) terminate any employees or agents who knowingly and willfully engage in such practices. CompTel also has called on carriers to avoid using deceptive, inappropriate or "high pressure" sales tactics, and to redouble their efforts to minimize instances of unintentional changes and pursue all appropriate remedies when slamming or cramming is attributable to the executing local carrier. The complete text of CompTel's "*Customer Choice" Principles* is attached.

CompTel and e.spire strongly support the consumer protection goals embodied in S.3888. e.spire, along with other CompTel members, does everything it can to prevent slamming. At great expense, e.spire mandates the training of all of our sales personnel by a reputable firm that verifies that all rules will be met. We have not had any complaints filed against us at the FCC. The handful of complaints against us at the local level have largely proven to be cases where a member of a household, or an employee of a business, has made a change without telling the authorized subscriber. When, after investigation, we have found this to be the case, we have settled the complaint with the subscriber without incident. Other CompTel members have had similar successes in combating slamming. Although we are working hard to realize the same goals as those reflected in H.R. 3888, we would like to point out a few areas of concern in the bill and make a few suggestions that would address these concerns—in particular, PIC freezes, liability for unintentional slamming, criminal liability, and national uniformity of the law.

Efforts to Address Slamming

First, we believe that, while PIC freezes can be an effective tool to empower consumers to prevent being slammed, they have the potential to be used in an anticompetitive way by the incumbent local carrier (ILEC) who physically performs the switch. Once a consumer agrees to a PIC freeze, it may be overly burdensome to provide the verification necessary to be allowed to switch to another carrier. In many cases, this creates too much of a hassle for consumers and they simply give up. PIC freezes also can create consumer confusion when they are marketed as a consumer protection safeguard. This kind of marketing can cast the ILEC as a regulator and obscure its role as a vendor.

Let me also mention that there is an important distinction between local and long distance PIC freezes. Right now, the regional Bells and GTE dominate the local market with 99 percent of all subscribers receiving their services. Although PIC freezes, marketed and performed by these incumbent carriers, more typically focus on reducing long distance slamming, they may also have the effect of securing the ILECs' competitive positions when they face competition in the local market. Thus, local PIC freezes could lock up almost all customers in the region to *one* company—the ILEC that performs the freeze. Thus, local freezes are likely to become a barrier to entry for local competitors. Further, as long as there is little or no competition in the local telephone market, PIC freezes for local service are premature and potentially dangerous to competition.

In order to prevent any potential abuses of the PIC freeze option, the FCC should be permitted to act to stop any *anticompetitive* use of PIC-freezes. Specifically, the FCC should adopt rules that prohibit ILECs from (1) engaging in discriminatory or otherwise anticompetitive PIC-freeze practices, and (2) using deceptive or misleading PIC freeze solicitations.

Further, H.R. 3888's PIC freeze position should be modified to clarify that, by guaranteeing the right to a PIC freeze, the bill nonetheless does not "limit the Commission's authority to prescribe the means or terms by which an exchange service provider solicits or markets such an option." This language would allow the FCC to guard against anti-competitive practices while still protecting a consumer's right to have her choice of provider frozen.

We are also concerned that the bill creates liability for unintentional slamming. H.R. 3888 could be clarified by adding a requirement of intent and knowledge to the provisions violation of which lead to penalties. The Senate recognizes this in its report on S.1618, the companion bill to H.R. 3888. The Senate report states that:

> the Commission will award damages where there is fault on the part of the carrier and will use discretion to not award or mitigate damages in cases, for example, where the complaint was a result of customer confusion, carrier error, or an unauthorized change by a carrier's unaffiliated reseller (in which case the reseller, but not the underlying carrier, may be liable for damages), an error by the local exchange carrier or interexchange carrier in keying in a change, or some other error.

These changes would ensure that the Commission and the courts could focus on punishing fraudulent carriers who seek to profit from changing a consumer's telephone provider without permission, while dispensing with complaints that have been brought in error or are unfounded.

For some of the same reasons that we are concerned about imposing civil penalties for inadvertent charges and the like, we are also concerned about the criminal provision contained in the Senate bill. Such a provision could subject to criminal liability responsible corporations who, for example, have a rogue sales agent who performs an unauthorized carrier change. Despite our best efforts to educate that employee to prevent such abuse, and our immediate termination of that employee, we could nonetheless be subjected to criminal liability. We applaud you for having the foresight to remove those provisions and hope that you will continue to maintain your position.

Finally, CompTel supports uniform federal and state verification requirements, noting that requiring providers to comply with differing requirements for interstate and intrastate services, as well as differing requirements among the states, will lead to customer confusion and increased costs of service. These increased costs of service ultimately will be borne by customers in the form of higher rates.

Thank you for the opportunity to testify here today. I would be glad to answer any questions you have.

ATTACHMENT A

Acceptable Use Policy

ACSI

This Policy represents ACSI's Acceptable Use Policy ("Policy") applicable to the customers ("CUSTOMER") of ACSI and its subsidiaries and supersedes any other written or oral Policy. Upon notice published on-line via ACSI's web page ACSI may modify the Policy, amplify the Policy, as well as discontinue or change services offered.

ACSI reserves the right to revise this Policy at any time. CUSTOMER may view the most up-to-date version of this policy at any time at www.acsi.net or www.gate.net.

By using any of the services offered by ACSI, CUSTOMER is bound by and must comply with this Policy in its entirety. Violations of the guidelines, delineated below, will result in cancellation of the CUSTOMER Policy or such other action as ACSI, in its sole discretion, may deem appropriate.

I. SYSTEM AND NETWORK SECURITY

1. CUSTOMER may not tamper with other accounts, or commit unauthorized intrusion into any part of ACSI's system, or use any of ACSI's machines, files, accounts, networks to intrude without authorization into any other system.

2. CUSTOMER may not use ACSI services not included in CUSTOMER's account, nor devise ways to circumvent security in order to access services CUSTOMER is not paying for. This clause includes, but is not limited to, the scanning of ACSI's or other networks with intent to breach and/or evaluate security.

3. CUSTOMER may not use the system in a manner that encumbers disk space, processors or other system resources beyond those allowed by the specific type of account. CUSTOMERS may not make deliberate attempts to interfere with a service, overload a service nor attempt to disable a host.

4. ACSI will react strongly to the use or attempted use of Internet services or systems without the owner's authorization. This clause includes, but is not limited to, password cracking, defrauding others into releasing their passwords, denial-of-service attacks (sending packets with an illegal packet size, UDP flooding, ping-flooding, half-open TCP connection flooding, etc.). Additionally, customers may not use programs, scripts, commands nor send messages with the intent to interfere with a user's terminal session.

II. EMAIL

1. CUSTOMER may not send unsolicited e-mail to any account that has not specifically requested such unsolicited information or that causes complaints from the recipients of such unsolicited e-mail. ACSI services should not be used to send unsolicited advertising messages to other network users. CUSTOMER may not flood/spam newsgroups with commercial or non-commercial postings.

2. CUSTOMERS may not continue to send commercial e-mail to a recipient if recipient has requested that CUSTOMER discontinue such communication.

3. ACSI prohibits the transmission of e-mail that is harassing, libelous, defamatory, legally obscene or pornographic, threatening, abusive or hateful to non-consenting recipients.

4. The forwarding or propagation of chain letters of any type (including charity requests or petitions for signatures) is impermissible.

5. "Mailbombing" (i.e. flooding a user or site with large or numerous e-mail messages) is strictly prohibited.

6. CUSTOMERS may not forge header information.

7. ACSI prohibits the use of CUSTOMER's account, or network connection, to collect replies of messages sent from any another provider that violates the rules of this Policy or those of the originating provider.

8. The rules and regulations contained within this Policy apply to other means of Internet-based transmissions, including, but not limited to Internet fax or Internet phone.

III. USENET

1. ACSI may provide CUSTOMERS with uncensored newsfeed. ACSI does not control newsgroup content nor is ACSI responsible for postings by ACSI's CUSTOMERS.

2. It is the responsibility of posters to determine a newsgroup's etiquette. Therefore, CUSTOMERS that submit content to newsgroups must refrain from posting advertisements or other messages that are not expressly permitted by a newsgroup's charter or FAQs. Posters are expected to submit messages relevant to the newsgroup's topic and agree not to submit the same message to large numbers of forums or newsgroups.

3. CUSTOMERS are prohibited from forging header information and from posting chain letters of any type.

4. CUSTOMERS may only post binary files to newsgroups designed for that purpose.

5. CUSTOMERS may not cancel nor supersede a posting of a message other than their own unless they serve as newsgroup moderators in the performance of their online responsibilities.

6. ACSI prohibits the use of CUSTOMER's account, or network connection, to collect replies of messages sent from any another provider that violates the rules of this Policy or those of the originating provider.

IV. INTERNET RELAY CHAT (IRC)

1. ACSI does not maintain an IRC server, however, CUSTOMERS may use their Internet connection to access the server of another provider. In such a case, CUSTOMER is obligated to abide by the rules set forth by that provider as well as follow proper IRC etiquette.

V. GENERAL

1. Internet connections and all other services provided to the CUSTOMER by ACSI may only be used for lawful purposes. Transmission or storage of any informa-

tion, data or material in violation of any U.S. Federal or state regulation or law is prohibited. This includes, but is not limited to, material protected by copyright, trade secret or any other statute, threatening material or obscene material. ACSI reserves the right to remove any and all materials that infringe on copyright work. Such materials may be removed at any time upon receiving a complaint and/or notice of alleged copyright infringement.

2. Certain Internet services may contain language, pictures or other content which some individuals may find offensive, inflammatory, or of an adult nature. ACSI does not endorse such materials and disclaims any and all liability for such content. Access to such materials is at CUSTOMER's own risk.

3. Use of any information obtained via ACSI is at your own risk. ACSI specifically denies any responsibility for the accuracy or quality of information obtained through its services.

4. Use of other organizations' networks or computing resources is subject to their respective permission and usage policies.

5. CUSTOMER agrees not to resell ACSI's products without the prior written consent of ACSI.

6. If ACSI cancels CUSTOMER's account for any reason, CUSTOMER agrees not to reregister without ACSI's written consent. In the event CUSTOMER reregisters without ACSI's prior written consent, ACSI will cancel CUSTOMER's account and all dues and fees paid to date regardless of whether service has been rendered will be forfeited. Additionally, any amounts owed in arrears, will be made due and payable immediately.

7. ACSI requires that CUSTOMER is qualified to contract. ACSI cannot accept payments from persons who are not at least eighteen (18) years of age. CUSTOMER will be held responsible for keeping all billing data for ACSI accurate and up to date. False data supplied for the contract between ACSI and CUSTOMER will be grounds for account termination.

8. ACSI exercises no control whatsoever over the content of the information passing through it.

9. The CUSTOMER agrees to defend, hold harmless, and expeditiously indemnify ACSI from any and all liability, claim, loss, damage or expense arising out of CUSTOMER's breach or violation of any covenant contained in this Policy, or resulting from the CUSTOMER's use of the service.

10. CUSTOMER agrees to waive and hold ACSI harmless from any claims relating to any action taken by ACSI as part of an investigation into a suspected violation of this Policy or as a result of its conclusion that a violation of this Policy has occurred. Therefore, CUSTOMER cannot sue or recover any damages whatsoever from ACSI as a result of the decision to remove material from its server, or to suspend or terminate CUSTOMER's account.

VI. POLICY ENFORCEMENT

1. When ACSI becomes aware of an alleged violation of its Acceptable Use Policy, ACSI will initiate an investigation. During the investigation the ACSI may restrict CUSTOMER's access in order to prevent further possible unauthorized activity. Depending on the severity of the violation, ACSI may, at its sole discretion, restrict, suspend, or terminate Customer's account and/or pursue other civil remedies. If such violation is a criminal offense, ACSI will notify the appropriate law enforcement department of such violation.

VII. COPYRIGHT INFRINGEMENT

1. If ACSI becomes aware of material that could be infringing on a third party's copyright, posted by CUSTOMER, it will initiate an investigation. If ACSI receives from a Complainant a claim with the applicable copyright or trademark registration number; a copy of the underlying copyrighted work along with the CUSTOMER'S materials; and, a good faith certification, signed under penalty of perjury, that the work is the property of the Complainant, that the work has been copied and that use of the work is not defensible, ACSI, in its discretion, may, at any time, deny access to the challenged material of CUSTOMER.

2. ACSI will notify CUSTOMER of the copyright infringement allegation and will allow CUSTOMER to respond to the allegation(s).

3. ACSI shall have no liability, directly or indirectly, to Complainants or third parties for CUSTOMER'S infringing copyrighted materials. CUSTOMER shall reimburse ACSI for all expenses associated with processing valid infringement allegations and defending any and all legal claims associated therewith.

IX. REPORTING NETWORK ABUSE

1. Any party seeking to report any violations of ACSI's policy may contact via e-mail: abuse@acsi.net.

Mr. TAUZIN. Thank you, Ms. Murphy.

We will now hear from Mr. Robert McDowell, Deputy General Counsel, ACTA, McLean, Virginia.

Mr. McDowell.

STATEMENT OF ROBERT M. McDOWELL, DEPUTY GENERAL COUNSEL, AMERICAN CARRIERS TELECOMMUNICATIONS ASSOCIATION

Mr. MCDOWELL. Good morning, Mr. Chairman, members of the committee. Thank you very much for having ACTA here today.

Founded in 1985, ACTA has a membership of over 230 telecommunications service providers and related vendors. The majority of ACTA's carrier members are facilities-based and not switchless resellers.

ACTA applauds those Members of Congress who are seeking a rational, market-based approach to solving the slamming problem. ACTA has been working with industry and government for several years to craft industry-driven solutions and reasonable government regulations to help solve the slamming problem. However, ACTA wants to make sure that the newly born baby named "competition" is not thrown out with the bathwater in any attempt to eradicate slamming. We must be wary not to resort to extreme measures because, after all, the best way to eliminate slamming is to have only one phone company, and I don't think anyone in this room is going to advocate that, at least not today.

Mr. TAUZIN. We have been there.

Mr. MCDOWELL. Yes. ACTA believes that slamming can be curbed while not harming competition by strengthening the twin pillars of all consumer protection policies: swift and vigorous enforcement of statutes and rules, plus the certainty of punishment through stiff fines and other penalties. Accordingly, ACTA suggests that the follow steps should be taken to curtail slamming:

First of all, clearly define slamming. The definition should include a "known or should have known" or mens rea or gross negligence element. Such a definition would eliminate a number of innocent factors that are often mistaken for slamming, such as spousal or household confusion where one family member does not tell the other that he or she switched the family phone to another long-distance company, and "fat fingers," where a carrier's data entry person inadvertently transposes the digits of a telephone number.

Second of all, written LOAs, letters of authority, or third-party verification should be the required verification methods for carriers to use. These two methods have proven to be the best antidotes against fraud.

On the other hand, as with any civil complaint, a mere allegation of slamming should not be sufficient to satisfy a complainant's burden of proof. A carrier must be faced with a preponderance of evidence that it knowingly, or with reckless disregard, switched a consumer's long-distance or local carrier. Because incumbent local exchange carriers will be both submitting carriers and executing carriers for these changes, they should be held to a higher level of scrutiny when they seek to change a subscriber to their local or long-distance networks—at a minimum, mandatory third-party verification.

Now, slammers should be forced to pay dearly and be subjected to criminal prosecution in extreme circumstances, but slammed consumers should not be absolved of all responsibility to pay any and all charges for services provided, lest Congress wishes to encourage a new form of fraud. ACTA contends that such fraud would not be perpetrated by honest consumers, of course, but by enterprising con artists exploiting a government loophole. Even though long distance rates have come down over 70 percent since the breakup of AT&T, that trend may cease if honest carriers are forced to subsidize unscrupulous members of our society. In the end, only honest consumers would be harmed by having to pay higher rates.

Slammers should also be required to pay the victimized ISP for lost revenue and the PIC change fee, while the consumer should pay his or her original carrier only for the charges that would have been owed had there been no slam.

ACTA is concerned that some proposed legislation calls for the evisceration of due process rights during administrative review of slamming complaints. ACTA wholeheartedly supports congressional efforts to streamline the complaint process at the FCC, but under the Constitution, carriers and consumers alike must have a fair and full opportunity to present their cases. ACTA firmly believes that due process rights can be preserved while protecting consumers from onerous wars of attrition against carriers. In short, the facts of some cases may call for limited discovery within a reasonable and very short period. Anything less would not survive a court appeal.

Furthermore, ACTA is concerned that proposed surety bond requirements single out resellers. Although ACTA is not opposed to the idea of some form of bonding requirement at this time, it recommends that such requirements be equitably applied to all carriers and be based on carriers' gross revenue. Proposed alternatives may possibly undermine previous congressional mandates to encourage resale and send the wrong message to the American people about the long distance and local resale community. We should all remember that WorldCom, which is poised to become the second largest long distance carrier in the country, started out as a switchless reseller. If it had been unfairly singled out as being part of an inherently suspect community, it and others like it might never have unleashed one of the greatest entrepreneurial explosions of creative brilliance ever witnessed in the American economy.

Thank you, Mr. Chairman.

[The prepared statement of Robert M. McDowell follows:]

PREPARED STATEMENT OF ROBERT M. MCDOWELL, DEPUTY GENERAL COUNSEL, AMERICA'S CARRIERS TELECOMMUNICATION ASSOCIATION

Mr. Chairman, members of the Committee, my name is Robert McDowell and I serve as Deputy General Counsel to America's Carriers Telecommunication Association also known as "ACTA." On behalf of ACTA's members, I thank you for the opportunity to speak with you on the increasingly-vexing problem of "slamming."

Founded in 1985, ACTA has a membership of over 230 telecommunications service providers and related vendors. The majority of ACTA's carrier members are facilities-based. ACTA applauds those members of Congress who are seeking a rational, market-based approach to solving the slamming problem. ACTA has been working with industry and government for several years to craft industry-driven solutions and reasonable government regulations to help solve the slamming problem. However, ACTA wants to make sure that the newly born baby named "competition," is not thrown out with the bath water in any attempt to eradicate slamming. We must be wary not to resort to extreme measures because, after all, the best way to eliminate slamming is to have only *one* phone company, and I don't think anyone here today sees merit in that idea.

ACTA believes that slamming can be curbed while not harming competition by strengthening the twin pillars of all consumer protection policies: swift and vigorous enforcement of statutes and rules plus the certainty of punishment through stiff fines and other penalties. Accordingly, ACTA suggests that the following steps should be taken to curtail the growing slamming problem:

- Clearly define slamming with a mens rea or "known or should have known" or gross negligence element. Such a definition would eliminate a number of innocent factors that are often mistaken for slamming such as spousal or household confusion where one family member does not tell the other that he/she switched the family phone to another long distance company, and "fat fingers" where a carrier's data entry person inadvertently transposes the digits of a telephone number.
- Written letters of authority ("LOAs") or third-party verification ("TPV") should be the required verification methods for carriers to use. These two methods have proven to be the best antidotes against fraud.
- On the other hand, as with any civil complaint, a mere allegation of slamming should not be sufficient to satisfy a complainant's burden of proof. A carrier must be faced with a preponderance of evidence that it knowingly, or with reckless disregard, switched a consumer's long distance carrier.
- Because incumbent local exchange carriers ("ILECs") will be both submitting carriers and executing carriers, they should be held to a higher level of scrutiny when they seek to change a subscriber to their local or long distance networks—at a minimum mandatory third-party verification.
- Slammers should be forced to pay dearly, and be subjected to criminal prosecution in extreme circumstances, but slammed consumers should not be absolved of all responsibility to pay any and all charges for services provided lest Congress wishes to encourage a new form of fraud. ACTA contends that such fraud would not be perpetrated by honest consumers, but by enterprising con artists exploiting a government loophole. Even though long distance rates have come down over 70% since the break-up of AT&T, that trend may cease if honest carriers are forced to subsidize unscrupulous members of our society. In the end, only consumers would be harmed by having to pay higher rates.
- Slammers should be required to pay the victimized IXC for lost revenue and the PIC change fee while the consumer should pay his/her original carrier only for the charges that would have been owed had there been no slam.
- Resellers should not be required to notify end-users of changes in underlying carriers as this would only confuse consumers and benefit large carriers. Furthermore, such decisions as the choice of the supplier of the underlying services should be solely that of the reseller—as it is in any other industry.
- ACTA is concerned that some proposed legislation calls for the evisceration of due process rights during administrative review of slamming complaints. ACTA wholeheartedly supports Congressional efforts to streamline the complaint process at the FCC, but under the Constitution, carriers and consumers alike must have a fair and full opportunity to present their cases. ACTA firmly believes that due process rights can be preserved while protecting consumers from onerous wars of attrition against carriers. In short, the facts of some cases may call for limited discovery within a reasonable period. Anything less would likely not survive a court appeal.
- Furthermore, ACTA is concerned that proposed surety bond requirements single out resellers. Although ACTA is not opposed to the idea of some form of bonding requirement at this time, it recommends that such requirements be equitably applied to all carriers and be based on carriers' gross revenue. Proposed alternatives may possibly undermine previous Congressional mandates to encourage resale and send the wrong message to the American people about the long distance and local resale community. We should all remember that WorldCom, which is poised to become the second-largest long distance company in the country, started out a switchless reseller. If it had been unfairly singled out as being

part of an "inherently suspect" community, it, and others like it, may never have unleashed one of the greatest entrepreneurial explosions of creative brilliance ever witnessed in America.

Mr. Chairman, members of the Committee, thank you for your time and I look forward to your questions.

Mr. TAUZIN. Those bells you heard are the signals that we are going to have a vote on the floor, so we will continue to hear our witnesses, but we may need to break in about 5 minutes.

We now welcome Mr. Cerasale, who is the Senior Vice President of Government Affairs of Direct Marketing Association.

Mr. Cerasale.

STATEMENT OF JERRY CERASALE, SENIOR VICE PRESIDENT, GOVERNMENT AFFAIRS, DIRECT MARKETING ASSOCIATION, INC.

Mr. CERASALE. Thank you, Mr. Chairman and members. It is an honor to be able to testify here today.

The DMA is focusing its testimony on unsolicited e-mail or spamming. The Direct Marketing Association represents over 3,600 companies who are direct marketers, both domestic and international, and their suppliers and support services.

The DMA believes that no method of communications for commerce should be eliminated or banned, but that doesn't mean that the DMA agrees that the current use of e-mail is appropriate for legitimate marketing. We think it is not. It should be curtailed, but it should be curtailed without eliminating the medium.

The e-mail of the future, as the medium matures, can be very different from today's fraudulent, many times fraudulent and adult-oriented offers. We can envision times of sending coupons and so forth from legitimate marketers which can meet much more customer acceptance.

One of the things that is true is that legitimate marketers want to create a long-term business relationship with its customers, and you don't do that by angering your customers. You don't do that by sending them lots of things that they don't want, or that really upset them or that cost them money; and we need time for the Internet, not just e-mail but the Internet in general, to mature before we can see the fallout of what happens. We want to make sure that government, well-intended, trying to correct problems, does not eliminate this means of communication which is growing, can change, and will improve as many legitimate marketers get into the business.

Right now, about 87 percent of our members are in electronic commerce, but very few of them are in the e-mail business. Most of our members have Web sites and so forth and are using that forum of electronic commerce, but they may very well, as e-mail grows and matures, find creative ways to use electronic mail to send to potential customers that will not anger them, that will not be fraudulent, and of course will not be fraudulent; and e-mail could then become part of the communications mix of marketers to customers or potential customers.

The DMA believes, first that all, e-mail marketers should honor the rules of the forum of the Internet service provider, that being the one that they use to send out an e-mail, and the service provider of the recipient. In that way, Internet service providers can control their costs and their capacity needs by setting up the rules of the forum that they be required to be followed.

Individual customers should have the opportunity to opt out. They can do that, as in H.R. 3888, by hitting the reply key potentially and saying, don't send me any more; and marketers should be required to honor that.

But the Direct Marketing Association believes there should be another prong to this opt-out approach, similar to the approach that it has for telephone and regular mail, known as "snail mail," that is, the Mail Preference Service and the Telephone Preference Service, which have been in existence since 1971 and 1985 respectively. Those are processes where individual consumers can put their names on a list and marketers will compare that list with their marketing list and remove the names of people who do not want to receive mail or telephone.

We believe the same should be true with electronic mail, and we are reviewing proposals right now and hope to have a contract awarded in the very near future for an e-mail preference service.

As we look at fraud, the government should increase, and is increasing, its law enforcement efforts to combat fraud on the Net; and we plan to work closely with the government to help them. Any complaints we receive or violations of law, we do now and we will continue to send to the Federal Trade Commission, the State's Attorney General and the postal inspectors. Fraud is a cancer on commerce and it should be eradicated, and we work closely to do that.

I thank you for this opportunity to testify today. We look forward to working with you and your staffs on this bill and this problem, and I am ready to answer any questions. Thank you.

[The prepared statement of Jerry Cerasale follows:]

PREPARED STATEMENT OF JERRY CERASALE, SENIOR VICE PRESIDENT, GOVERNMENT AFFAIRS, DIRECT MARKETING ASSOCIATION, INC.

Good morning, Chairman Tauzin and members of the Subcommittee. It is an honor to be asked to testify today on behalf of the Direct Marketing Association concerning unsolicited commercial e-mail, its current use and potential use in the marketplace, and the effort to keep the Internet free from fraud and abuse.

I am Jerry Cerasale, Senior Vice President, Government Affairs for the Direct Marketing Association (The DMA). The DMA represents over 3,600 corporate members who are direct marketers, both domestic and international, and their suppliers and support services.

The DMA is very interested in any regulation of electronic commerce. Fully 87 percent of DMA members are involved in some form of electronic commerce.

While most established marketers are using interactive media in the form of Internet-based sites, many of which are now conducting transactions profitably, very few at this time are using e-mail for marketing to prospective customers.

Yet the interactive marketplace is extremely dynamic. Marketers are poised to capitalize on unsolicited commercial e-mail as a communication to potential customers. While the consumer and business-to-business marketplace will undoubtedly determine the future effectiveness of this channel, our members want to preserve the freedom to test and integrate unsolicited commercial e-mail.

We strongly believe that no method of communication for commerce should be eliminated—including unsolicited e-mail.

Currently, e-mail has proven to be popular and vital for servicing current customers. With the rapid changes in communications technology, we foresee businesses that have established relationships with customers by way of other media, testing e-mail as part of the communication mix. We see possibly household American brands—names that consumers know and trust—testing e-mail as a sales, service, marketing or other information-based communication vehicle.

However, The DMA does agree that many current uses of unsolicited e-mail are not appropriate for legitimate marketing and must be curtailed. We believe that Congress should examine approaches to eliminate inappropriate uses without eliminating the medium of e-mail altogether. We can envision, for example, the use of e-mail to deliver coupons to consumers, a very different and far more positive use of e-mail than the current stream of often fraudulent and adult-oriented offers that have no other target than an e-mail address.

Marketers have been very creative in providing products that American consumers want through the traditional media of mail, telephone, and direct advertising. The DMA wants to keep the new option of electronic communication open, not eliminate it by government regulation, either domestically and internationally.

We also believe that there are market forces that discourage legitimate companies from engaging in mass unsolicited e-mailing. The direct marketing field is very customer-oriented, and legitimate companies must provide good customer service, not anger their customers. Legitimate marketers are interested in a long-term business relationship with customers, and a means of communications which angers them is not financially viable.

Direct marketing is a growing business which meets the needs of time-pressed consumers. It is also growing rapidly in the business-to-business market as businesses discover the time-saving convenience of ordering directly. The economic impact of direct marketing in the United States is $1.2 trillion annually, creating over 12 million American jobs. Direct marketing-generated e-commerce alone is likely to top $4 billion this year, and $30 billion by 2002. We're all familiar with this astonishing growth, and measure of marketplace acceptance.

Direct marketing is also growing rapidly internationally. American companies can export products without the need to build any infrastructure in foreign countries. All that is needed are a means to solicit orders, accept orders, and deliver the product. Electronic commerce is a new medium that offers companies and customers throughout the world the convenience of at-home or at-the-office shopping. Any attempt to regulate electronic commerce must be tempered by consideration for its vast potential for commercial growth, convenience to customers, and new jobs created.

Electronic commerce, of which e-mail is a part, is new. It must be allowed to mature—with all its growing pains. The government, however good its intentions, should not strangle electronic commerce at birth. There are ample means to combat fraud in existence, and there are bills in Congress now which can provide American consumers with the mechanisms to avoid unsolicited e-mail.

The DMA position on unsolicited bulk e-mail is that individuals should be able to opt out from receiving it. The DMA has established principles for marketing on-line in conjunction with the Interactive Services Association. Those principles are attached to my testimony today. One section of these principles is "Unsolicited Marketing E-Mail". The principles state:

- Solicitations posted to news groups, bulletin boards, and chat rooms must be consistent with the forum's stated policies.
- On-line e-mail solicitations should be clearly identified and should furnish a means to opt out.
- Individuals whose e-mail addresses have been collected from on-line activities should be offered a means to opt out.
- Operators of chat areas, etc., should inform individuals that any information disclosed in the chat area may result in unsolicited messages.

The DMA envisions a two-pronged opt-out program. First, however, any e-mail marketer should *abide by the "rules of the forum"* unless the marketer has an existing relationship with the addressee. Thus, the rules on e-mail established by Internet service providers, AOL, for example, would apply to all e-mails sent to an AOL address. This approach is contained in a Senate bill, S. 875, introduced by Senator Torricelli, and we have spoken with your staff, Mr. Chairman, about this approach. We understand that unsolicited e-mail can increase costs and use up server capacity. This approach gives Internet service providers some control over the use of their capacity and costs.

The first prong of any opt-out plan is that the recipient of an unsolicited bulk e-mail *should be able to request that the marketer not send any more e-mails* to that address. This could be done *via* the reply key. This is the approach taken in H.R. 3888. Consumers must also know with whom they opt-out as required in H.R. 3888. Thus, e-mail marketers must tell consumers who they are. This is also part of any legitimate marketer's program. You cannot create a long-term business-customer relationship if the potential customer does not know who you are.

The DMA is actively working on the second prong for opt-out. We are now reviewing proposals to create an "e-mail preference service" (e-MPS) and hope to announce the award of a contract in the near future. An e-MPS would allow consumers to add their e-mail addresses, on line, to a list *at no charge; marketers would then use this list to delete the addresses from their e-mail list*. This is similar to The DMA's mail and telephone preference services, which have been working in the marketplace for many years (MPS began in 1971 and TPS in 1985). This approach is also in S. 875. In addition, starting in July 1999, DMA members will be required to use e-MPS as well as MPS and TPS as a condition of membership.

With these two prongs, consumers can limit all e-mail through e-MPS or company specific e-mail through the reply key opt-out. Moreover, Internet service providers can create and then market different "rules of the forum" concerning e-mail.

This approach is far superior to banning the use of e-mail to reach prospective customers. E-mail, the Internet, and the World Wide Web are still new means of communications for most Americans. They are also ever-changing technologies. The DMA believes that these new forms of communication should be allowed to grow and mature. Prohibition of e-mail will not allow the growth of the medium. New filtering technologies, more rapid access, and new means of connection to the Internet could alter the use and efficacy of e-mail solicitations. Electronic commerce, e-mail in particular, will continue to evolve and change. A ban on the use of commercial e-mail is premature at best and may be counterproductive by "chilling" advancement of certain new technologies.

The DMA applauds the government, especially the FTC, Postal Inspectors and the state attorneys general for enhancing their efforts to combat fraud on the Internet and, specifically, in e-mail. The DMA will continue its efforts to cooperate with these law enforcement efforts. The DMA has consistently referred fraud or other violations of law found in any ethics complaint to the appropriate law enforcement agency, state or federal. Fraud should be severely punished whether made on paper, over the air waves, over phone lines, or on the Net. It is a cancer to all commerce regardless of the medium used, and it should be eradicated.

Again, I thank you for the opportunity to be here today, and I am available to answer any questions.

Mr. WHITE [presiding]. Thank you, Mr. Cerasale.

Ms. Mulligan.

STATEMENT OF DEIRDRE MULLIGAN, STAFF COUNSEL, CENTER FOR DEMOCRACY AND TECHNOLOGY

Ms. MULLIGAN. Good morning. I really am pleased with the opportunity to be here. I represent the Center for Democracy and Technology, a nonprofit civil liberties organization that works to preserve First Amendment freedoms and privacy and democratic values in this new medium.

I want to thank the Chairman, although he is absent, and Representative Markey for not only their leadership on consumer protection issues, but also their effort to set a marker in the sand on the issue of data privacy. And I want to acknowledge that we look forward to working with the subcommittee on that issue; and also to thank Representative Wynn and Representative Eshoo for their work on Internet issues in general, and encryption particularly.

Over the past few years, as many of the witnesses today have said, the Internet and particularly e-mail have brought a rapid change in our communications structure. The ability to communicate both one-to-one and one-to-mass have proven an enormous boon to our democratic values, allowing people to exchange information, ideas and cultures across the globe. Unfortunately, the ease with which this medium, particularly e-mail, facilitates communication has proven a boon to the First Amendment, but also a boon to some of the people who would choose to use this medium in a rather unscrupulous fashion.

Unsolicited commercial e-mail, known as "spam," in many areas of the Internet is causing problems, and as people have recognized today and as the Federal Trade Commission in their hearings over a year ago on this issue recognized, unsolicited commercial e-mail is a problem not just for users that find it to be a nuisance and an annoyance, but also to Internet service providers, to ISPs, to the commercial backbone providers, because this does allow people to shift costs in ways that traditional mail does not.

However, unsolicited commercial e-mail is not fax, it is not postal mail, and it is not a broadcast. I think, if anything, what the Communications Decency Act being struck down by the Supreme Court tells us is that the Internet is a new medium, and it needs to be looked at and examined carefully; and that restrictions put on speech in this medium have to be as unintrusive as possible, but meet the needed goal.

It is for this reason that we think the approach taken in H.R. 3888 and mirrored by the Senate in S. 1618 is an appropriate first step. It steers clear of many of the thorny First Amendment issues. It does not unduly burden speakers, it does not unduly burden ISPs; and the definition, while we think it needs to be tweaked a little bit to ensure that it does not prohibit anonymous, noncommercial speech, which is clearly constitutionally protected, that it is narrowly tailored to deal with the problem today, which is the use of e-mail to send uncommercial messages in a way that frustrates users' attempts to cease receiving those messages.

While we move forward in this medium, I would encourage the subcommittee to continue to study this issue. Even if H.R. 3888 became law, this is a new medium, it is an incredibly difficult medium to regulate. It is not going to be controlled by U.S. law alone; it is going to require technical applications, it is going to require self-regulation; it is going to require, probably, international cooperation.

So we look forward to working with the committee. We think this is a very reasonable and appropriate first step, and we thank you for your effort.

[The prepared statement of Deirdre Mulligan follows:]

Prepared Statement of Deirdre Mulligan, Staff Counsel, Center for Democracy and Technology

I. Introduction and Summary

The Center for Democracy and Technology (CDT) is pleased to have this opportunity to testify on the issue of unsolicited commercial email (UCE).

CDT is a non-profit, public interest organization dedicated to developing and implementing public policies to protect and advance First Amendment freedoms, individual privacy, and democratic values on the Internet. CDT is pleased that the Congress has recognized the important implications for these issues raised by the growth and prevalence of UCE.

Over the past few years, the Internet has rapidly become the cornerstone of an immense, global, multimedia communication network for culture, science and commerce. The Internet has proven wildly beneficial not only in fomenting free speech, but in facilitating the operations of the commercial marketplace as well. The first, most popular, and widely used application on the Internet is electronic mail, or email. Across the globe, email is spanning distances and cultures by easing the exchange of knowledge, information, and resources.

Unfortunately, the very popularity and efficiency of email has created several problems. The one we address today is that of unsolicited commercial email. Because of the effortlessness with which one sender can transmit a message to hundreds, thousands, or even millions of recipients, sending unsolicited commercial inducements to vast email address lists has been an irresistible temptation to some businesses.

Unlike postal mail, which is paid for piece by piece by the sender, the full cost of unsolicited commercial email is not borne by the sender. The current system of allocating the costs of moving information, including email messages, on the Internet allows the costs of sending bulk missives to be shifted from the sender to intermediaries, such as Internet service providers (ISPs), and to the recipients. While each individual email message only requires a minimal amount of Internet resources, when multiplied by the millions, such bulk messages can easily clog data pipelines and force both ISPs and recipients to spend time and resources to deal with what are frequently unwanted messages. Additionally, UCE, which can flood an individual's home or office email accounts, is viewed by many recipients as the computer equivalent of unsolicited telemarketing pitches.

However, responding to the problems caused by UCE is not simple. Not only does this very complicated issue touch upon First Amendment and privacy concerns, it also involves regulating a decentralized and global technical infrastructure. Both the frustrations of the Internet community and the complexities of addressing UCE were aired at the Federal Trade Commission's half-day workshop on UCE held last June. At its conclusion, and at the request of then-Commissioner Varney participants agreed to undertake a collaborative effort to explore possible responses to the growing problems associated with UCE.

For the past year CDT has coordinated a diverse group of organizations and businesses to explore the problems associated with UCE and identify potential solutions. Participants in this effort include representatives from all my fellow panelists organizations this morning—America Online, the Coalition Against Unsolicited Commercial Email, the Direct Marketing Association—and many others. The work of the Ad-hoc Working Group on Unsolicited Commercial Email is detailed in the report to be delivered to the Federal Trade Commission in July.

While the report of the working group is not yet public, I believe that the detailed review of legislative, technical and self-regulatory approaches to this issue and the broad recommendations of the working group will provide a useful roadmap to those seeking solutions to the problems associated with UCE.

Of course, the Senate has already taken some action by passing the amendment targeted at UCE, sponsored by Senators Murkowski and Torricelli, to the Telephone Anti-Slamming Bill, S. 1618. These amendments require creators and senders of UCE to provide accurate contact and routing information as well as permitting recipients to request removal from mailing lists. The bill empowers the Federal Trade Commission, state governments, and ISPs to enforce its provisions. This identical approach is taken in H.R. 3888, introduced by Chairman Tauzin and now pending before this committee.

CDT believes that this approach is a good first step that will reduce the problems caused by UCE. We believe the bill, unlike other approaches, steers clear of many of the thorny First Amendment issues, and does not unduly burdens speakers or ISPs. However, we do believe that the current definition of commercial email is overbroad and may unconstitutionally prohibit anonymous, non-commercial speech—clearly not the intent of its drafters.

CDT believes that, if enacted, these provisions will begin to address the problems of UCE. However, CDT believes that the impact of legislation, particularly in an environment like the Internet, must be monitored. CDT appreciates the Committee's effort to focus on this issue and encourages the Committee and Congress—whether or not the provisions of H.R. 3888 and S. 1618 become law—to monitor this issue. CDT and other members of the Ad-hoc Working Group individually, and perhaps as a group, will also be carefully monitoring the implementation of both state and federal laws. The Working group's report will be available soon. We look forward to working with you and thank you for your effort to address this important issue.

II. UCE IS A GROWING PROBLEM FOR THE INTERNET

The unique characteristics of the Internet offer the potential to greatly facilitate free speech and foment democratic values. As the recent Supreme Court decision Reno v. ACLU recognized, the Internet offers new opportunities to maximize individuals' ability to choose the opinions and ideas worthy of attention and adherence. However, the aspects of email that make it a boon to organizers, advocates and others seeking to spread their message and make common cause also enable individuals and corporations to nearly effortlessly send unsolicited commercial messages by the hundreds of thousands into email in-boxes across the globe.

In an ironic twist, the flood of this particular form of speech—unsolicited commercial messages—has effectively chilled other speech in several significant ways. The unbridled use of email by commercial entities to send unsolicited messages, and pass along the cost of those messages, to end users may undermine the very First

Amendment values that enable UCE. Sobering evidence is provided by Usenet news groups "ongoing email discussions on specific topics—where discussion once flourished, but have grown silent due to the influx of UCE and the harvesting of participants' email addresses.

The speech of some commercial entities has been chilled as well. Several companies have called CDT seeking assistance in communicating with customers who have actively requested to be contacted via email. Other businesses have refrained from using email at all because in the current environment it is viewed by the majority of email users as a bad business practice. Aware of the pervasive negative feelings toward UCE, companies are anxious to ensure that recipients of their requested messages can distinguish them from UCE.

In response to abuses of their email system, some ISPs have set terms of service agreements that go beyond limiting UCE and set rules more broadly to limit or prohibit unsolicited bulk messages regardless of their content. As a result, individuals engaged in non-commercial speech have been cut off by ISPs.

Because of its cost-shifting nature, UCE places a burden on those who transmit and receive it. For users, UCE inappropriately imposes costs in the form of connection time and server and disk storage space, not to mention the time wasted identifying and deleting unwanted messages. Increased costs for ISPs are similar. Soft costs include the expense of network bandwidth and processing email. Hard costs encompass additional staff and storage demands. Additional costs and damage results from messages with inaccurate routing and sender information. These costs are not nominal. Estimates of the volume of email have been as high as 30% of total email volume, costing ISPs and users real dollars each month.

UCE is unfairly shifting costs onto ISPs and recipients, chilling some users' speech, and undermining the viability of email itself.

III. THE RESPONSE SHOULD BE TAILORED

The cost to Internet users, Internet service providers and the burden on the network as a whole has placed the issue of UCE on the agendas of Internet users, ISPs and, most recently, policy-makers.

Informal estimates indicate that today roughly half of unsolicited commercial email messages contain fraudulent or deceptive content. Fortunately, there are already laws on the books to combat fraud, regardless of whether it is conducted through the mail, over the phone, or on the Internet. However, regulating unsolicited commercial email messages that provide accurate information is a more complex issue. On the one hand such messages are truthful speech entitled to certain First Amendment protections. On the other hand, the government does have a substantial interest in reducing the harms associated with this form of commercial speech.

Acknowledging the real costs and privacy considerations raised by UCE, we must be cautious in regulating commercial speech in this new medium. It is, of course, important to note that although commercial speech may be regulated by the government, such speech still maintains substantial First Amendment protection. In addition, the Constitution requires that we consider the potential chilling effects and increased burdens on non-commercial speech posed by any such regulation.

Care and deliberation is appropriate not solely because of the potential impact on speech, but also due to the evolving nature of email and its uses. The impact of regulation in the decentralized and global medium of the Internet is unclear. The implementation of any regulation on speech in this medium must be carefully monitored and assessed. The ultimate results must be reviewed in light of the goal. Will efforts to regulate unsolicited commercial email messages be successful and lead to increased control by users and Internet Service providers over UCE—lowering and eliminating costs and allowing users to avoid unwanted messages? Or will it unintentionally invite more commercial actors to partake in sending UCE, encouraging what it was meant to reduce by leading to larger numbers of UCE messages and an increase drain on Internet resources? These answers and others equally important are as yet unknown.

The issue and the solutions ultimately chosen to address UCE, touch on core civil liberties concerns and have ramifications for the future of the Internet. An improper policy or technical resolution to the UCE issue could have a negative impact on online free speech and individual privacy, or have unintended consequences for the Internet. While the stakes are high, the current situation is intolerable to many. Precisely because the impact of legislation in this dynamic and evolving medium is difficult to predict, CDT is pleased that thus far Congress has chosen to tread carefully and narrowly in this area.

IV. LOOKING TOWARD POSSIBLE SOLUTIONS

At the conclusion of the Federal Trade Commission's June 1997 session on Unsolicited Commercial Email (part of a three day Workshop on Consumer Privacy), then-Commissioner Varney urged participants to undertake a collaborative effort to identify workable solutions to the problems arising from UCE. Over the past year, CDT has shepherded an open process, the Ad-hoc Working Group on Unsolicited Commercial Email—to explore the problems associated with UCE and identify potential solutions. Participants in the FTC's workshop, joined by other interested parties, have explored the issue of UCE, reviewed proposals, and identified a range of potential solutions.

In July the group will deliver its report to the Federal Trade Commission and make it publicly available. The report documents the progress, findings and recommended first steps to address UCE of the Ad-hoc Working Group on Unsolicited Commercial Email. The goal of the group and the report is twofold: to provide a factual basis for efforts to address UCE; and, set forth initial recommended actions, established through rough consensus of the group, that should be taken to address UCE. We look forward to sharing the report with the Sub-committee and to continuing this dialogue.

As a convener and primary drafter of this report, CDT will defer a discussion of the general issues until the final report is released. However, we will put forth three guidelines which should inform the framework of any legislative response to the harms of UCE. We have found that there is a widespread consensus to:

a) maximize individual email users' control over the information that enters their inbox;
b) ensure that costs are not imposed unfairly upon end users, and Internet service providers; and
c) increase enforcement of existing FTC regulations, and state laws, regarding unfair, deceptive and misleading commercial statements in a way that protects the First Amendment right to free speech.

These guidelines are broad and permit substantial flexibility in crafting legislative proposals with regard to UCE.

V. A GOOD FIRST STEP

CDT believes the approach taken by Chairman Tauzin in H.R. 3888 are an appropriate first step toward addressing the problems associated with unsolicited commercial email.

H.R. 3888 requires those who send UCE to:

- identify themselves and provide accurate contact information within the body of their email message;
- provide accurate routing information; and
- stop sending email messages upon the request of a recipient.

The bill also gives several different parties the right to bring legal action against the senders of unsolicited commercial email. Those parties include:

- The Federal Trade Commission, which may fine anyone who violates the law up to $15,000, and may seek an injunction that prohibits the violator from sending more UCE;
- State Attorneys General, who may bring lawsuits on behalf of the residents of their state to get an injunction against the transmission of more unsolicited commercial email, force the sender to comply with the law, and obtain damages and 'other appropriate relief' from the sender for the harm it caused by sending unwanted commercial email; and
- Internet Service Providers who have been harmed by people who use their services to send UCE may also bring a lawsuit to get an injunction and to obtain damages and other appropriate relief. ISPs may be awarded up to $15,000 for each violation of the law through the use of their service. The court may also force the violator to pay the ISP's attorney fees, as long as they are reasonable, and court costs. By allowing the courts to shift the cost of a successful lawsuit off ISPs, and onto the shoulders of the UCE senders themselves, the bill may encourage more ISPs to pursue senders of UCE.

The bill gives the FTC, the State Attorneys General and the Internet service providers the power to enforce the law's provisions. The bill also retains the states' abilities to enact additional legislation or to employ existing consumer protection laws to address unsolicited commercial email.

It is important that the scope of any attempt to reduce unwanted or abusive uses of email be carefully limited in order to prevent unconstitutional and unnecessary (for at this time UCE is the source of problems) limitations on speech. Indeed, any overly broad legislation might ultimately destroy email's usefulness in a misguided attempt to save it.

H.R. 3888 attempts to avoid this conundrum by specifically limiting the scope of the bill to electronic mail that contains advertisements or solicitations. It also provides exceptions for email sent at the request of the recipient or for email sent within the context of an ongoing business relationship.

CDT believes therefore, that the basic thrust and scope of H.R. 3888 moves in the right direction. However, we are concerned that the specific definition used is overly broad, and could unconstitutionally restrict email messages that contain a solicitation but who's primary purpose is not commercial. (For example many non-profits and individuals have solicitations or pitches in their email signature. The signature file may request donations, advertise services, or hawk a product—but the core message of the email may be clearly non-commercial.) One of the central impositions of this bill is that it requires those who create and send UCE to provide accurate contact information. If this requirement were applied to messages whose primary purpose is political or personal, but contain a solicitation or advertisement, it would be in conflict with the general freedom to publish anonymously recently affirmed by the Supreme Court. (McIntyre v. Ohio Elections Comm'n)

It is critical that legislation aimed at UCE steer clear of regulating other forms of speech. Unlike commercial speech which can be subjected to disclosure requirements like those in H.R. 3888—contact information—under existing legal precedents, such requirements on speakers of literary and political messages (and potentially others) have been rejected by the Supreme Court. (See, Talley; McIntyre)

We have a long tradition of both publishing anonymously and defending the right to do so. In the context of politics, political movements, and organizing, anonymity has played a critically important role enabling unpopular views and controversial opinions to be espoused and judged on their merits without placing the speaker in harms way.

To ameliorate our concerns, we suggest that the statute incorporate the legal definition of commercial speech as articulated through Supreme Court cases:

> Unsolicited Commercial Electronic Mail Message—The term "unsolicited commercial electronic mail message" means any electronic mail message whose primary purpose is to propose a commercial transaction, not including messages sent by persons to others with whom they have a prior relationship.

CDT also notes that H.R. 3888 must be narrowly interpreted in order to conform with recent Supreme Court cases regarding commercial speech. Certainly the State is asserting a substantial interest by protecting the free speech enhancing value of the Internet. However, it is important that the means chosen are in proportion to that interest, and are carefully drafted to achieve their goal.

One of the most important qualities of the Internet is that the barriers to entry are extremely low. As a means of communicating cheaply to a broad audience, the Internet, specifically email, is unsurpassed in economic efficiency. The Supreme Court recognized this fact implicitly in Reno v. ACLU, in which the Court was very concerned with the burdens imposed on speakers by the Communications Decency Act.

CDT believes that H.R. 3888 is a first step towards addressing the problems associated with UCE. The requirements for the creators and senders of UCE are limited to those that will directly aide Internet Service Providers and users in filtering out unwanted messages, limiting the damage caused by bounced messages, and allowing users to prohibit future advertisements and solicitations from annoying them. No burden is placed on the ISPs, nor do individual speakers bear excessive costs. Most importantly, with our suggested change to the definition, we believe that H.R. 3888 will narrowly focus on UCE and steer clear of regulating other forms of speech.

VI. WHAT SHOULD CONGRESS DO NEXT?

While it is unclear whether H.R. 3888 will on its own prove to be the silver bullet, we believe that if enacted into law it would reduce the number of unsolicited commercial email messages. Some anti-UCE activists believe that the only way to combat UCE is for Congress to enact a ban. However, in light of recent Supreme Court decisions on commercial speech, it is questionable whether such a ban would withstand a legal challenge. More importantly, CDT believes that the approach taken in H.R. 3888 will reduce UCE without banning any form of speech. If the history of UCE and its practitioners behavior tells us anything, it tells us that senders choose to conceal their identity and to frustrate the ability of users to quickly, easily and automatically respond. Why? Because if recipients can respond history tells us that they do so quickly, forcefully, and with a fairly resounding "NO more UCE."

The most telling example of the potential power of the tailored regulations contained in H.R. 3888 come from the infamous Internet tale of Canter & Siegel. Martha Siegel and Laurence Canter in one journalists words, "have the distinction of being the most detested husband-and-wife team in the history of the Internet. And we are talking global hatred... true internationalism." ("A Net.conspiracy so immense: Chatting with Martha Siegel of the Internet's Infamous Canter & Siegel," K.K. Campbell) Canter & Siegel, immigration attorneys, sent an unsolicited message advertising a service to nearly 6,000 Usenet newsgroups. Unlike many of today's "spammers" Canter & Siegel's return email address appeared on the message. Within hours their Internet service provider was bombarded with angry messages. According to reports the ISP's system crashed numerous times and Canter & Siegel's account was canceled. As known "spammers" Canter & Siegel, like Sanford Wallace after them, discovered that its difficult to find an Internet Service Provider. When Netcom found that Canter & Siegel had opened an account with them they quickly canceled it stating that, "Our position is that NETCOM can be compared to a public restaurant where a customer may be refused service if the customer is not wearing shoes. for the health of the other customers and the good of the restaurant, that customer may be turned away. NETCOM believes that being a responsible provider entails refusing service to customers who would endanger the health of the community."

The story of Canter & Siegel, the recent alleged conversion of Sanford Wallace, other anecdotal stories of uninformed "spammers" experiences with angry recipients, and the high number of "spammers" who disguise their identity and the message origin, suggests that a little light on the subject—and the sender—may go a long way toward reducing UCE.

CDT believes that if UCE is identified with a sender and can be easily responded to that a likely impact will be a reduction in UCE as senders are forced to bear the costs of receiving responses, removing individuals from their lists, and handling the angry messages of millions of disgruntled email users whose efforts to be heard have been frustrated for years.

Wisely, H.R. 3888 does not preclude states from passing additional legislation to reduce UCE. Many states have already begun to take such action. A wide variety of pending legislation at the state level indicates that a diversity of approaches are emerging to respond to this problem. Congress should continue to allow states to experiment with alternative legislative schemes if they feel it is necessary and Congress should monitor the effectiveness of such action.

On example of state action is legislation passed by the state of Washington in March, which recently went into effect. The language of the Washington legislation is very similar to that of H.R. 3888. Of course, like H.R. 3888 such legislation will not directly eliminate UCE. However, as Washington State Attorney General Christine Gregoire said, "This is not a perfect law, but it will start a process for changing the behavior of those who use the Internet to market their products and services."

It is the same here. While it may not solve all of the problems associated with UCE, we believe H.R. 3888 is a first step worth taking and that as Justice Brandeis said, "sunlight is often the best disinfectant."

For these reasons CDT suggests that Congress continue to monitor this issue. We will provide you with the report of the Ad-hoc Working Group as soon as possible. CDT looks forward to working with the Senate and House as they move forward on this issue. Thank you for the opportunity to share our views with the Sub-committee.

Mr. WHITE. Thank you, Ms. Mulligan.

Our next speaker is Ms. Grant. I will remember to push the button for Ms. Grant, I didn't for Ms. Mulligan. So she probably shortened her testimony.

STATEMENT OF SUSAN GRANT, VICE PRESIDENT FOR PUBLIC POLICY, NATIONAL CONSUMERS LEAGUE

Ms. GRANT. Thank you for asking the National Consumers League, the oldest nonprofit consumer organization in the United States, to talk about the epidemic of slamming.

Our National Fraud Information Center, which is a hotline for consumers to call to get advice about telemarketing solicitations and to report fraud, has received more complaints about slamming so far in 1998 than in all of 1997. But we know that what we are hearing about is just the tip of the iceberg, and in fact, the best figures for the epidemic of slamming is from the local phone companies themselves who are the gatekeepers of the system. Just in 1997, Ameritech, for instance, in the five States that it covers, had over 115,000 slamming complaints and tells me that the problem is continuing to increase.

I want to focus my remarks on what I think needs to be done to give consumers back control over their telephone service, which is the problem here. So these are our suggestions for slamming the door on slamming.

Banning negative option sales of phone service is contained in both the bills that you are discussing today, and we certainly think that that is a good move. Those are abused because consumers receive them, thinking that they are just promotions for phone service and toss them, without realizing that they need to do something affirmatively in order to prevent their phone service from being switched.

We also think that contests should be banned in connection with sales of phone service. That is not reflected in either of the bills yet, but it is one of the largest areas of abuse that we see, and we don't think that people should play games of chance when it comes to their phone service.

We also think that it is really important for consumers to get immediate notice when their phone service has changed, and by "immediate," we mean within 3 to 5 days of the change being effected.

We also think that that notification should come from the local exchange as the gatekeeper, the one that actually effects the change, and not from the slammer. We don't think that we can rely on these fraudulent companies to send consumers the notice that they need to realize that their phone service has been switched. What we found from a survey that we have conducted is that most consumers don't realize that they have been slammed until they get their phone bill with exorbitant charges on it.

We also think that we need to improve the PIC freeze system. That is the option that consumers can choose to say to their local exchange, don't change my phone service from one company to another unless you hear from me directly saying that that is okay.

We know that there are two problems with the PIC freeze presently. One is that if the consumer is slammed by the reseller of the consumer's original carrier, it seems that, at least in some cases, PIC freeze protection is not triggered because the system doesn't recognize that there has been a change; the service is still being provided by the same underlying carrier.

The other concern that we have is a decision in the State of Michigan by the Public Utilities Commission that seems to put the PIC freeze system in peril, which essentially says that if the telephone carrier has followed one of the FCC's prescribed methods for verification and that carrier requests the change through the local exchange, the local exchange has to make the change, even if the customer has a PIC freeze and the customer has not contacted the local exchange directly. We are very concerned about this, because in attempting to give consumers back control over their telephones, it seems as though that PIC freeze is the best way to do that, and yet it is not necessarily a given that that is going to be there to protect consumers.

We think that one of the most important things that Congress could do to reduce incidents of slamming is to take away the economic incentive by giving consumers the right to refuse to pay slamming charges, just the same as they have the right to refuse to pay unauthorized 900 number charges, for instance. We think that this would not only reduce the incentive to slam, but it would relieve consumers of a terrible hassle when they are slammed, it is really only the beginning of their problem. We don't think that consumers should have to get their bills recalculated in order to pay either the slammer or their original carrier what the call should have cost.

We also think that consumers' complaints have to be handled much more expeditiously, and one of the keys of doing that is having information on the phone bill about who the service provider is, as well as who the billing aggregator is, if there is one.

If I can just make a brief comment about the time periods that are in one of the bills for dealing with consumers' complaints, I think that 120 days is far too long for a carrier to resolve a consumer slamming complaint, and that 150 days for the FCC to take action is also too long. That adds up, if my math is right, to 9 months. You could have had a baby in that time, and I really think that carriers should resolve consumers' complaints in no more than 30 days, and that the FCC perhaps should have longer, 60 or 90 days to take action.

Another thing that I want to point out to the committee is the important role that States play in fighting slamming. They are often more easily able to act quickly than the Federal Government, and for that reason, I am concerned that there should be no preemption for either intrastate or interstate service in terms of the States' abilities to protect their consumers.

Finally, we certainly do approve of schemes to provide additional penalties to slam the slammers. Thank you very much.

[The prepared statement of Susan Grant follows:]

PREPARED STATEMENT OF SUSAN GRANT, VICE PRESIDENT FOR PUBLIC POLICY, NATIONAL CONSUMERS LEAGUE

The National Consumers League appreciates the opportunity to comment on the rising problem of "slamming," the unauthorized switching of consumers' telephone carriers. NCL is a private, nonprofit organization that has represented consumers in the marketplace and the workplace since its founding in 1899.

NCL'S ROLE IN FIGHTING TELEPHONE-RELATED FRAUD AND ABUSE

NCL has taken an active role in educating consumers and advocating for appropriate consumer protections concerning telephone-related fraud and abuse. In 1992, NCL created the National Fraud Information Center, a unique hotline service, 1-800-876-7060, which consumers can call for advice about telephone solicitations and report possible fraud and deception. The NFIC's services were expanded in 1996 with the launch of its web site, http://www.fraud.org, through which consumers can make inquiries and report fraud. With the advent of scams in cyberspace, the NFIC now also offers advice about and takes reports of fraud perpetrated through online services and the Internet. Consumers can report telephone-related fraud to the NFIC by calling its toll-free hotline, using its online reporting form, by e-mail, or by writing.

Consumers' fraud reports are uploaded daily by the NFIC to the data base maintained by the Federal Trade Commission and the National Association of Attorneys

General. The NFIC also relays selected fraud reports to over 160 individual federal, state and local law enforcement agencies, including the FCC.

NCL also coordinates the Alliance Against Fraud in Telemarketing, which is comprised of representatives from consumer groups, law enforcement and regulatory agencies, trade associations, telephone carriers, credit card companies, and other business interests. The AAFT conducts meetings and produces materials designed to educate its members and the public about telephone-related fraud, including unauthorized or misrepresented carrier switching. In addition, NCL works with the media, and in partnership with other groups, to raise public awareness about the benefits of telephone competition and deceptive practices of which to be wary.

COMPLAINTS ABOUT CARRIER SWITCHING REPORTED TO THE NFIC

Increasing Number of Complaints

NFIC has seen an alarming increase in carrier switching complaints. By the end of 1997 we had received 807 reports about carrier switching, making it the 5th most frequent subject of fraud reports made to the NFIC last year. In just the first five months of 1998, we have already received 825 slamming reports, elevating its ranking to the #2 fraud. Cramming, another telephone-service related fraud, is currently #1.

However, we know that what we are hearing is just the "tip of the iceberg." A Louis Harris & Associates survey commissioned by the League to look at the affects of telephone competition in three Midwest markets, Chicago, Detroit/Grand Rapids, and Milwaukee, revealed that nearly one-third of the respondents had been slammed themselves or knew someone who had. Only 7 percent complained to a government agency, 2 percent to a group such as ours. Most consumers complained to the slammer, the original carrier, or the local exchange carrier.

Nature of Carrier Switching Complaints

In analyzing the slamming reports we received in 1997, we found that only a small number of the carrier switching reports made to the NFIC, less than 10 percent, are from consumers who agreed to switch their service based on alleged false promises of lower rates or other incentives that were never delivered. Most of those incidents involved major, well-known carriers.

However, in the vast majority of the reports made to the NFIC, consumers complained that they never authorized their service to be switched. Most of the complaints concern long-distance service, but some consumers also reported unauthorized switching of local telephone service in areas where competition now exists. Complaints about unauthorized service switching were made against dozens of different companies, most of them resellers of telephone service. Many consumers noted that they'd never even heard of these companies until the names appeared on their phone bills. In fact, the Harris survey showed that 80 percent of the respondents with slamming experience discovered the problem when they received their bills.

Some consumers are mystified by how their service was switched, since they contend that they never had any conversation or other contact with the companies. In other cases, consumers said that they believed they were switched as a result of:

- receiving calls from companies claiming to be their regular carriers, or to be affiliated with their regular carriers, offering to consolidate their billings;
- signing up to receive coupons for products such as cigarettes;
- being offered discount plans by companies falsely claiming to be their regular carriers;
- entering car raffles or other contests at malls, county fairs, etc.;
- someone in the household who was not the account holder signing a promotional form;
- a minor in the household calling a pay-per-call number;
- receiving a call from someone supposedly conducting a survey;
- using a calling card to make calls from a hotel phone.

The creativity of slammers is boundless. In one case, the consumer said that he was contacted by someone who told him that he had reached his credit limit with his regular carrier and had to switch to another in order to keep making long distance calls. More than one consumer reported service being switched after someone who was purportedly from the FCC called to notify them about "new telephone regulations." In one especially inventive scam, the consumer was lured to calling a number in response to an advertisement for doing telemarketing work at home. He later received a notice that his service was switched and that, in addition to his calling charges, he would be assessed a $10 monthly fee for "tracking" his work. We have also received a few reports recently from consumers who say that they have been contacted by companies claiming to have purchased their old debts, unrelated to phone services, and threatening to proceed with collection unless they switch their phone service to those companies.

Consumers report being slammed multiple times—one man was slammed by the same company seven times. Some also report being billed by the unauthorized carrier for other unwanted services, such as voice mail and paging. Most consumers were unaware that their service had been switched until they received their bills, and some did not realize it until several billing periods had transpired. Even after they thought that they had resolved the problem and gone back to their original carriers, they were slammed again.

Difficulty Reaching the "Slammer"

Consumers report having difficulty reaching the companies to which they have been switched. Either there is no answer at the company's number, or the consumer simply gets a recording, or the company hangs up on the caller. Often the company name;and number on the bill is that of a billing agent who may be acting on behalf of several different carriers. Even the local telephone companies cannot tell consumers the names of the carriers or how to reach them, making resolving complaints and reporting slamming incidents to law enforcement difficult.

Problems with Proof of Authorization

When consumers question the authorization for switching, the proof that is offered is often fabricated. For instance, consumers report that:

- the signature on a written authorization form was forged;
- the claim that someone else at their business authorized the switch was false;
- on the date that the company said the switch was authorized, the consumer did not even have service at that number;
- the switch was purportedly authorized by someone who was deceased;
- the taped authorization was not the voice of the account holder;
- if they agreed to switch initially and then canceled, they were switched again without their permission and the original agreement was presented as authorization;
- the taped response to a so-called survey was presented as authorization;
- the person from whom authorization was obtained was not the account holder;
- the consumer received a "negative-option" notice of switching but did not understand that failure to respond constituted authorization.

Sometimes the companies simply refuse to produce any documentation of authorization.

Difficulty Resolving Billing Disputes

In addition to being charged exorbitant amounts, consumers have reported to the NFIC that they were charged for the same time period by more than one company, that they had difficulty getting adjustments for overcharges, and that they were threatened with collection or loss of telephone service for refusal to pay disputed charges. If they already paid the charges, they could not get refunds.

Consumers have also complained about inability to be reinstated in special calling plans or programs by their original carriers, and losing other premiums as a result of unauthorized service switching. In some cases, they also have difficulty getting switched back to their original carriers, and are required to pay switching fees, even though the FCC rules provide that they should be able to switch back at no charge. Furthermore, many consumers do not know that they have the right to pay only the amount that their original carriers would have charged.

In our Louis Harris survey, 80 percent of the respondents said that their slamming problems were resolved, but a third described the process as very difficult or somewhat difficult. Twenty-six percent said it was somewhat easy, while another third said it was very easy.

Victims of slamming are outraged and frustrated. People rely on their home and business telephone service and they feel strongly that their right to choose their carriers should be protected. They do not believe that they should have to spend their time and energy going around in what often seems like endless circles to resolve problems that are not of their making.

SUGGESTIONS FOR FIGHTING SLAMMING

Verification

Based on the consumer complaints that the NFIC has received, it is clear that there are problems with each of the present verification procedures. In light of this and in anticipation of even more competitive pressure as the market for telephone services expands, we believe that stronger measures are needed. In comments we have filed with the Federal Communications Commission we said that the "negative option" notice of carrier switching should be banned. Consumers fail to grasp the fact that this is not just another solicitation.

We also believe that contest entry forms should be banned as a means of promoting telephone services.

We also told the FCC that the same verification procedures should be required no matter whether the initial contact with the consumer was an in-bound or outbound call. We are aware of instances in which unauthorized carrier switching resulted from calls that consumers made, and we believe that protection is just as necessary in that case as with inbound calls.

Notice of Carrier Change

Notice separate from the bill should be sent to the consumers by the billing agent immediately after a carrier change has been processed. The slammer cannot be relied on to provide this notice.

Carrier Freezes

Carrier freezes give consumers the choice of having added protection in regard to their desired phone service. We believe that the option to freeze one's service, local and long-distance, should be freely promoted, as long as it is described fairly and accurately. Consumers' carrier freeze requests must be honored and strong penalties levied on companies that fail to do so. Legislation should clarify that if a carrier claims to follow one of the FCC's prescribed verification procedures, it does not negate the fact that a consumer requested PIC freeze protection and that the service cannot be changed until and unless that consumer has directly notified the local phone company of the desired change in service. The PIC freeze system must also be improved so that it works even when the slammer is a reseller of the original carrier.

Liability for Payment

None of this is enough, however. We believe that the most effective way to deter slamming is to prevent companies that change consumers' service without authorization from being able to reap the financial reward for doing so.

PAYMENT OBLIGATIONS

To remove the economic incentive to slam and help the innocent victims of this crime, Congress should provide that consumers have no obligation to pay any charges assessed by unauthorized carriers. Furthermore, they should be refunded any payments they have made to companies who slammed them. Consumers should not be obliged to have their bills recalculated to what their original carriers would have charged—they should simply have no liability for unauthorized charges.

Dispute Resolution

Thirty days is adequate time for carriers and their billing service providers to resolve consumers' slamming complaints. The name, addresses and phone numbers of the carriers and the billing service providers, if any, should appear on the bills, along with instructions for questions and complaints. If satisfactory authorization cannot be shown and the consumer continues to dispute the charges, they should be removed from the bill and the carrier that assessed them can pursue the matter through collection or other lawful means. The FCC should have no more than 90 days to resolve slamming complaints.

State Action

States can generally act more quickly to stop illegal practices and obtain redress for their constituents. Congress should not preempt states from pursuing intrastate or interstate carrier switching abuses. We support provisions to allow states to help enforce federal antislamming rules while at the same time being able to use state procedures where appropriate.

Increased Penalties

We also support increased penalties for slamming. Private rights of action may be useful for class action suits, but state and federal agencies should also be able to seek restitution and punitive damages.

CONCLUSION

Finally, as our Harris survey shows, consumers are barraged by telephone, mail and advertising solicitations for telecommunications products and services. They need more objective information about their choices and education about their rights.

The problem of slamming has reached critical proportions. If adequate action is not taken to curb it, the marketplace for local and long distance telecommunications services will be a quagmire instead of the cornucopia that was envisioned as a result of increased competition. We look forward to working with the Congress and others to ensure that the telecommunications marketplace is fair and offers the benefits that consumers expect and deserve.

Mr. TAUZIN. Thank you very much, Ms. Grant.

Finally, Ms. Barbara Dooley, Executive Director of the Commercial Internet Exchange Association.

Ms. Dooley.

STATEMENT OF BARBARA A. DOOLEY, EXECUTIVE DIRECTOR, COMMERCIAL INTERNET EXCHANGE

Ms. DOOLEY. Good morning, Mr. Chairman and members of the subcommittee. Thank you for inviting me to testify this morning on Title III of H.R. 3888, introduced by Chairman Tauzin.

CIX is the oldest international trade association of Internet service providers in the world. Our members range in size from companies like UUNet, PSINet, IBM, AT&T, ATT and Bell Atlantic to national and regional providers in the U.S. and around the world.

We are grateful that you have sought the views of ISPs in public hearings before marking up legislation on this important subject that has stimulated so much emotional debate within the Internet community.

The last few years have witnessed a rapid growth in the volume of unsolicited bulk commercial electronic mail, UCE, commonly referred to as "spam" or "junk e-mail." Last week before the Senate one service provider estimated that about 30 percent of its e-mail consists of these unwanted e-mail messages. Some of this UCE consists of sexually oriented advertisements. Much of it also consists of misleading, deceptive or outright fraudulent advertising.

UCE is, first and foremost, a network integrity issue, though it also concerns protection of free speech. Often overlooked in this debate is the growing number of small home or office businesses built on e-mail or the Internet whose revenues literally depend on using the Internet to communicate with their customers.

To determine the severity of the UCE problem, CIX and the Internet Law and Policy Forum, a respected, not-for-profit legal and research body, recently undertook a worldwide survey of ISPs, including U.S. service providers, on this issue. We are still analyzing survey results, but our preliminary data results of U.S. ISPs show the following:

Ninety-four percent report that their customers are irritated with the practice; 79.5 percent say that UCE slows system performance; 33.7 percent say that it causes system crashes; 58.5 percent report that they must deal with it daily or more frequently; 28 percent say they must deal with it weekly; 27.7 report they have witnessed 100 percent or more growth in UCE; and 15.7 percent report growth of 50 to 99 percent in UCE traffic.

The alarming result is that 28 percent of reporting ISPs state they are losing revenue from this practice. Many of the thousands of ISPs are small- or medium-sized businesses. They make little or

49-326 98 - 3

no profit to date, and to them, UCE is literally a life-or-death matter.

UCE affects other network providers besides CIX's members and the 6,500 or so commercial U.S. service providers. It afflicts literally hundreds of thousands of private network providers, like schools and libraries, corporations, hospitals, even the House of Representative's e-mail systems.

ISPs employ a number of weapons against spammers. Technological weapons include filters, terms of service agreements, interprovider agreements, and legal action against abusers.

The CIX supports vigorous enforcement of existing consumer protection laws by the FTC and State attorneys general against initiators of UCE. In addition, we believe that there is a limited, but valuable place for new laws against those who take advantage of the technology to shift costs to providers, consumers and e-commerce businesses. There is no magic bullet that will eliminate UCE. We are making some headway against the practice, but more needs to be done. But I would like to note and emphasize that what technology created, technology can help fix, if given a chance.

CIX would be pleased to work with members of the subcommittee, its staff and personal staff to develop appropriate responses. Among the steps we propose would be to provide ISPs and consumers with legal weapons, clarify our rights and obligations, and begin to shift the cost back onto initiators.

I appreciate this invitation to testify, and I am prepared to answer any questions you have. Thank you.

[The prepared statement of Barbara A. Dooley follows:]

PREPARED STATEMENT OF BARBARA A. DOOLEY, EXECUTIVE DIRECTOR, COMMERCIAL INTERNET EXCHANGE ASSOCIATION

Mr. Chairman, Members of the Subcommittee, I am honored to be invited to testify before you on Title Three of H.R. 3888, introduced by Subcommittee Chairman Tauzin. My name is Barbara Dooley. I am the Executive Director of the Commercial Internet eXchange Association (CIX) http://www.cix.org/, the world's oldest trade association of Internet Service Providers (ISPs) and industry stakeholders, organized to facilitate the profitability and utility of the ISP industry by—

- Promoting Internet relevant policy forums and markets;
- Encouraging Internet universal connectivity.
- Disseminating information on industry growth and responsiveness;
- Working to maximize the social benefits of the Internet and seeking fair commercial environments.

CIX's members are highly diverse, reflecting the vast range within the ISP sector itself. ISPs build the Internet's infrastructure and connect consumers to the Internet. Our members range in size from large global backbones like UUNet, Teleglobe, and PSINet, national providers such as Epoch, Verio, and e.spire to regional dialup providers. Some of our members provide direct full time connections to the Internet for corporations, while others specialize in small businesses or residential dial-up accounts. They include such recognizable names in the data networking and communications business as IBM, AT&T, Bell Atlantic, and Netcom to name just a few. Our members also span the globe and include non-US headquartered providers such as Fujitsu and BT.

PART I

A. Introduction. The issue that I shall address this morning—unsolicited commercial electronic mail (UCE), also commonly referred to as "spam" or "junk e-mail", afflicts non-commercial Internet access providers as well, including private corporate networks; governmental providers; educational institutions such as schools and libraries; and non-profit institutions. Indeed, Members of the Senate Communications

Subcommittee noted last week that they receive UCE at their Senate mailboxes, some of it of a highly dubious nature.

Mr. Chairman, I am pleased that your bill H.R. 3888 addresses the problem of UCE in addition to "slamming" and "cramming", for it is a major concern to the Internet community. The term "spam" has become somewhat of a joke, sounding almost innocuous and humorous. Because the word has a humorous connotation derived from a renowned Monty Python skit, the problem is sometimes dismissed and ignored. It is anything but a joke to service providers who connect users to the Internet.

Some view UCE as a consumer or civil liberties issue. It is partly both these issues, but it is first and foremost a network problem that threatens to undermine the integrity of the Internet. Left unchecked, its growth could seriously impair the Internet's commercial prospects through the following: clogging the network with vast quantities of unwanted messages; discourage corporations from using the Internet for mission critical communications and applications, make the Internet inefficient and more costly than market needs should dictate; and deter consumers from becoming subscribers.

CIX has the following observations about UCE and attempts to resolve this problem:

1. The problem of unsolicited commercial e-mail cannot be resolved until the costs of UCE are shifted back onto the initiator of such mail.
2. There is no "magic bullet" that alone can defeat UCE. Action in many areas is required, including technology, vigorous law enforcement, public education, exposure and condemnation of abusers, adoption of new laws, protective actions by ISPs, and international cooperation. New laws alone, no matter how well-intended, will be insufficient to deter this practice especially by those who are judgment-proof, defrauders or technologically adept, but they can be helpful if they arm service providers and Internet subscribers with the appropriate legal tools to pursue and combat abusers.
3. Local networks that provide Internet access are private property, and their owners should be accorded the full legal rights of other property owners.
4. Deliberate interference with network operations should be treated identically as other torts and criminal actions.

B. International Survey. As this problem grew in severity, CIX and the Internet Law and Policy Forum (ILPF), the leading international forum for analysis and debate of Internet legal issues, undertook an international survey of ISPs in the last quarter to determine the severity of their UCE problems and examine the means ISPs use to protect their networks and defeat "spammers". Reports are still being collected and analyzed, and the final results will be tabulated and published by the ILPF.

Our preliminary findings show the following with regard to US ISPs: 94.0% reported that spam irritates their subscribers; 79.5% reported that UCE slows system performance; 75.9% stated that it increases operating costs; 33.7% said it creates system outages, while 22.9% reported other effects such as staff costs and a tarnished image.

When questioned about the frequency of the impact, 58.5% reported daily or more frequent impact; 28% said weekly, 8.5% said monthly, 3.7% said infrequent, and only 1.2% said never.

Regarding growth of the problem, 27.7% of US ISPs reported 100% or more growth; 15.7% reported growth between 50-99%, 27.7 reported 10-49%, 9.6% reported the same amount of UCE, and only 2.4% reported a fall in UCE.

Fully 27.9% of US ISPs reported that they are losing revenue as a result of UCE.

C. Why is UCE an ISP Concern? There are several reasons for their concern. First is the matter of customer service. Customers don't like it and are particularly offended when such mail advertises pornographic services and products. They are particularly dismayed if the intended recipients are their children. During last week's Senate hearings, witnesses failed to note that many of the victims are small businesses and telecommuters who rely on electronic mail communications and the Internet to connect them to their customers or main offices. Whenever their communications links are severed or slowed because of UCE, these small businesses lose opportunities, revenues, and profits.

Another operational problem is that UCE degrades ISPs' quality of service by consuming limited network resources like bandwidth or computer equipment (mail server) capacity. By falsely assuming the identity of legitimate providers, UCE initiators cause disagreements among service providers and disrupt inter-provider relations.

UCE raises the cost of doing business by causing systems to crash if the mail servers must absorb sudden increases in mail [1], resulting in extra hours by ISP employees, reduced productivity as employees' are diverted from serving customers to restoring service, and costs for extra equipment and software. During congressional testimony last week, an online service provider (OSP) estimated that approximately thirty percent of its e-mail was "junk" mail or UCE.[2] companies like AOL or AT&T have the resources to divert to combat UCE, but many of the more than 6300 ISPs are small to medium-sized businesses operating with little or no profit. The extra costs caused by UCE could be literally a life or death matter for them.

UCE has also blossomed into an international problem. A recent British report estimated its cost to British and Irish users, providers, and businesses at five billion pounds annually.[3] Its use and presence are spreading around the world as more users connect to the Internet.

There have also been reports of malicious sabotage of ISPs' networks through "mailbombs". In one recent case, it was reported that an ISP was the object of multiple disruptive unsolicited messages for cooperating with the police in an investigation of child pornography.[4]

C. What Makes This a Complex Issue? UCE raises many difficult issues that must be addressed as we craft solutions. There are legitimate advertisements in which subscribers might be interested as well as fraudulent, deceptive or offensive advertising. One must also take care not to prohibit all forms of unsolicited communications, which would include constitutionally protected political speech and legitimate messages.

UCE is economically rational because the cost of mail software programs and the mailing lists is inexpensive to the initiator of the mail. The costs of "spam" are borne by the service provider, recipient, and small business user who relies on the provider. It is essential that this cost-shifting be re-balanced so that senders cannot avoid the consequences of their actions.

Commentators agree that consumers should have the option not to receive unwanted messages or solicitations but often disagree whether it is preferable to have an "opt-in" or an "opt-out" option. Under the former, a consumer could receive UCE only by affirmatively expressing a willingness to receive such communications, while with an "opt-out" solution, a recipient must express a desire to receive no further unsolicited commercial e-mail.

The last, and possibly most problematic, issue involves enforcement of solutions. Dishonest e-mail users will continue to abuse the practice and will not comply with the requirements of any statute requiring accurate return addresses or an opt-out option. Or they may have no assets against which one could recover in any suit.

D. Crafting Solutions. There is no easy answer or single solution. Instead the Internet community is employing a variety of devices. Technologically, providers and users can use filters that detect and dispose of messages from well-known domains used by "spammers".

Service providers have also successfully gone to court to seek injunctions against initiators of UCE. They have also been quite successful in such legal actions although such tactics are predicated on locating the sender, obtaining jurisdiction and service. Providers also invoke their terms of service agreements with customers prohibiting their networks from being used to send UCE to terminate service for abusers.

In still other cases, providers have entered into agreements with other providers to detect and restrict the transmission of UCE. The Netizen community as a whole has found "spamming" to violate fundamental tenets of the Internet and has vigorously opposed the practice, sometimes by confronting abusers personally, exposing abusers or retaliating against practitioners.

CIX believes that legislation has a limited but valuable and legitimate place in this fight against UCE abuses and recommends some actions in Part II of our testimony.

---

[1] Several instances of network failures caused by UCE have been recorded in the online media. These include failures or slowdowns involving PacBell, AT&T, Netcom and others. See testimony of Ray Everett Church, Subcommittee on Communications, Senate Commerce Committee, June 17, 1998.

[2] Testimony of Robert Boe, Associate General Counsel, America Online, June 17, 1998, before the Senate Communications Subcommittee.

[3] CNET News 4/28/98), http://www.news.com/News/Item/0,4,21493,oo.html/

[4] CNET News (4/12/98), http://www.news.com/News/Item/0,4,21493,00.html/

PART II. COMMENTS ON LEGISLATION

CIX is pleased that your bill H.R. 3888 addresses this problem and has several suggestions to improve the effectiveness of your proposal. In particular, I am delighted that this Subcommittee has decided to hold hearings on the issue before attempting to craft legislation unlike the situation in the Senate, when the ISP industry was not consulted before S. 1618 was debated and passed.

Title Three of H.R. 3888 would require initiators of UCE to provide the correct routing information, return address, and an opt-out for recipients. Failure to comply with these provisions will open up the senders of non-compliant mail to civil action by the FTC and state attorneys general.

In the Senate, the focus was on the needs and obligations of spammers and secondarily on recipients' interests, while the needs of infrastructure providers like ISPs and OSPs and electronic commerce received less or no attention. The House has an opportunity to review S. 1618 and adopt appropriate changes based on a hearing record.

In particular, CIX would recommend the following:

- Acknowledgement of service providers' rights and obligations with respect to UCE.
- Recognition of ISPs' right to protect the integrity of their private networks.
- Full recovery for damages caused to ISPs' network, including legal fees and penalties for deliberate interference.
- Right of recovery for damages by individuals engaged in electronic commerce who rely on ISPs and OSPs for communications to their customers and to obtain commercial information.

Conclusion. In summary, Chairman Tauzin and Members of the Subcommittee, CIX would like to work closely with the Subcommittee, its professional staff, and your personal staff to develop appropriate remedies to this problem. CIX does not advocate one solution—first we must clearly identify the problem. The one area in which the Internet and stakeholders has distinguished itself is its ability to self-regulate and solve problems. Small successes have been achieved, and we look forward to attacking this difficult issue in cooperation with our industry colleagues and government.

Thank you. I would be happy to answer any questions you may have.

Mr. TAUZIN. Thank you very much. The Chair will recognize himself for a round of questions. We are waiting for other members to return from the vote.

Let me maybe get a conversation going between you, Mr. Strickling, and some of the other witnesses at this point. We have heard some concerns about the FCC enforcement, a timetable. Could you kind of comment back to some of the concerns you heard expressed about FCC enforcement in this area?

Mr. STRICKLING. Why, I think as my opening statement indicated, we are moving as aggressively as we can to improve our performance in that regard. In particular, I think, by not waiting until we get the complaints from the consumers and getting the response from the carrier before we actually undertake our own investigations, we are now doing that much more on a real-time basis so that we are able to go after the slammers much more at the time of the actual event as opposed to what, in many cases, could be 6, 9, 12 months later.

So—these are new changes that have just gone into effect, so I don't think consumers yet have seen the benefit of that. But we are very concerned about how fast we do these things, and we will improve in that area over the next several months.

Mr. TAUZIN. In terms of the referee issue, Mr. Schultz has pointed out correctly that Mr. Dingell has a different approach, but perhaps the two may not be as incompatible as they first appear.

Talk to me just a bit, Mr. Strickling, about Mr. Dingell's concept about giving the FTC some authority in this matter and how that might work in conflict or in coordination with your own efforts.

Mr. STRICKLING. Well, I think whatever the Congress decides, we will find a way to work without friction and without conflict with our sister agency. We feel, however, that since we are, in the case of slamming, dealing with carriers, those are people we understand, we understand the industry, and we feel well equipped to do what is necessary to protect consumers in this area.

I think when you move to the issue of cramming is perhaps where the question of jurisdiction becomes more of an issue, because in the case of cramming, a number of the charges that are being passed on to consumers' bills are coming from people who are not really officially part of the telecommunications industry, and I think there the FTC has exercised jurisdiction, as they should.

And if more clarification is needed in that regard, we would certainly support that.

Mr. TAUZIN. Well, one of the ways in which the two agencies can work well with an informed consumer base is in the area of clarity and disclosure on telephone bills. We have heard a lot of suggestions about what we might want to prohibit, for example, contests whereby telecommunications services are switched as a result of somebody signing on to a contest or getting involved in a contest. That is one approach, going in and prohibiting certain specific forms of activities that tend to be sites where fraud is occurring frequently.

Another approach is simply more clarity in the billing, more immediate and direct information to the customer, more rights for the customer in not allowing someone to profit from those kinds of practices, all of which have been discussed by some of our consumer groups here.

Can you exchange a little bit? What is the better approach? Should Congress go in and actually prohibit specific marketing practices just because some use those practices to commit fraud, whereas others may not; or should we aim more at full disclosure and notification and penalties or perhaps take the money out of the people who defraud people using those practices, which might otherwise be legitimate practices in a good marketplace?

Mr. STRICKLING. I think, first and foremost, you have to follow the money. If the money wasn't getting to the slammers, they would have no incentive to engage in this behavior. That is why in previous testimony from the chairman, the Commission has indicated that we favor an approach that allows the consumer to be absolved of making payments for one or two billing cycles, because that will force a revolution in the way the industry has organized itself and will prevent slammers from ever getting the money. That is what puts them into business to begin with, so we think that is the top priority, to take the profit out of this.

The rest of it in terms of more disclosure to consumers, we certainly support that, and it is a good idea and it should be part of any comprehensive program to combat slamming. But the top priority has got to be to stop the money from getting to these people.

Mr. TAUZIN. In terms of the money, here is where I would like you to please come back, in terms of taking the profit out of it and not allowing someone to literally put the consumer in the position where they have to pay the bill and then fight over it later, the suggestion is that we have to give more authority to the consumer not to pay the bill, not to be responsible for the bill or to get a refund for a billing that occurred in a slamming situation.

The reverse concern comes in; what about reverse fraud? What about consumers taking advantage of these provisions to defraud telephone companies constantly signing on to contests, switching and then complaining that they really didn't know what they were doing and, therefore, not paying their telephone bills, never having to pay them. We get into those balances all the time. Comment on those, please.

Ms. GRANT. My understanding in talking to members of the telephone industry about 900 number charges is that telephone companies share information about people who are known abusers of the system, and I would imagine that would go on for the small minority of consumers who might abuse it.

My concern is that consumers are told by the slammers in particular that their service will be disconnected if they refuse to pay, and that is a very powerful tool to get them to pay, because consumers are very concerned about maintaining that lifeline to the world.

We think that it would be simplest and fairest if we could say to consumers, you don't have to worry about it, you don't have to pay. We don't think that it would lead to widespread abuse. I can't really think of any other instance in which consumers are obliged to pay for service that they never authorize.

Mr. TAUZIN. We brought a show-and-tell today. Obviously, it sort of makes the case for part of this hearing today, the mysterious meat, Spam.

The question arises—John Kennedy figured out the power of television and effectively used television to defeat his chief rival, Mr. Nixon, for the presidency. The question is, when will we reach a point in Internet ubiquity that someone will figure out that political spam becomes an effective tool for success in the political world.

Ms. Mulligan, I see you are primed to go. I want to hear your comments on that. How do we deal with that? Because I suspect politicians are going to catch on to this notion very soon, that as long as you can shift the cost to somebody else rather than using the mail system to communicate in a political campaign, why not spam the dickens out of your potential voter base, particularly when regional ISPs and local lists can be obtained?

I understand we have some testimony which indicates that data bases of e-mail addresses are available $10 per million, per million targets. We are getting into some very cheap forms of political campaigning all of a sudden. How do we deal with that, Ms. Mulligan?

Ms. MULLIGAN. Well, I am going to give you my take on it, and then I am also going to share a story with you that perhaps illustrates the point that as a politician or as a reputable business, the thing that you have is your brand, and the last thing you want to do is send out a message through a mechanism that is going to alienate 99 percent of your constituents.

Mr. TAUZIN. That is a good point.

Ms. MULLIGAN. I think that what you have here is, in a marketplace where an unscrupulous marketer or somebody who doesn't already have a large brand can send out an e-mail and get a 1 percent return, but have invested nearly nothing, they don't care if they alienate the other 99 percent of the population.

Mr. TAUZIN. That is sort of what television did. Airwaves are flooded with television commercials now, and I assume a lot of people are alienated by that, and yet it works.

Ms. MULLIGAN. That's right. And there is a lot of indication that political, politicians, campaigners are definitely looking at spam and seeing that there are some downsides to kind of sending broadcast e-mail messages.

A political organizer out on the West Coast in California was going to send out a mass, unsolicited campaign message, and was actually talked out of it by other folks using the Internet to organize. They said, look, you are going to tarnish this medium. None of us are ever going to be able to send out a political message, solicited or not. You are going to ruin it; don't do it.

So I think that where there are responsible actors, where there are people who are concerned about their image, as politicians are, that the market forces are a little bit different; and what we are talking about right now is a lot of very unscrupulous actors that are already engaged in illegal activity. We are talking about fraud. We are talking about garden variety pyramid schemes, chain letters, et cetera.

Mr. TAUZIN. Well, it is obviously a problem we have to think about it, and I think one of the suggestions we heard today about making sure that this doesn't become synonymous with people calling you on your mobile phone with all sorts of telemarketing, because in essence, that was a good analogy. That is essentially what is happening, because the cost gets shifted over to the ISP consumer; and it seems to me that maybe reversing that cost in some way, in some respect, might be very useful. That is food for thought. I thank you for that.

The Chair will now yield to the gentleman from Michigan for a round of questions.

Mr. DINGELL. Thank you, Mr. Chairman.

Mr. TAUZIN. Let me also commend the gentleman from Michigan for his legislative efforts in this area and suggest to him that the witnesses have favorably commented on many features of the legislation you drafted, Mr. Dingell, with the hope that you and I can perhaps bring some of these issues together in a final draft; and I want to thank you for your good work here, sir.

Mr. DINGELL. Thank you, Mr. Chairman. I, first of all, commend you for the hearings; second of all, for your leadership and the introduction of meaningful legislation in this matter; and third of all, Mr. Chairman, I certainly look forward to working with you on this matter and to coming forward with a piece of legislation on which you and I can work together on the House floor. I believe that is very much in the public interest. I think this slamming situation is a very bad one and requires forceful and immediate action.

I am reading here from the GAO's analysis of what has transpired. It says, "FCC has taken little punitive action against the slammers. In 1997, FCC obtained consent decrees against nine companies nationwide that paid $1,245,000 in fines because of slamming." It goes on to discuss the State regulatory agencies which have not done better.

It discusses then, it says, "The FCC, State regulatory agencies, and the telecommunications industry rely on others to be the main forces against intentional slamming;" however, with regard to the FCC's anti-slamming measures, they "effectively do little to protect consumers from slamming."

[The prepared statement of Hon. John D. Dingell follows:]

PREPARED STATEMENT OF HON. JOHN D. DINGELL, A REPRESENTATIVE IN CONGRESS FROM THE STATE OF MICHIGAN

Thank you, Mr. Chairman, for holding this important hearing today on the subject of slamming. Slamming is the illegal practice of switching a customer's local or long distance service to another carrier without their knowledge or consent. It is becoming an increasingly widespread problem. Offenders are using craftier and more sophisticated methods than ever before to perpetrate this fraud on consumers. A recent survey commissioned by the National Consumers League revealed an astounding statistic: nearly ⅓ of the respondents were either victims of this crime or knew someone who had been.

What has been done to stop this growing epidemic? The FCC first issued rules on this subject back in 1985, and it has updated the rules several times since then. Unfortunately, these regulatory forays have yielded precious little in terms of protecting consumers. In the Telecommunications Act of 1996, Congress instructed the Commission to issue new rules to deter slamming. More than two years later, these new rules remain tangled in a regulatory morass on M Street. Meanwhile, the rate of slamming continues to climb.

Recently the FCC took a bold step and issued the largest fine ever against a company engaged in slamming—$5.7 million—and revoked its license to provide telecommunications service in the United States. Unfortunately, not one customer was provided an avenue for relief from the fraudulent charges. Many of them actually had to pay the company that defrauded them. This is an outrageous affront to innocent consumers and must not be tolerated.

Consumers need relief from slammers. They need to know that if they are slammed, they will not be required to pay those who partake in this illegal activity. The slamming legislation I have introduced, H.R. 3050, accomplishes this by relieving consumers from any liability for unauthorized charges for up to three months after they are slammed. It would also allow consumers to collect $500 for each slamming violation if they choose to pursue the matter in small claims or other State court. Furthermore, it gives the FTC and State Attorneys General greater authority to investigate and prosecute the bad actors who prey upon our constituents to make a fast buck.

I commend you, Mr. Chairman, for your efforts in addressing the slamming issue as well. Your bill, H.R. 3888, has some excellent provisions in it, including those dealing with PIC freezes and improved verification procedures. However, I do not share your level of confidence in leaving the process of consumer relief to a 13 month bureaucratic effort at the FCC. I think it is imperative that consumers get immediate relief from unauthorized charges, and that the Federal Trade Commission be given the authority to remedy this problem using its extensive experience in dealing with fraudulent business practices.

Ultimately, I hope that we can work together, with the help of information provided by our fine witnesses here today, to produce legislation that truly addresses the scandal of slamming and provides a quick and painless remedy for the consumer.

I thank the witnesses for coming today, and look forward to hearing their testimony. I yield back the balance of my time.

Mr. DINGELL. Now to Mr. Strickling, in how many slamming cases has the FCC perfected and leveled fines against the parties that have done the slamming?

Mr. STRICKLING. I think prior to April of this year, we had brought forfeiture cases against approximately 20 carriers.

Mr. DINGELL. Approximately 20. Obviously, there are more slamming cases going on in the country than 20.

Mr. STRICKLING. No question.

Mr. DINGELL. Now, I note the big one at which you leveled fines at $5.7 million, has that been collected?

Mr. STRICKLING. Not yet. We are still pursuing Mr. Fletcher.

Mr. DINGELL. You haven't found him?

Mr. STRICKLING. Not yet.

Mr. DINGELL. The company has collapsed; it no longer exists. Since your proceeding was against the corporation, it is against a corporation that no longer exists, so the $5.7 million, in all probability, will never be collected; is that right?

Mr. STRICKLING. It is, I think, too early to say that. The fine could also be collected from Mr. Fletcher directly.

Mr. DINGELL. Well, if you can find him. We must assume he is down somewhere in Rio de Janeiro sitting there with a fine, cool drink, enjoying the sights and sounds of Rio and the good life that goes with it.

Mr. TAUZIN. Eating Spam sandwiches, probably.

Mr. DINGELL. No, he will be doing much better than Spam, Mr. Chairman. Spam was for the infantry in World War II, as I well remember.

But having said that, we now find ourselves in this awkward position. Somebody goes out and slams a citizen, let's say Mr. Bliley, because they slammed him. So Mr. Bliley now has been slammed and he seeks redress.

If we say Mr. Bliley doesn't have to pay his bill, that means that he is effectively protected, the slammer is deterred, with no bureaucratic efforts or no quagmire or no cost for the taxpayers. Is that a fair statement, Mr. Strickling?

Mr. STRICKLING. As you have stated it, I think so. And we do support the idea of having——

Mr. DINGELL. Now, having decided that, let's assume that my dear friend, Mr. Bliley, has been slammed, and he is outraged, but let's assume that my legislation is in place. But let's analyze who benefits and who hurts.

Mr. Bliley pays his carrier, that is, the regularly authorized carrier. The regularly authorized carrier is providing those services, so he gets a windfall; is that right?

Mr. STRICKLING. That's right.

Mr. DINGELL. If, however, Mr. Bliley doesn't pay the slammer, the slammer doesn't get a windfall, the slammer doesn't get to defraud Mr. Bliley, and the slammer suffers an economic loss that deters him from further misbehavior; is that right?

Mr. STRICKLING. We hope so, yes, sir.

Mr. DINGELL. So then Mr. Bliley gets a modest windfall. He is not compelled to pay somebody for services that he did not want from a provider that he had no contractual relationship with; is that right?

Mr. STRICKLING. That's right, and I am sure Mr. Bliley——

Mr. DINGELL. Does that strike you as being absolutely fair?

Mr. STRICKLING. Absolutely. We support it.

Mr. DINGELL. I am curious. Is there anybody that finds this to be an unfair resolution at the witness table?

Mr. MCDOWELL. I just want to make sure I understand you correctly.

I think you said that the subscriber, Mr. Bliley in this case, did not desire a certain type of service when, in fact——

Mr. DINGELL. That's right.

Mr. McDOWELL. [continuing] when in fact what it was he was desiring was the long distance service, but from a different carrier.

Mr. DINGELL. Let's say that he had a contract with Southern Bell, or let's say he had a contract with AT&T. Let's say he had a contract with AT&T. So along comes the slammer; and let's say that this is Slippery Communications, Incorporated, and Slippery Communications, Incorporated, slams Mr. Bliley and then proceeds to insist that he pay them. No contractual relationship, Mr. Bliley has been taken advantage of; and so what do we do here about making Mr. Bliley whole?

Do we make him pay the slammer? If he pays the slammer, the slammer gets money that he is really not entitled to, because he is profiting then from his own wrong. Mr. Bliley pays AT&T, but he had no contractual relationship. AT&T has provided no service. So Mr. Bliley is paying AT&T for services they have not provided him. Mr. Bliley is a man who has been wronged.

My question is, should Mr. Bliley be compelled to pay either the slammer or his carrier, which has provided no services; or should he perhaps receive some modest recompense for the wrongdoing that was done to him by Slippery Communications, Inc.?

Mr. McDOWELL. As I understand your scenario, let me clarify something.

Mr. DINGELL. I have tried to clarify it as much as I can. I have only 5 minutes, and I am just wondering what concern you have about this. What is your quarrel with this approach?

Mr. McDOWELL. We are concerned——

Mr. DINGELL. You want Slippery——

Mr. McDOWELL. No, sir. We want Slippery to lose money from that, have absolutely no financial incentive. But what we are concerned about is free long distance, free by the mere allegation of saying you were slammed. That would produce a whole new industry of fraud that the Congressman may not be anticipating.

Mr. DINGELL. I think maybe we have to take a look at that. But basically in that particular trilogy, the slammer should get nothing——

Mr. TAUZIN. Without objection, the gentleman's time is extended by several minutes.

Mr. DINGELL. I thank you, Mr. Chairman. I am going to respect the Chair and my colleagues.

Mr. Bliley has been wronged. Now, it may be that this has been accompanied by cramming, which is another nefarious practice which this committee is going to have to address also; and if that be the case, then there is still more reason for Mr. Bliley being compensated because he has then been wronged additionally by matters not currently before the committee, and Slippery, Inc., is in here saying, oh, my, he might—Mr. Bliley might have gone out to defraud us out of our fully justified returns from our slamming activities.

Mr. McDOWELL. I agree with everything you have said. I am concerned that there might be an overzealous hope that the long distance community has an uncanny ability to share 100 percent accurate information regarding very creative con artists out there who might take your good intentions, which will be embodied in a statute, and then run away with fraud, spend hundreds of millions of dollars a year calling Tokyo or the Cayman Islands or whatever the case might be, and that will only be passed on, those costs will be passed on to the honest consumers.

Mr. DINGELL. Well, let's look at that, because let's take this. How different is Mr. Bliley's relationship between these two carriers than, let's say, a credit card purchaser? Mr. Bliley is buying on a credit card, and he is subject to fraud, he simply refuses to pay, and the person who has to address the question of fraud is not the credit card company, but rather, it is the merchant. Now, how is that different?

We have a clearly established precedent in law, and I am curious, I am curious as to how establishing this well-settled precedent for a second time in connection with fraud is essentially wrong.

Mr. MCDOWELL. As I understand it, in this case, Mr. Bliley is receiving a service. It is from a company that he did not wish to contract with. And he is certainly entitled to some recompense for the duress and whatever that he might have experienced as a result of being slammed, and we think we should be compensated in some form. But I want Congress to ask the question, how can we prevent the reverse fraud that the Chairman referred to earlier?

Mr. DINGELL. I think that merits consideration, but at this particular minute, my sympathies lie with the guy that has been defrauded. I am very sorry for Mr. Bliley.

Now, you are sitting there in your—at your kitchen table going through your mail, and all of a sudden you find somebody who has sent you a pair of fur-lined underwear. You have not ordered this pair of fur-lined underwear, and you are not the kind of person who would buy fur-lined underwear. You are immensely offended.

Now, under Federal law, you are not compelled to return this wonderful fur-lined underwear, particularly since it is summer, nor are you compelled to pay for this fur-lined underwear. You may use it, you may throw it away, you may give it to Goodwill, or you may give to it a friend down the block who happens to like fur-lined underwear.

Mr. TAUZIN. Let's not carry this too far, Mr. Dingell.

Mr. DINGELL. But in no event are you compelled to pay for this fur-lined underwear.

Mr. MCDOWELL. No, sir.

Mr. TAUZIN. The gentleman's time has expired.

Mr. DINGELL. And I thank you, Mr. Chairman. Neither you nor I wear fur-lined underwear, and I think neither does Mr. McDowell. So thank you.

Mr. TAUZIN. You can, of course, respond and the Chair will also make additional time available once I have gone to other members. The gentleman may respond.

Mr. MCDOWELL. I want to make it perfectly clear, ACTA believes that aggrieved, slammed consumers should be compensated for that wrong, and the slammer should be forced to pay dearly. However, we have to remember, in your analogy there, the consumer did not want the fur-lined underwear, but with long distance services, the consumer did place the call, cramming aside, cramming aside.

Mr. DINGELL. And he didn't want to be slammed, either.

Mr. MCDOWELL. But he did receive the service.

Mr. DINGELL. Nor does he want to go to the FCC and wait 13 months while the FCC adjudicates a matter on which they have literally thousands or perhaps tens of thousands—how many thousands of these cases do you have in your backlog at the Commission?

Mr. TAUZIN. The gentleman's time has expired.

The Chair will recognize the gentleman from Washington State, Mr. White, and we will make additional time for other members who wish to come back.

Mr. White.

Mr. WHITE. Thank you, Mr. Chairman. I appreciate it very much.

This discussion of slamming is interesting. I would like to focus on spamming a little bit, and in particular, I would like to find out from Ms. Murphy and Ms. Mulligan and others on the panel how far we have to get into it at a governmental level. We get spam here, too; in fact, we get a ton of spam in the U.S. Congress. It has got to be one of the key targets of spammers across the United States.

I have kind of spent my career here, short as it has been, trying to keep the government out of the Internet business any more than absolutely necessary; and I am really reluctant to get us involved unless there is no other solution to the problem.

I have been very encouraged recently to see the efforts that industry has been making on privacy issues, just very recently, and I think there are even efforts in terms of content, such as pornography, of developing standards that come up from the Internet community, that are enforced privately, kind of the FASB modeling or the modeling that accountants use where the government has some oversight, but it is really the accountants themselves that set the standards and figure out the best way to make these things work.

I guess my question for Ms. Murphy and Ms. Mulligan is, how much do we really need to have a governmental solution here, and wouldn't we be better off if the industry and the community itself could come up with some self-policing mechanisms that they will understand far better than we will ever understand that may allow us to solve the problem in a little better way?

Mr. SCHULTZ. Congressman, first I would like to ask a clarifying question. Which industry are you talking about? Are you talking about the spamming industry? The ISP industry? The backbone industry?

Mr. WHITE. I am talking about the Internet community at large, and I think one of the things that that community desperately needs, and I think is starting to develop in some areas, such as the area of privacy and the area of—perhaps in the area of content pornography, are some industry- or community-wide organizations that can set some standards and, over a period of time, move people into complying with those standards.

It may be, and maybe this is what you are going to tell me, that the industry is too diverse, so you can't do that. But what I am really asking, is there a way to do that, and if not, are you going to be stuck with something that we come up with?

Mr. SCHULTZ. Well, if you consider spammers to be part of the industry, then I guess I would have to disagree with you. There are a lot of bad actors that take advantage of the Internet to send fraudulent and pornographic materials, and I am not sure that they are the types of businesses that would be relied upon to self-police.

Mr. WHITE. I totally understand that, but you don't see anything that the community itself can do to, you know, at least set some standards and figure out some ways to solve the problem that don't require our intervention?

Mr. SCHULTZ. Well, the strongest recommendation that I made in my testimony was to let the control of the network lie with the network providers, so that we can, by contract, determine what is good for our network. It is a network integrity issue, it is not a content issue, to determine what is good for our network. And who knows, if the marketplace wants to support some spammers, maybe there will be some network providers out there that are willing to allow that kind of communication to take place.

But my focus is that, by contract, we should be able to control what is on our network.

Mr. WHITE. Thank you. Ms. Mulligan.

Ms. MULLIGAN. I think your question is an excellent question. As you know, we are very anxious to make sure that the Internet develops in a way that really respects its global medium and its decentralized nature, and that government intervention—you have to look and see, if you push on this piece of the bubble, where does it go?

That said, we have been, at the behest of the FTC, hosting an ongoing series of meetings over the past year that have been attended and participated in by a very broad range of organizations from the Coalition Against Unsolicited Commercial E-mail, the Direct Marketing Association—Sanford Wallace participated for a very short stint. But I think that the general notion is that there is much that has to be done through the marketplace.

For example, right now, e-mail is not costed out on a per-message basis. There are good sides to that, and there are also downsides to that. I think that many people who are responsible network carriers are looking at different ways to allocate costs. There are filtering mechanisms that allow individuals to block out messages if those messages are easily identified, and one of the things that H.R. 3888 would do is to help ISPs and help consumers identify messages that are likely to be spam.

So I think that what you are hearing from a very large number of the Internet community is that, yes, self-policing, technical fixes, good industry policies are part of the solution, but that it has been really impossible to deal with the bad actors, and the bad actors are gumming up the network in a way that is causing problems for people accessing information they want, which is interfering, for example, with the First Amendment values that this medium can support, and is actually burdening the network in ways that are causing real infrastructure problems. So I think it is a both, it is not an either/or.

Mr. WHITE. Mr. Chairman, could I ask unanimous consent for one more question?

Mr. TAUZIN. The gentleman has unanimous consent for an additional question.

Mr. WHITE. Thank you.

One thing I need to understand, is the idea that the spam recipient, who has to pay the cost of receiving it, what is the incremental cost that they receive? You don't have to pay for an additional e-mail, so is it just having your system available and having it be overloaded and having to worry about that; or is it your problem, Ms. Murphy, your network has to pay the cost of having too many messages? How does that work?

Ms. DOOLEY. I could answer that from a wider ISP perspective, and it is different around the world, but the basic benchmark is that recipient pays and networks pay, and that is because on the one side, although there is general flat-rate pricing in the industry here, in fact in many places in the world there is per-minute charging, so that means that the user pays a cost for the download of the mail. So if there is a lot of mail that the user doesn't wish to receive and the user or the network is not using filtering technology, these costs can become very high.

There are other unintended costs for many kinds of companies that run mail service, for example.

There are other unintentional consequences for many kinds of companies that run mail services, for example, where they are taken over to use, to send spam so that the initiator of spam never pays any of those real costs themselves. There are many ways that this cost-shifting passes on to network providers, who then, because they have to take the customer calls, increase personnel, all of the things that we are finding in the survey that we did. That is a widespread, unintended consequence.

Mr. WHITE. I understand that. I know that these guys are going to have to move.

Let me make sure that I understand. The primary cost is borne by the network providers, the people who have to police the networks. I get a zillion e-mails from people from around the United States who all press the button for 435 members of the House of Representatives, and we have a filtering device to get that out, but it doesn't cost me to get that. It costs me time to go through it.

If I were downloading at home, it may cost me a little additional telephone time to get those messages. But the primary cost is borne by you or the network people, so it is not quite the same as having e-mail on your cellular phone. It is more like the cellular telephone provider getting clogged up because they can't handle all of this traffic, but I think I understand that.

Ms. DOOLEY. That is true right now, and it is our position that the costs are primarily borne by network service providers. On the other hand, we are finding increasingly that businesses suffer real loses because of incoming mail that they cannot control and police, and the efficiency of their employees is negatively impacted by the fact that they cannot actually do proper e-mail filtering.

Mr. TAUZIN. The gentleman's time has expired.

If the business is experiencing losses and costs are going up to the business, sooner or later the customer ends up in a competitive marketplace having to pay a higher rate. That is a real problem.

Mr. WHITE. I understand that. We will have this discussion later, Mr. Chairman.

Mr. TAUZIN. The Chair recognizes the gentleman from New York for a round of questions, Mr. Engel.

Mr. ENGEL. Thank you. Can I ask unanimous consent to insert a statement into the record?

Mr. TAUZIN. Unanimous consent has already been granted, and it is made a part of the record.

Mr. ENGEL. Thank you.

I wanted to first ask anyone who would care to answer, the two bills before us, the chairman's bill and Mr. Dingell's bill, there have been concerns raised about the process by which customers can appeal to recover what they feel are unauthorized costs incurred after being slammed. The FCC has no formal process to address the situation as we stated currently.

Mr. Dingell's bill allows a customer to sue in State court. Mr. Tauzin's bill sets up a new process at the FCC for the customer to appeal. I am wondering if we can have some comments on the best way to deal with the problem, which process might be better.

Mr. STRICKLING. I will take a stab.

Again, I think it comes back to first trying to prevent the money ever getting to the slammer. That is a preferable situation to be in than to be in either of two alternatives, which are trying to get the money back from the slammer, which is why some of the proposals, which would have absolved the consumer of the liability tc begin with, probably are the best way to deal with this, because the money never gets to the slammer.

When you are dealing with the question of getting the money back from the slammer after the fact, I think either process might work. Obviously, going into State court puts the burden on the complaining party to actually bring a court action for what in all likelihood will be a fairly small amount of money.

I think the concern at our end is that to the extent that would fall to the FCC to handle, it would just be a question of the work load of handling the thousands of complaints that would come in. Again, if the more efficient way to do this would be to allow the customer never to pay the money in the first place, that could avoid all of the bureaucracy either in the State court or at the FCC. At the same time, we would be free to bring these larger forfeiture cases against the bad actors who have engaged in this activity with large numbers of customers, where we can seek million dollar fines and revocation of operating authority. I think that is a far better place for us to put our efforts.

Mr. ENGEL. Would it take a year, or 13 months has been mentioned in case there was a process for the customer to appeal?

Mr. STRICKLING. That is entirely a function of how many complaints we have and how many resources we have at the Commission we have to respond to them.

Mr. ENGEL. Ms. Grant, I know that you also wanted to answer.

Ms. GRANT. I think slamming is a complex problem. People are slammed by legitimate telecommunications carriers as well as the fly-by-night people, and because it is a complex problem and there are all different entities involved, not only the slammer but possibly a billing aggregator, I think that it calls for a multifaceted solution. I think there is room for everybody to play a role in that.

I think that the idea of having the FTC have jurisdiction over the advertising and promotion aspects of this is really a good one. I think that—no offense to my telecommunications friends, anybody can call themselves a telephone company now and offer services without really knowing anything about the business and basically have other people taking care of the business end of it. I think that the FTC does have an important role to play in terms of the promotional aspects and I think the States do, too.

I would like to see something where the FTC and the FCC share jurisdiction, where the States are able to help with this problem as they do with other kinds of telemarketing fraud.

Mr. ENGEL. You mentioned the FTC, so let me follow up on that. I understand that your organization works closely with the FTC in an effort to maintain the National Fraud Information Center and the Alliance Against Fraud in Telemarketing; is that true?

Ms. GRANT. That is correct. Our National Fraud Information Center, which collects information from consumers about slamming and other telemarketing frauds, contributes that information to a database that is maintained by the FTC for the use of law enforcement agencies, so we have a very important relationship.

Mr. ENGEL. Could you shed some light on the FTC's efforts to prevent consumer fraud? And you obviously do see consumer advantage to be gained by authorizing the FTC to enforce rules to prevent slamming?

Ms. GRANT. Right. The FTC is the main Federal cop on the beat going after companies for deceptive acts or practices, and has civil jurisdiction as opposed to criminal jurisdiction that other agencies have.

I have seen over my years in consumer protection the FTC being more and more active in going after a wide variety of abusive practices. I don't think that it makes any sense at this point for the FCC not to have jurisdiction in this case simply because a company has gotten the status of being a telecommunications carrier, which the GAO report illustrated is a very easy status to attain. It doesn't really mean anything these days in terms of what you are doing in promoting your services.

I don't think that there should be any difference between the FTC's ability to go after somebody for abusive practices in that area as opposed to all of the other businesses that are concurrently taken to task.

Mr. ENGEL. Thank you.

Generally it has been my impression, and I wish anyone on the panel would correct me if I am wrong, a lot of the victims of slamming are senior citizens, perhaps at a disproportionate ratio to the general public. Is that true or not true?

Mr. TAUZIN. Perhaps Mr. Schultz with the AARP can respond.

Mr. KELLY. I would like to offer one thought on that, and the victims are really twofold; they are not only the users but also the carriers which had been previously selected to provide those services, many being small businesses.

Mr. SCHULTZ. In terms of the victims, this goes across all generations. It is not restricted to older Americans, but I would guess—I don't have statistics, but I would assume that perhaps a larger percentage would be older Americans. But certainly it is not restricted to that segment.

Mr. ENGEL. Mr. Kelly, you have expressed concern about the surety bond provisions in H.R. 3888. I am wondering if you can expand further your concerns with the provision.

Mr. KELLY. Our principal concern is that the surety bond is really, in our view, unnecessary in this legislation. We think the stepped-up enforcement, the additional education reporting requirements, the increased penalties and the other considerations will go a long way toward dealing with the slamming problem.

The problem with the surety bond issue is that it is designed only for the smallest competitors in the industry. The so-called switchless resellers; and thereby it would give—it would impose additional costs by the government that they would have to recover, but their larger and better capitalized competitors would not have to bear such a responsibility.

Mr. ENGEL. Since some of the switchless resellers are thought to be slamming customers, what would be the alternative to the surety bond? What would you propose as the alternative?

Mr. KELLY. I believe the surety bond provision is completely unnecessary in the legislation. I think that the other elements that I described will do the job, particularly stepped up enforcement and increased penalties. We think that is where the focus ought to be, and that is where these bills are headed.

Mr. ENGEL. Thank you, Mr. Chairman. I believe my time is up.

Mr. TAUZIN. I thank the gentleman.

The AOL decision which just came down, how does it affect the issue of slamming—of spamming, rather, and the question of contractual capabilities?

Are the providers common carriers?

Can you contract people out who have been abusing the system? If you are not a common carrier, what are you, fish or fowl here?

Ms. MURPHY. There have been a handful of decisions which dance around these issues, and I am not sure which decision you are referring to.

Mr. TAUZIN. I thought there was a decision on the news today. It hit CNN today that AOL was very pleased that the Supreme Court ruled in their favor that they were not responsible to an individual who complained about receiving information or—

Ms. DOOLEY. The Supreme Court refused to review a lower court decision which dealt with a complaint from an AOL user who had been—

Mr. TAUZIN. Who had been ridiculed?

Ms. DOOLEY. Correct.

Mr. TAUZIN. As I recall, advertisements went out under this man's name, advertising T-shirts which ridiculed the Oklahoma City bombing a week after it occurred, and the man was vilified by this fake presentation on the Internet and received hate mail, threats against his life even for having the audacity to advertise such T-shirts, when it was fake and he had nothing to do with it.

He sued AOL, claiming AOL should have been a better gatekeeper. AOL apparently won the lower court decision.

Ms. DOOLEY. The Internet service provider industry welcomes the Supreme Court decision in that because we do believe that

Internet service providers should be monitoring or gatekeepers for content and that we do have the court and judicial system.

Mr. TAUZIN. So do the common carriers. That is the question that we are asking.

Ms. DOOLEY. We are not common carriers.

Mr. TAUZIN. What are you? If in fact you are not obligated and you have—you see, Mr. White asked you a good question a while ago. He asked if the Internet community could come together and straighten this out, so we didn't have to legislate in this First Amendment area, and the answer you gave him then was, Ms. Murphy, that the spammers are bad players and they are not part of an agreement.

We were talking about, in television, the networks and the cable companies do have some sort of content control. They decide what is on the networks and in the cable systems, but AOL and other providers are saying here that we shouldn't have to be responsible because we are not gatekeepers about what comes over our system, but at the same time we are not going to help you in getting those same people to sit down with us and resolve it in a way that you don't have to step in and create either the responsibility or the liability for becoming gatekeepers. And so if you don't police content yourself, why aren't you a common carrier?

Ms. MULLIGAN. May I make some stab?

Mr. TAUZIN. Please try.

Ms. MULLIGAN. What you have is an emerging medium. If you look at—many of the members of CIX, for example, are purely conduits. They help people get their own messages out and enable people to develop web sites. They develop no content on their own. They are not publishers. Each individual can use this medium to spread their message far and wide. Many of the members of CIX have never seen the content and don't care what the content is.

There are areas where there are State laws and Federal laws that require them, where they have knowledge, to help law enforcement, like State law enforcement dealing with child abuse. If there is some information that someone is doing harm, they have a duty to report and that has been carved out by the States.

Mr. TAUZIN. What Mr. White is sort of, I guess, laying on the table for you is somewhat of a choice. How much do you want us to continue to carve out in the way of legislative requirements and responsibilities, and how much are you willing industry-wide to work out protocols and technologies that will put more power in the hands of consumers without the necessity of us creating all of these carve-outs?

We can go a long way on this. Ms. Murphy, I would like to hear your comments.

Ms. MURPHY. Yes. I just wanted to clarify one point.

Our company certainly acts as a conduit, the dumb pipe. We are even one step further removed than the Internet service provider.

The AOL decision, and I am familiar with the lower court decision, and I have not read the paper yet, so I have learned something about the decision coming out, but it doesn't solve my dilemma. In reading the AOL decision—

Mr. TAUZIN. Give me your dilemma one more time.

Ms. MURPHY. The dilemma is, we are a common carrier. We don't have any visibility, what goes over our pipes; it is a bunch of data bits. At no time is it resonant—you can't pinpoint where the data is at any one point in time. We have no idea what the content is.

That is the focus of my comments, and I had hoped to make that clear to Congressman White.

Our concern is, contract is the way to go. We want to be able to set policies that ensure the integrity of our network, to put those policies in contractual form so that the Internet service providers that are our customers know what we accept as far as use that impacts network integrity. To me, that is somewhat of an industry solution.

Mr. TAUZIN. I am going to suggest that—I am going to leave the record open for all of you to elaborate on your comments today. I am going to suggest that whole question that you elaborated—I am not sure that admitting you are a common carrier is quite a good idea at this point. Maybe you want to, maybe you don't, but there are universal service requirements on common carriers and access charges, and there are some big issues out there.

I am going to give you a chance, if you want to respond in writing and further elaborate on the points. But—so let me lay it out as Mr. White tried to lay it out to you.

It is an emerging form of communications. It is emerging so rapidly we don't have policy to fit it, and we don't want to regulate it. At the same time, Mr. Shimkus and many of the consumer groups have correctly pointed out that people are being abused and defrauded and charged the wrong way for services. And you can argue about whether they got a benefit that they should pay something for or not, but clearly people are being charged for services that they didn't ask for and, in some cases, at higher rates than they bargained for, and they are being abused with the spamming instances.

And Mr. Schultz, you are right, often it is people who are less attentive to some of the fine print, and very often it is the senior citizens or young people or groups of busy people in our society who don't check or understand what every bill says or means.

We have a lot of problems here, and we can really get into a lot of legislating in this area or we can count on this emerging industry and all of its players to come together, like in the privacy area where we encouraged them to do so and to present to us some real protocols and some agreements on technology that is going to put more power in the hands of consumers here without the necessity of us writing all of the rules in Washington, DC.

Having laid that on the table, if you have suggestions for us, please come back in writing. Your admonitions to us on the legislation, Mr. Strickling, the concerns that you have raised with us about improving our draft, we deeply appreciate that.

You have made some good points. I am particularly intrigued with the PIC freeze problem in Michigan. I want to know more about that. If you can please supply that to us, Ms. Grant.

And to the extent that you are going to submit written statements, we will also keep the record open for further questions which we may want to submit to you, and we will ask you to have them in by July 2 if you are going to submit additional clarifications. That is next Thursday.

If there are no further questions by any members of the committee, let me again thank you very much, with our commitment to move as rapidly as we can in these areas as we try to continue to thoroughly understand them. And we thank you for this hearing, and the hearing is now adjourned.

[Whereupon, at 12:37 p.m., the subcommittee was adjourned.]

[Additional material submitted for the record follows:]

SUPPLEMENTAL TESTIMONY OF RILEY MURPHY, VICE PRESIDENT, E.SPIRE COMMUNICATIONS

Thank you, Mr. Chairman, for this opportunity to elaborate further on e.spire's status as a common carrier and information service provider. We are in fact both, and under the law our regulatory status depends on the service we are offering to the customer and the facilities that we use to provide our services. As amended by the Telecommunications Act of 1996, e.spire is treated as a common carrier under the Communications Act of 1934 (the Act) only to the extent that it provides telecommunications services. To the extent that e.spire is providing information services, then the Federal Communications Commission (the Commission) has ruled that we are not a common carrier. Yet your entire network gets 251 access where an ISP alone could not.

The core of e.spire's business is the provision of telecommunications services as both a competitive local exchange carrier (CLEC) and as an intrastate and interstate packet-switched data and voice backbone provider. In both of these capacities we hold our service out to the public, and the customer contracts with us to transport their information without change in the form or content (other than for transmission purposes) between whatever points the customer specifies. A customer might be an individual or a business, including a business as an information service provider (ISP). In some cases we transport the customer's information entirely on facilities that we own or lease from another common carrier (mostly incumbent local exchange carriers (LECs) or a long distance backbone provider). In other cases we transport the information part of the way to its destination, and then hand it off to another common carrier with whom we have interconnection agreements (for example Bell Atlantic or AT&T) for delivery to its final destination. When we provide either of these transport services neither e.spire nor the other common carrier to which we hand off the information has any control over or knowledge of what that information is. It could be an e-mail, a file, a voice conversation, or picture of some kind.

A secondary but growing portion of e.spire's business is information service. In our capacity as an ISP the customer contracts with us to enhance their information in certain ways, for example by enabling the customer to read, store, and edit information obtained from a database or an Internet web page, and then forward that revised information to a friend. In most cases today, the customer must also contract with a common carrier (usually the incumbent LEC) to have the information they want enhanced transported to and from e.spire. The customer may also contract directly with e.spire for both transport and enhancement, a situation I will address in a moment. Once the customer's information reaches e.spire, e.spire in its ISP capacity becomes a customer, and contracts with a common carrier (for example WorldCom) for a dedicated line to carry the customer's enhanced information from our data switches to and from the data switches and data bases of other ISPs. As an ISP that enhances the customer's information, and in generating our own information for use by our customers, e.spire may have some limited knowledge of and control over content. However, the volume of information that customers ask us to enhance increases daily, and effective review or monitoring, even if Constitutional, would be practically impossible.

In our capacity as an ISP e.spire agrees with the Chairman and Congressman White that some form of industry agreement, rather than government regulation, is needed to prevent spamming from injuring our customers. As I summarized in my oral presentation, e.spire has dealt effectively with spamming in our common carrier role by including contractual provisions that allow us to refuse to transport the spammer's information, regardless of its content, whenever an ISP identifies one of our customers as the source of spamming, in order to protect the integrity of the e.spire network. Any legislation should make it clear that both the common carrier that provides the transport and the ISP that enhances a customer's information have the right to limit or terminate service as a matter of contract if spamming occurs.

Let me turn now to why e.spire is both a common carrier and an ISP in the current regulatory and legal environment. The Act, as amended by the Telecommunications Act, establishes certain rights and obligations that apply to telecommunications carriers and to LECs. These rights and obligations are important not only to e.spire, they are what make accelerated deployment of the Internet and the Information Age possible. These rights include non-discriminatory access to, and resale of, services provided by common carriers and LECs, as well as the right to interconnect with and use the networks of other common carriers and LECs. The obligations include the requirement to provide service to any customer that requests it and to contribute to universal service when providing telecommunications services, so that all persons have affordable access to a ubiquitous, national telecommunications system.

Critical to e.spire's ability to provide competitive telecommunications and information services to our customers are the rights given to telecommunications carriers under section 251(c) of the Act[1] to interconnect with, and obtain unbundled network elements from, incumbent LECs that control the physical networks and electronics that make it possible to economically reach every home and business in the country. As a telecommunications carrier e.spire has the legal right to connect to the incumbent LEC network at cost based rates, which is what allows e.spire to provide competitive transport services to ISPs and other subscribers. These rights also allow e.spire to be a one-stop provider of both information and telecommunications services, a packaged service that an increasing number of subscribers want to have provided.

A telecommunications carrier is defined as "any provider of telecommunications services,"[2] which in turn is defined as "the offering of telecommunications for a fee directly to the public . . . regardless of the facilities used."[3] The term "telecommunications" is defined to mean "the transmission, between or among points specified by the user, of information of the user's choosing, without change in the form or content of the information as sent and received."[4] Similarly, the Act defines "information service" as "the offering of a capability for generating, acquiring, storing, transforming, processing, retrieving, utilizing, or making available information via telecommunications . . ."[5]

Clearly, when an ISP or anyone else hires e.spire to transport their information between points without change in the form or content, e.spire meets the definition of a telecommunications carrier. Similarly, when someone hires e.spire to provide the capability to "generate, acquire . . . or make available information via telecommunications," e.spire meets the definition of information service. To the extent e.spire is engaged in providing information services, we are not a common carrier, which is the position several of the other witnesses, who are themselves ISPs, and the Commission strongly support. However, to the extent that e.spire or anyone else is providing telecommunications services, we or they are a common carrier.

A review of typical ISP business arrangements with common carriers and customers reveals that e.spire's position does not raise the spectre of regulation of the Internet or other information services. There are three common arrangements in use today, in each of which there is no need, either as a matter of law or public policy, to impose common carrier regulation on the ISP. A fourth arrangement is beginning to emerge that could raise strong public policy concerns, but only if the Commission fails to fully implement the requirements added by Congress in section 251 of the Act which were intended to ensure competitive access by CLECs (and ISPs served by those CLECs) to the local exchange facilities of incumbent LECs.

The first, and most common, scenario today is one in which a residential or business subscriber and an ISP both contract to be customers of an incumbent LEC. Both the subscriber and the ISP have a legal right to the transmission services offered by the incumbent LEC on a common carrier basis. In addition, the residential or business subscriber contracts separately with the ISP for information services. The incumbent LEC provides the facilities that transport information without change in the form or content (other than for transmission purposes only) between its two customers (the subscriber and the ISP), makes universal service contributions based on revenue from both customers, and fulfills the public responsibilities mandated by the Act. To the extent that a residential or business subscriber cannot

[1] 47 U.S.C. 251(c).
[2] 47 U.S.C. 153(44).
[3] 47 U.S.C. 153(46).
[4] 47 U.S.C. 153(43).
[5] 47 U.S.C. 153(20).

get information services from one particular ISP, the incumbent LEC will connect them to another that will provide the service, and neither the subscriber nor the ISP can be legally prevented from reaching each other using the incumbent LEC's network facilities.

In the second, and increasingly common, scenario the ISP contracts with a CLEC like e.spire to transport information to and from the incumbent LEC's central office, while the business or residential subscriber contracts with the incumbent LEC to transport their information to and from the central office that the CLEC connects to. Again, the business or residential subscriber also contracts separately with the ISP for information services. As in the previous scenario, both the ISP and the residential or business subscriber have a legal right to contract with the CLEC and the incumbent LEC for the transmission services they each offer on a common carrier basis. Both the CLEC and the incumbent LEC make universal service contributions and discharge the other public responsibilities imposed by the Act. There is no need to impose those responsibilities on the ISP, because the public interest is already being adequately served by both common carriers, and common carrier rules ensure that neither the subscriber nor the ISP can be denied access to the other party.

The third common scenario is where an ISP contracts with a packet switched backbone provider, such as e.spire or AT&T, to transport the enhanced information of the ISP's customers to other ISP data switches, data banks, or customers. Here again the public interest is protected, and the requirements of the Act fulfilled, by the presence of the backbone provider. The backbone provider offers to transmit the ISP's information without change in the form or content as sent and received, i.e., it is providing a telecommunications service and is therefore a common carrier to that extent. As a result, the backbone provider makes universal service contributions and carries out the other public responsibilities to the extent required by the Act. Since the backbone provider is a common carrier, albeit a deregulated one, it cannot discriminate among ISPs, therefore ensuring that all ISPs and their customers can transmit their information throughout the country or the world, eliminating any legal or public policy reason to impose a redundant common carrier obligation on the ISP.

The fourth scenario is one that is only just emerging, but it too demonstrates that there should be no need for common carrier regulation of information services provided by ISPs as long as the Commission fully implements section 251(c) of the Act so that CLECs, and thus the ISPs served by those CLECs, have competitive access to business and residential subscribers using the local exchange facilities and equipment of the incumbent LEC. The convergence of computers and digital telecommunications technology, along with declining costs for new infrastructure and the enactment of the Telecommunications Act, have now made it possible for incumbent LECs to also be the ISP. This condenses the three or four party transaction involved in connecting the residential or business subscriber with an ISP into a two party transaction, namely the incumbent LEC/ISP and the residential or business subscriber. This new arrangement should function much the same as the first scenario presented, as long as the LEC half of the combined incumbent LEC/ISP operation and its local exchange facilities and equipment remain subject to the provisions of the Act, such as section 251, that are intended to ensure that all subscribers can reach and be served directly by the competitive provider of their choice.

In conclusion, Mr. Chairman, e.spire hopes that this explanation has been helpful in highlighting our position as both a CLEC and an ISP. e.spire must be a telecommunications carrier under the Act in order to get access to local exchange facilities and equipment owned by the incumbent LEC. e.spire and other CLECs need at least some of the incumbent LEC facilities and equipment in order to provide competitive telecommunications and information services to business and residential subscribers. We are the conduit through which many ISPs are able to reach their customers at competitive rates. e.spire firmly believes that there is no need for common carrier regulation of any information services when those services are provided to subscribers using networks that are open to competitors. Congress has provided the legal framework in the Telecommunications Act to ensure that competitive telecommunications carriers have access to the local exchange facilities and equipment needed to offer services to the subscribers reached by those networks, regardless of the entity that may, singly or in combination with an affiliate, operate those networks.

SUPPLEMENTAL TESTIMONY OF BARBARA DOOLEY, COMMERCIAL INTERNET eXCHANGE ASSOCIATION

Thank you, Mr. Chairman, for the opportunity to supplement our testimony in support of the conclusion that Internet service providers ("ISP's") are not common carriers under the Federal Communications Commission's ("Commission") regulatory framework. CIX is a trade association that represents over 150 Internet Service Providers ("ISPs") who handle over 75% of the United States' Internet traffic. CIX works to facilitate global connectivity among commercial ISPs in the United States and throughout the world. CIX has been an active participant in the Commission's proceedings implementing the Telecommunications Act of 1996 in order to provide the perspective of ISPs and to ensure a regulatory framework that continues to promote the healthy development of this revolutionary new medium.

Consistent with law and public policy, the Commission has correctly found that enhanced or information service providers, including ISPs, are not common carriers. As such, ISPs are not subject to the panoply of the Commission's common carrier regulations, which would otherwise inhibit market entry and make the market more complicate to operate in for midsize and small businesses.

The dichotomy between basic and enhanced services was defined almost 20 years ago in the Commission's *Computer II* decision, where the Commission held that enhanced service providers were not Title II common carriers under the Communications Act of 1934. With the Telecommunication Act of 1996, Congress added the terms "telecommunications service" and "information service." With considerable deliberation on the issue, the Commission has found that these terms reflect the Commission's long-standing decision not to subject information service providers to common carrier Title II regulation.

In its *Non-Accounting Safeguards Order* the Commission reaffirmed that information services are distinct from telecommunications, and thus not subject to Title II common carrier regulation. The Commission held that telecommunications "only includes transmissions that do not alter the form or content of the information sent." Because information service providers "alter the format of information through computer processing applications such as protocol conversion and interaction with stored data," such providers are not properly deemed to be telecommunications service providers.

In its recent April 10 *Report to Congress,* the Commission once again reviewed the issue and, after much comment, it reinforced that the regulatory dichotomy between telecommunications and information services, including Internet access service. The Commission's based these conclusions on both the nature of Internet access service offerings, as well as Commission precedent. As the *Report to Congress* stated, "[T]he provision of Internet access service crucially involves information-processing elements . . ." and as such . . . "it is appropriately classified as an information service."

The Commission's decisions on this issue are unequivocally in the public interest. Information services including the Internet are distinctly different from telecommunications. As such, applying common carrier regulations designed for telecommunications services to Internet service providers would result in a wide variety of negative consequences that would threaten the continued development of the Internet and the deployment of high bandwidth services. In Section 230 of the 96 Act Congress clearly directed the Commission to not regulate Internet services by making it the policy of the United States and the Commission "(1) to promote the continued development of the Internet . . .;[and](2) to preserve the vibrant and competitive free market that presently exists for the Internet . . ., *unfettered by Federal or State regulation.*" Without subjecting Internet service providers to common carrier regulation, the Internet continues to grow at an unprecedented rate and especially for small businesses, which brings immeasurable benefits to society.

Finally, I would note that the issue of some incumbent local exchange carrier ("ILEC") practices vis-a-vis their wholly-owned subsidiary ISP are an entirely separate issue. There are certainly legitimate concerns in the ISP industry as to the ILECs' provision of underlying telecommunications services, including services to facilitate efficient data transport. Moreover, with the ILEC offering both the underlying telecommunications and participating in the ISP market, there is significant concern of ILEC abuse due to its monopoly control over the essential telecommunications needed by all ISPs in a competitive market. As you can see, these telecommunications issues directly impact ISPs and should continue to be an important and focal area of FCC regulation.

CIX again thanks the Chair for this opportunity and reiterates it interest in participating in further proceedings on this and related issues.

PREPARED STATEMENT OF THE FORUM FOR RESPONSIBLE AND ETHICAL E-MAIL BY MICKEY CHANDLER, CO-FOUNDER AND PRESIDENT [1]

Thank you, Mr. Chairman, Mr. Markey, and members of the Committee. I am very grateful to have been asked to speak to you today on behalf of the Forum for Responsible and Ethical E-mail, also known as FREE.

FREE is an all-volunteer, ad hoc group of owners and operators of Internet-based businesses, Internet service providers (ISP's), technology professionals, and consumer activists. We are the newest Internet advocacy group dealing with e-mail issues in the United States at just over three months old. We have also begun assisting citizens of other nations to form similar organizations in their own homelands. Our organization was formed to advocate a legislative solution to the problem of "junk e-mail," [2] because it has become clear to us that technical and self-regulatory solutions have proven to be no solution at all. We are an international proactive organization that has engaged in on-site protests of junk e-mailers and have attracted national media coverage.

The Forum represents a wide range of Internet users and Internet-based businesses. Our Board of Directors include long-time Internet users, such as: a world-renowned programmer of anti-junk e-mail software, a paralegal, an embedded systems consultant, a research associate in a developmental biology laboratory, a housewife, a technical writer, the owner of a small, start-up Internet Service Provider, the system administrator for a newspaper, and the moderator of a USENET newsgroup. The Abuse Desk supervisors of two of America's fastest growing mid-sized Internet Service Providers Erols Internet Services, and Mindspring Enterprises, advise our board. What we all have in common is our love of the Internet. Some of us make our living on-line, while others see a problem that demands a legislative solution. We welcome the presence of businesses on-line and we want to do business on-line. We do not want to subsidize, unwittingly and unwillingly, industries that choose to do their business in cyberspace.

Our founder, Jim Nitchals, passed away quite unexpectedly a little over two weeks ago. Jim was my best friend, colleague, and closest advisor. Jim is best known for his willingness to talk to, and convince those who engage in what we call "net-abuse" to change. He was responsible, in large part, for Apex Global Information Systems, Inc's, policy change last November from a pro-spam policy to a no-spam policy. He is, perhaps, best known for his role in convincing Sanford Wallace and Walt Rines to become responsible Internet citizens. For all of his accomplishments, Jim often spoke of the need for a legislative solution to the problem presented by unsolicited broadcast e-mail. I know Jim was very much looking forward to these hearings, as he would often ask me about what progress I was making toward having FREE represented when they happened.

The Problem

On one recent evening, I came home to find included amongst the mail in my e-mailbox was an advertisement that read: "Our research indicates that this message is of interest to you . . . If you are under 18, please delete this message now. Another member of FREE's board received a mail with a subject line of "George is no longer with us." It was an advertisement for international drivers' licenses.

These messages illustrate some of the reasons why many members of the Internet community have requested legislation to put a stop to bulk e-mail. The sender has no way to know and no incentive to find out if the service or product being advertised is actually of interest to the recipient. Further, knowing that it is unlikely to be of interest, the mailers hide their advertisements behind misleading subject lines to induce the unwilling into reading the unwanted.

For traditional bulk mailing through the United States Postal Service, businesses must pay a per-piece cost for the mailing. This cost provides strong incentive to carefully target mailings. Even then, the Marketing industry has an abysmal record of honoring requests to opt-out of lists,[3] even though not honoring the requests in-

---

[1] This testimony was prepared with the advice and assistance of the FREE Board of Directors: Mickey Chandler, Steve Atkins, Ian Hayes, Leah Roberts, Clifton Sharp, Jr., Steve Sobol, Laura Tessmer, and Kelly Thompson. Some portions have been excerpted from the testimony of David H. Kramer, Esq., before the Washington State Legislature. Mr. Kramer may be contacted at Wilson Sonsini Goodrich & Rosati, Palo Alto, CA 94304, (650) 493-9300. Some portions have also been excerpted from the testimony of Ray Everett-Church, Esq., before the United States Senate Communications Subcommittee. Mr. Everett-Church may be contacted at (202) 588-0426.

[2] Also called "Unsolicited Commercial E-mail" (UCE), or more broadly, "Unsolicited Broadcast E-mail" (UBE), or in the vernacular, "spam."

[3] Bob Van Voorhis, "I'm not trying to kill this dog. I'm trying to save its life!" *TeleProfessional Magazine,* Advanstar Communications Inc., Vol. 11, Number 6, June 1998, pp. 32-36.

49-326 98 - 4

creases their costs. E-mail, on the other hand, uses a trust-based system of economics wherein each recipient pays for his or her own e-mail. Further, because of the cooperative nature of the Internet, the other customers of the ISP must also share in the cost. Indeed, the entire community of Internet users pays the cost of the bulk e-mailer's advertising. In the words of one long time Internet citizen, "The 'net is community. Everything else is implementation of details." Junk e-mail has forced devastating costs on that community. This shows no sign of slowing. Why should it? The marketing industry refuses to honor requests to opt-out of lists for which they must pay actual and incremental costs, and in some cases already have a statutory duty to honor. Can they be expected to honor requests to remove individuals from mailings for which the marketers do not pay?

The effect on the marketplace of ideas has been staggering. Broadcast e-mailers "harvest" e-mail addresses from USENET newsgroup posts and web pages and by joining opt-in mailing lists for the sole purpose of obtaining working addresses. This has caused people to remove or alter their personal information, including e-mail addresses, to escape the onslaught of junk e-mail. In many cases people stop adding new ideas to any forum and in some have abandoned the medium altogether. This has had the effect of ending true freedom of speech and the open exchange of ideas for millions of Internet users.

The Solution

The Internet is the greatest marketplace of ideas the world has ever seen. We must not legalize the abuse that is stifling this forum, and call that legalization a solution. So, what is the solution? Because the costs of E-mail depends on a trust-based, "everyone pays their share" system of economics, it is imperative that the solution gives control to the people who bear the cost, and allows them to decide what is appropriate. The solution proposed by Rep. Smith gives control back to each user.

Is This a First Amendment Issue?

The marketing industry will sell you the idea that bulk e-mailers have a constitutional right to ply their wares at the expense of others. I implore you to look at the true issues here. The issue is not whether a business may engage in advertising on the Internet; indeed, there are many options available to any business wishing to advertise. These options range from mailing only to people who have requested it, to purchasing advertising banners on other's webpages, to reciprocal links between businesses.

Instead, there are several issues involved. Foremost among them are my rights to be left alone and to not be forced to pay for the advertisements of others. The marketing industry, to protect its own interests, will tell you that I, the consumer, do not have these rights. They will tell you that their right to speak, to force their advertisements on us, anyone with an e-mail address, outweighs our right to privacy and our right to control our property. However, we believe that the loss of bulk, junk e-mail most assuredly will not spell the end of legitimate online business, just as the passage of the junk fax law did not spell the end of all advertising that uses the telephone or the facsimile machine.

Although some have questioned the constitutionality of Representative Smith's approach, let me assure you that there is ample precedent for supporting his legislation. When addressing a similar issue of unsolicited advertisements, the Supreme Court said it best in the case of Rowan v. U.S. Post Office:

> Nothing in the Constitution compels us to listen to or to view any unwanted communication... We categorically reject the notion that a vendor has a right under the Constitution or otherwise to send any unwanted communication into the home of another. If this prohibition operates to impede the flow of even valid ideas, the answer is that no one has a right to press even 'good' ideas on an unwilling recipient... We repeat, the asserted right of a mailer stops at the outer boundary of every person's domain.[4] Further, the Rowan court appreciated the fact that content decisions, which H.R. 3888 would force the Federal Trade Commission into making, should be left to the recipient.[5] Courts have generally held that it is acceptable for legislatures to enact restrictions on the time, place, and manner of advertisements.

In addition to these fundamental precepts, every court that examined the junk fax law upon which H.R. 1748 is based has upheld its constitutionality. In Destination Ventures v. FCC,[6] the Ninth Circuit, after noting that commercial speech receives less protection than political or religious speech, concluded that the statute served

[4] 397 U.S. 728 (1970)
[5] Id., at 733, 736, and 737
[6] 46 F.3d 54 (9th Cir. 1995)

a substantial government interest in preventing recipients from having to bear the cost of third party advertising. It found that the prohibition on junk faxes directly advanced that interest. That is the very same interest served by H.R. 1748.

H.R. 3888 and S. 1618 Are Signals of Disaster for the Internet

Just as we find H.R. 1748 a clear, legitimate, and constitutional solution, we find that Title 3 of H.R. 3888, and Senator Murkowski's amendment to its Senate counterpart S. 1618, is a tremendous threat. Although FREE, like the Coalition Against Unsolicited Commercial E-mail (CAUCE), endorses the intent behind Senator Murkowski's amendment to the anti-slamming bill, we are deeply concerned that this proposed law will increase the burden on businesses and consumers.

As written, the bill sets basic standards of legality that are easily met. The legislation would allow marketers to indiscriminately send massive amounts of e-mail with no recourse for the victim other than begging to be taken off the list. Furthermore, placing enforcement solely in the hands of a faceless governmental bureaucracy is an unworkable solution. The Federal Trade Commission's plate is already full to overflowing, we feel it is unreasonable to expect they will be able to ferret out thousands of violators operating out of their basements and in boiler rooms. This is especially true in light of the fact that the Federal Trade Commission has already shown unwillingness or inability to deal with spam which advertises services or products that are already illegal.

By setting such a low threshold for legitimacy, we fear it will cause increasing volumes of junk e-mail. In fact, FREE has already received numerous reports of junk e-mailers making slight modifications to their tactics and proclaiming that their mail "is protected by Federal Law." It is a very bad sign when the "remedy" for a problem empowers the very abusers it is designed to inhibit.

S. 1618 and H.R. 3888 make the strong presumption that people should assume the costs of advertising which they did not ask for, do not want. Both S. 1618 and H.R. 3888 force people to spend time and money getting themselves removed from thousands of mailing lists they never asked to be added to. The present legislation would force us to subsidize the advertising of any business that chooses to advertise by junk e-mail without our permission, without our knowledge, and without the exchange of any consideration. This legislation potentially requires us to remove ourselves from more than 23,300,000 mailing lists, one list at a time.

Conclusion

Legislation is desperately needed to stop the cost-shifting problem inherent in junk e-mail. Because the nature of junk e-mail is so similar to junk faxes, FREE agrees with CAUCE that amending 47 USC 227 is a well-tailored solution to the problem. Like the fax law, it defines a deceptive and unfair business practice that is damaging and costly to consumers and sets statutory damages. In doing so, it returns the economics of junk e-mail to a proper balance and places enforcement in the hands of the consumer, rather than the hands of any government agency.

Thank you, Mr. Chairman. I would be happy to answer any questions the committee might have.

PREPARED STATEMENT OF RAY EVERETT-CHURCH,[1] CO-FOUNDER AND COUNSEL, COALITION AGAINST UNSOLICITED COMMERCIAL EMAIL

Thank you Mr. Chairman and members of the Committee. I am very grateful to have been asked to speak to you today on behalf of the Coalition Against Unsolicited Commercial Email, also known as CAUCE. CAUCE is an all-volunteer, ad hoc group of owners and operators of Internet-based businesses, service providers, technology professionals, and consumer activists. We are now the largest Internet advocacy group in the United States with over 10,000 registered members in nearly every state. Our coalition was formed to advocate for a legislative solution to the problem of "junk email," because it has become clear to us that technical and self-regulatory solutions have proven to be no solution at all.

The Coalition represents a wide range of Internet users and Internet-based businesses. Our Board of Directors includes long-time Internet Users, owners and operators of ISPs, a marketing and public relations professional, a lawyer, a college stu-

[1] This testimony was prepared with the advice and assistance of the CAUCE Board of Directors: Scott Hazen Mueller, Chairman, John Mozena, John Levine, Doug Muth, J.D. Falk, Edward Cherlin, Corey Snow, George Nemeyer, and Ray Everett-Church. Some portions have been excerpted from the testimony of David H. Kramer, Esq., before the Washington State Legislature. Mr. Kramer may be contacted at Wilson Sonsini Goodrich & Rosati, Palo Alto, CA 94304, (650) 493-9300.

dent, and the author of the best-selling book *The Internet for Dummies.* What we all have in common is that we make our livings, to some degree or another, from the Internet. We all want the Net to thrive, and we want to do business online. We are willing to pay our own way, but we are not willing to subsidize the advertising of others.

I should note that I have been authorized to say that this testimony also represents the views of our Coalition partner, the Internet Service Providers Consortium. It also generally represents the views of our colleagues at the Forum for Responsible and Ethical Email (FREE).[2]

Unsolicited Commercial Email Threatens the Future of Online Commerce

Let there be no mistake that this is an important day for the Internet; you are taking up an issue of tremendous importance for the future of online commerce. As a greater and greater percentage of our gross domestic product revolves around the explosion of computer-related and Internet-related commerce, I do not exaggerate when I say that junk email has the potential to harm our economy in ways that terrorists could only dream about.

The technology news media reports with alarming frequency system crashes and network outages caused by junk email attacks. Junk email has knocked out systems belonging to major Internet service providers such as AT&T,[3] @Home,[4] Pacific Bell,[5] Netcom,[6] GTE,[7] and literally hundreds of smaller ISPs serving rural communities across the nation. And the volumes of junk email are increasing every day.

If junk email were as innocuous as the mail ads you get through the U.S. Postal Service, we would probably not be discussing this here today. But the fact that your committee is holding these hearings today is testament to the fact that junk email—also called UCE, unsolicited commercial email, and "spam"—is a very different animal with tremendous costs and consequences for the future of the Internet. There are some who would have you believe that junk email is no different from any other type of advertising media, but I urge you not to believe that. There is no other medium quite like junk email in its ability to damage Internet systems and impede legitimate Internet commerce. I know of no more efficient means of consuming the time, money and resources of millions, against their will.

Unsolicited Commercial Email Shifts Tremendous Costs Onto Recipients

Unlike virtually every other communications medium, the majority of email costs are paid by the recipients—not the sender. This is, for better or for worse, the nature of the Internet. It grows out of the cooperative arrangements upon which the Internet was created, where each participant pays for their portion of the infrastructure. This means that once an email is sent, whether it is an advertisement or a letter from a college student to her parents, the costs for relaying, transmitting, receiving, storing, and downloading the message borne by any number of people, *except* the sender. When you are not paying the freight, as is the case with the sender, it is only natural to be less concerned with the costs involved. And therein lies the problem.

Even if the problem were limited to just one or two messages a day, forcing a recipient to pay for receiving advertising would be unacceptable, but we are not talking about just a few messages. I know this first hand: During calendar year 1997, the email account I use for my business received over six thousand pieces of junk email, weighing in at 41 megabytes of data. That is an average of sixteen (16) pieces of junk email each day. Indeed, the economics of junk email create a strong incentive to send such mail as frequently and as broadly as possible. Given that the cost of sending one hundred messages is the same as one million, a mailer has every incentive to send his message to as many email addresses as possible. With such a minuscule investment, even if only one out of every million recipients buys the mailer's miracle cure or multi-level marketing scheme, not only will he have recovered his tiny investment, he may well have turned a handsome profit.

---

[2] FREE has also filed its own supplementary testimony to more fully discuss the concerns of their constituency.

[3] "Spam Slows WorldNet Mail"—C|Net News (7/16/97) http://www.news.com/News/Item/0,4,12512,00.html

[4] "Spam Snags @Home Mail System"—C|Net News (2/25/98) http://www.news.com/News/Item/0,4,19487,00.html

[5] "Pacific Bell Suffers Slowdown"—C|Net News (3/13/98) http://www.news.com/News/Item/0,4,20046,00.htmi; "PacBell Fights Spam Explosion"—ZDNet (3/13/98) http://www.zdnet.com/zdnn/content/zdnn/0313/294405.html

[6] "Spam Clogs Netcom Lines"—C|Net News (4/29/97) http://www.news.com/News/Item/0,4,10204,00.html

[7] "Sprint Down for 5-hour Count"—C|Net News (9/3/96) http://www.news.com/News/Item/0,4,3039,00.html (discussing problems at both Sprint and GTE).

The problem with junk email stems from the realization by unscrupulous mass marketers that they can force unwanted and unwelcome messages on millions of consumers, with just the touch of a button, at virtually no cost to themselves. For less than a hundred dollars, you can outfit your computer with all the necessary hardware and software to generate a million pieces of junk email each day. You can even buy databases of email addresses on CD-ROM; the going rate right now is under $10.00 per million addresses. Top it off with an unlimited Internet account for $19.95, and junk emailer is born.

While the costs are small for the junk mailers, the same cannot be said for the people who have to transport, process, store, and retrieve that email. Millions of Internet users, businesses and consumers alike, pay for their access to the Internet in increments of time. Many more, particularly those in rural communities and those who travel extensively, must make toll calls to obtain a connection. For these individuals, each unsolicited commercial message they receive is like a telemarketer's call to their cellular phone—they pay to receive messages they did not ask for and inevitably do not want. Like many millions of people, I pay for my Internet access by the minute. I estimate that the Internet connection time alone for those six thousand unsolicited messages cost me in the hundreds of dollars—and that is before I even begin to calculate the amount of time wasted in sorting through all that junk to find my important email.

It also presents a problem for those who do not immediately review their email. When these individuals do check their electronic mailboxes, they find they must wade through dozens of unsolicited advertising messages in order to find their legitimate email. During that time, their company or service provider has been forced to store that tremendous volume of mail until the user can retrieve it. Just a few days worth of junk email for a service provider the size of America Online would easily fill all the disk storage space of all the computers in all of the offices on Capitol Hill.

Junk email forces Internet users to become a captive audience for whatever advertising message anyone wishes to send them, at any time, any number of times. Yet the hard costs are minuscule when compared to the non-monetary costs of junk email. Unlike direct mail from the post office, junk email arrives throughout the day at home and at work, and there is no effective technical means of blocking it.[8] Junk email in the workplace interrupts employees who must wade through pornographic ads and "get rich quick" schemes to find work-related email. Parents and their children often have no choice but to accept, pay for and dispose of these unwanted and sometimes highly offensive messages. Major junk email campaigns can also knock out Internet systems, resulting in lost data, lost business, and lost productivity.

The Economics of "Junk Email" Encourages Massive Abuse

When turned into an advertising medium, the skewed economics of email turn traditional notions of advertising on their head. In virtually no other advertising medium does the advertiser get to force the recipient to bear more costs than they do. At least with television, print ads in newspapers, or advertisements in the U.S. Mail, the sender incurs significant initial costs and is forced to target their advertising carefully because each additional ad bears in incremental cost. But in the world of junk email marketing, it costs no more to send the first email than it does to send the ten millionth email. Thus, there is every incentive for the marketers to cast their advertisements as widely and indiscriminately as possible.

Not only is there no incentive to carefully target the mailing lists, there isn't even an incentive to reduce duplication. So today many people, myself included, regularly receive multiple copies of the exact same advertisement.[9] And why not? When ad-

---

[8] Blocking and filtering of junk email has proven extremely ineffective in combating junk email. In order to block or filter email, you must first know where it is coming from. Then once you implement a block for that location, a junk mailer can rapidly change their location. For example, they may send mail via an America Online connection, then once that route is blocked, they will reconnect via CompuServe, then via Netcom, and so on. In Internet parlance, these kinds of mailers are called "whack-a-moles," a reference to the popular carnival arcade game where you strike the mole with a mallet only to have it reappear somewhere else. Junk mailers obtain throw-away Internet accounts for one-time usage, bouncing from one ISP to the next, making up an address and launching their messages. While a receiving site can add that address to its filters, the spammer will seldom use that address again. Senator Murkowski's original bill, S. 771, proposed a mandatory "tag" on commercial email. However, filtering based upon advertising tags would not relieve the burden on Internet services providers or businesses whose facilities are already overwhelmed with massive quantities of junk email.

[9] One particular junk mailer has permutations of my email address on his list no less than five times. Whenever they take on a new client, I always get five copies of each and every ad. From the complaints received from CAUCE members, such situations are not at all uncommon.

vertisers pay so little of the costs involved, there is no incentive for them to be careful; indeed, time spent on editing a mailing list is time wasted.

You will undoubtedly hear from representatives of the marketing industry who will say that electronic mail represents a low cost method of marketing which will put mass advertising into the hands of even the smallest businesses. That is certainly true. But what they never acknowledge is that what makes junk email so inexpensive is that every recipient is forced to subsidize that advertising whether they want to or not. I am continually astonished that the marketing industry defends the need for junk emailers to steal money and resources from their would-be customers. No other industry would dream of stealing from potential customers in this fashion, and no other industry would dare come before Congress and ask that their right to steal from the public be protected.

For this reason, many people have called junk email a form of "postage due" marketing. I am not so charitable. Quite simply, I call it theft. It is stealing the time, money, and resources of others against their will. And any legislation that sanctions the sending of unsolicited email, however well-intentioned, does nothing short of legalizing a kind of theft. Therefore I urge the members of this committee to reject any so-called solution which would permit the practice of theft by email to continue.

The Threat to Businesses and Service Providers is Enormous, and Growing

I am sure you will hear horror stories from many Internet Service Providers about the volumes of junk email coursing through their systems, but some larger companies have publicly estimated that upwards of 30% of their daily email traffic is junk email. As a former consultant to America Online's email administrators, I can tell you that they have made major investments in equipment and personnel to keep their systems running in the face of the onslaught. Companies like Hotmail, AT&T, Earthlink, UUNet, Netcom, CompuServe, and Erols also invested millions and hired numerous full time administrative staff to do nothing but combat the effects of junk email.[10]

But I am not here today to tell you about the problems of large ISPs—they will tell you that themselves. I am here to tell you that even a fraction of AOL's daily junk email dose is more than enough to put small businesses and small Internet Service Providers out of business. With more and more companies conducting their critical business over the Internet, junk email is costing those businesses millions. Moreover, junk email threatens to put hundreds of small ISPs out of business, particularly the kinds of small, local service providers who provide the only cost-effective Internet access to thousands of consumers, businesses, and schools in rural areas all across the United States. Even as I speak, this committee and others in Congress are debating whether FCC-imposed fees should subsidize Internet access for schools and libraries. As you wrangle over that issue, let me remind you of this fact: junk emailers peddling porn sites and miracle potions are already subsidizing *themselves* on the backs of schools, libraries, businesses and consumers all across this nation.

CAUCE has heard from many dozens of small and mid-sized ISP all across this country, all of whom are crying out for relief from the damaging and costly practices of unscrupulous advertisers. Technology shows little promise of solving the problem, and hauling junk mailers into court on cuttingedge theories in cyber space law is just not a reasonable or affordable answer. Small ISPs exist on notoriously tiny profit margins. Seemingly little things, such as the number of milliseconds it takes for a computer to process a piece of email, become looming problems when you are facing the demands of Internet services. For an Internet Service Provider, the processing capacity of their mail servers is a precious commodity and when their systems are tied up processing junk email, it creates a drag on *all* of the services they provide to their customers.[11]

The problem is also compounded by the fact that ISPs purchase bandwidth—their connection to the rest of the Internet—based on projected usage by their prospective user base. For most small and midsized ISPs, bandwidth costs are among one of the

---

[10] A May 4, 1998, news article from *Internet Week* surveys the many millions of dollars spent by numerous service providers in coping with the problems caused by junk email. The article, "Postage due on junk email—Spam costs Internet millions every month" is on the web at: http://www.techweb.com/se/directlink.cgi?INW19980504S0003

[11] Small ISPs are often unable to afford the massive redundant systems that larger companies can afford. Thus, processing junk email can slow down all of the functions on servers that might be filling multiple critical functions such as a mail server, a web server, and a domain name server. Constraints on server capacity are also one of the reasons "filtering" schemes are not viable solutions for many ISPs; filtering email consumes vast amounts of processing capacity and is the primary reason most ISPs cannot implement it as even a partial strategy for eliminating junk email.

greatest portions of their budget and contributes to the reason why many ISPs have a tiny profit margin. Without junk email, greater consumption of bandwidth would normally track with increased numbers of customers. However, when an outside entity (e.g., the junk emailer) begins to consume an ISP's bandwidth, the ISP has few choices: One, let the paying customers cope with slower Internet access, occasional crashes, and degraded services; two, eat the costs of increasing capacity; or three, raise rates. No matter the choice, the recipients are still forced to bear costs that the advertiser has avoided.

The Nobel Prize-winning economist Ronald Coase has written eloquently about the damage done to the economy when these kinds of costs are chronically externalized onto an ever-widening base. In his writings, Coase has discussed the dangers to the free market when an inefficient business—one that cannot bear the costs of its own activities—distributes its costs across a greater and greater population of victims. What makes this situation so dangerous is that when millions of people only suffer a small amount of damage, it becomes too costly for the victims to recover their tiny share of the overall damages. Such a population will continue to bear those unnecessary and detrimental costs unless and until their individual damage becomes so great that those costs outweigh the transaction costs of fighting back.

The classic example is pollution: It is much cheaper, in raw terms, for a chemical manufacturer to dump its waste into the local river. Such externalities allow one person to profit at another's—or everyone's—expense. Certainly those who are harmed might have a cause of action under civil law to recover their actual damages. But for the vast majority of victims, there are significant transaction costs involved in bring individual lawsuits. For most, those costs will prohibit them from ever seeking redress. As a result, the skewed economics of pollution will give incentive to the polluters while making it prohibitive for victims to seek a remedy. Much is the same when it comes to junk email. While some companies have successfully sued junk emailers for the damage they have caused, very few ISPs can afford to fight these kinds of cutting edge cyberlaw battles.[12] As a result, the economics favor the abusers and disfavor those victimized. Indeed the mailers are counting on the fact that their incremental theft will not be noticed or that people will just hit the "delete" key and move on. They hope that if they steal only a tiny bit from millions of people, very few will bother to fight back.

As Coase pointed out, this is a prescription for disaster. When inefficiencies are allowed to continue, the free market no longer functions properly. As we all remember from our college Microeconomics classes, the "invisible hands" that would normally balance the market and keep it efficient cannot function effectively when the market is carrying dead weight and perpetuating chronic inefficiencies. Unchecked, businesses that are otherwise unprofitable will indefinitely leech off the indirect subsidies they extract from the public at large.

In the context of the Internet, the costs of these externalities can be seen every time you have trouble accessing a web site, whenever your email takes 3 hours to travel from AOL to Prodigy, or when all your email is lost in an ISP server crash.

---

[12] In fact, in nearly every lawsuit on junk email-related issues, the actions of junk emailers have been found unlawfulin one form or another. See, e.g., *Cyber Promotions, Inc. v. America Online, Inc.*, C.A. No. 96-2486, 1996 WL 565818 (E.D. Pa. Sept. 5, 1996) (temporary restraining order), rev'd (3d Cir. Sept. 20, 1996), partial summary judgment granted, 948 F. Supp. 436 (E.D. Pa. Nov. 4, 1996) (on First Amendment issues), reconsideration denied, 948 F. Supp. 436, 447 (Dec. 20, 1996), temporary restraining order denied, 948 F. Supp. 456 (E.D. Pa. Nov. 26, 1996) (on antitrust claim), settlement entered (E.D. Pa. Feb. 4, 1997); *America Online, Inc. v. Over the Air Equipment, Inc.* (E.D. Va. complaint filed Oct. 2, 1997), preliminary injunction entered (Oct. 31, 1997), settlement order entered (Dec. 18, 1997); *Bigfoot Partners, L.P. v. Cyber Promotions, Inc.* (S.D.N.Y. complaint filed Oct. 6, 1997); *In re Canter,* No. 95-83 1-O-H (Term. Bd. Prof. Resp. Feb. 25, 1997), disbarment order entered (Tenn. June 5, 1997); *CompuServe Inc. v. Cyber Promotions, Inc.*, No. C2-96-1070 (S.D. Ohio Oct. 24, 1996) (temporary restraining order), preliminary injunction entered, 962 F. Supp. 1015 (S.D. Ohio Feb. 3, 1997), final consent order filed (E.D. Pa. May 9, 1997); *Concentric Network Corp. v. Wallace,* No. C-96 20829-RMW (EAI) (N.D. Cal. complaint filed Oct. 2, 1996), stipulated judgment entered (Nov. 5, 1996); *Earthlink Network Inc. v. Cyber Promotions, Inc.*, No. BC 167502 (Cal. Super. Ct. L.A. County May 7, 1997) (preliminary injunction), consent judgment entered (Mar. 30, 1998); *Expert Pages v. Universal Networks, Inc.,* No. 97-1542 SI ENE (N.D. Cal. May 2, 1997) (temporary restraining order); *Parker v. C.N. Enterprises,* No. 97-06273 (Tex. Travis County Dist. Ct. complaint filed May 26, 1997), temporary injunction entered (Sept. 17, 1997), permanent injunction entered and damages awarded (Nov. 10, 1997); *People v. Lipsitz,* 663 N.Y.S.2d 468 (N.Y. Sup. Ct. 1997); *Prodigy Services Corp. v. Cyber Promotions, Inc.* (S.D.N.Y. filed Oct. 18, 1996), settlement entered (Dec. 13, 1996); *VNZ Information & Entertainment Services* (S.D. Cal. complaint filed Nov. 13, 1997), default judgment entered (Apr. 15, 1998); *Web Systems Corp. v. Cyber Promotions, Inc.,* No. 97-30156 (Tex. Harris County Dist. Ct. complaint filed June 1997), temporary restraining order entered (June 6, 1997).

But the costs do not stop there. With junk email already the number one complaint of most Internet users, consumers have deserted many public discussion forums for fear that their email addresses will be "harvested" and added to junk mail lists. Customers are afraid to give their addresses out in legitimate commerce for fear of being added to and traded among thousands of mailing lists. Legitimate businesses are afraid to use email to communicate with their existing customers for fear of being branded "net abusers."

Congress Has Acted to Stop Cost Shifting Before

In the pollution context and in many other situations where the marketplace has failed to maintain its own natural equilibrium, governments have appropriately stepped in to alter the skewed economic balance. By enacting substantial fines and penalties as a matter of public policy, governments have remedied the marketplace failure and made responsible behavior more cost effective. A perfect case in point is the federal statute that outlawed the sending of unsolicited advertisements via fax machine.

Email is increasingly becoming a critical business tool in much the same way as the fax machine became an indispensable took during the late 1980s. As more and more businesses began to use fax machines, marketers decided that they could fax you their advertisements. For anyone in a busy office in the late 1980s, you will undoubtedly remember the piles of office supply catalogs and business printing ads that came pouring out of your fax machine. On far too many occasions, you had to shut off the fax machine in mid-advertisement so your business colleagues could try and send their fax before the advertiser could redial.

The similarities between junk faxes and junk email are many: both forms of advertising shift the costs onto recipients, both of them tie up expensive resources without compensation to the victims, and both require federal legislation to cure. There are also some compelling differences that make email more pernicious than taxing. Certainly the average email costs a recipient less than a fax, however you cannot easily send ten million faxes at the touch of a button the way you can with email. In addition, the fax advertiser must bear some marginal cost for each fax sent, particularly if a long-distance call is involved. But with junk email, recipients and ISPs bear most of the cost while the advertiser bears little—and with a few keystrokes, you can quadruple the amount of damage done. With greater and greater abuse not merely a possibility, but an everyday reality, a legislative solution as strong as the junk fax prohibition becomes a necessity.

When looking for a legislative solution to the problem of junk email, we found that the fax statute, 47 USC 227, has been tremendously successful at virtually eliminating the problem of junk faxes and points the way to a real and meaningful solution to the problem of junk email. Therefore we strongly urge the passage of Representative Smith's bill, H.R. 1748. The bill is a model of logic and simplicity. It assures that those who wish to receive such mass mailings can continue to do so by simply asking, while those who do not want them, will not get them, or will have a legal remedy if they do.

S. 1618 and H.R. 3888 Portend Disaster for the Internet

Just as we find H.R. 1748 a clear solution, we find S. 1618 and its House counterpart H.R. 3888 to be a tremendous threat. Although CAUCE endorses the intent behind Senator Murkowski's and Senator Torricelli's amendment to the anti-slamming bill, we are deeply concerned that this proposed law will, if anything, make the burden on businesses and consumers even greater.[13]

As written, the bill sets basic standards of legality that are easily met, even by today's current crop of disreputable scammers and brazen porno spammers. The legislation would allow marketers to indiscriminately send massive volumes of email with no recourse for the victim other than begging to be taken off the list. Furthermore, by placing enforcement solely in the hands of government bureaucracies, we believe it is unreasonable to expect that the Federal Trade Commission will ever be able to ferret out thousands of violators operating out of their basements. Finally, the legislation could be seen to preempt state laws on junk email.[14]

---

[13] CAUCE expressed our concerns with that language directly to Senator Murkowski prior to the amendment's introduction. A copy of our letter to Senator. Murkowski is attached and I wish to incorporate that letter into my testimony by this reference.

[14] Washington and Nevada already have measures on the books dealing with problems created by junk email. And numerous other states are considering legislation to address the harm done to businesses. Bills are pending in California, Colorado, Connecticut, Kentucky, Maryland, Massachusetts, New Hampshire, New Jersey, New York, Rhode Island, Texas, Virginia, and Wisconsin. Professor David Sorkin from the John Marshall Law School in Chicago maintains a web site tracking current legislation at: http://wwwjmls.edu/cyber/statutes/email/.

By setting such a low threshold for legitimacy, we fear it would allow for increasing volumes of junk email. In fact, CAUCE has already received numerous reports of junk emailers making slight modifications to their tactics and proclaiming that their mail is protected by the Murkowski-Torricelli amendment. It is a very bad sign when the "remedy" for a problem gives cover to the most egregious abusers.

We should not presume, as S. 1618 and H.R. 3888 appear to do, that people are willing to incur both direct and indirect costs for advertisements that they did not ask for and invariably do not want. These bills would force people to continuously incur out-of-pocket monetary costs, unless and until they spend more time and money getting themselves removed from thousands of mailing lists they did not ask to be on in the first place. Because of the almost limitless potential for continued abuse under S. 1618 and H.R. 3888, CAUCE believes that this legislation has the consequence of legitimizing massive abuse, making things worse than the status quo, thereby contributing to the demise of email.

H.R. 1748 is an Effective, Narrowly Tailored, and Constitutional Approach

Legislation is desperately needed, as it was in the case of junk faxes, to stop the cost-shifting problem inherent in junk email. Because the cost shifting nature of junk email is so similar to junk faxes, CAUCE believes that amending 47 USC 227 is a well-tailored solution to the problem. H.R. 1748 amends the anti-junk fax statute to prohibit the sending of unsolicited commercial advertisements by email. Like the fax law, it defines a deceptive and unfair business practice that is damaging and costly to consumers and sets statutory damages. In doing so, it counterbalances the economics of junk email and places enforcement in the hands of the consumer, not in the hands of any government agency.

Although some have questioned the constitutionality of H.R. 1748's approach, let me assure you that there is ample precedent for supporting Representative Smith's legislation. When addressing a similar issue of unsolicited advertisements, the Supreme Court said it best in the case of *Rowan v. U.S. Post Office:*[15]

> Nothing in the Constitution compels us to listen to or to view any unwanted communication... We categorically reject the notion that a vendor has a right under the Constitution or otherwise to send any unwanted communication into the home of another... We repeat, the asserted right of a mailer stops at the outer boundary of every person's domain.

In another Supreme Court case, *Breard v. Alexandria,*[16] the Court upheld the constitutionality of a local ordinance prohibiting door-to-door solicitation, stating that it is a misuse of the guarantees of free speech to force anyone to admit solicitors against their will. In *Bland v. Fessler,*[17] the Ninth Circuit upheld California's ban on the use of automated dial and delivery devices, ruling that advertisers had no right to turn consumers into a captive audience, forcing them to receive any message the advertiser wished to send. The Ninth Circuit concluded such a prohibition was a reasonable time, place and manner restriction and was reasonably tailored to serve the state's substantial interest in protecting peoples' right to be left alone.

In addition to these fundamental precepts, every court to look at the constitutionality of the junk fax law, upon which H.R. 1748 is based, has upheld its constitutionality. In *Destination Ventures V. FCC,*[18] the Ninth Circuit, after noting that commercial speech receives less protection than political or religious speech, concluded that the statute served a substantial government interest in preventing recipients from having to bear the cost of third party advertising. It found that the prohibition on junk faxes directly advanced that interest. That is the very same interest served by H.R. 1748.

Finally, and most importantly, in *CompuServe v. Cyber Promotions,*[19] one of the first cases directly discussing the constitutional question of junk email, a Federal District Court held that:

> "Defendants' contention... that there are no adequate alternative means of communication is unpersuasive. There is no constitutional requirement that the incremental cost of sending massive quantities of unsolicited advertisements must be borne by the recipients."

In this and other regards, H.R. 1748 is the antithesis of the Communications Decency Act. The approach in H.R. 1748 comes from the Internet community, by their request, rather than being enacted over the objections of an unwilling Internet community. As was argued in the CDA challenge, the government should not be in the

---

[15] 397 U.S. 728 (1970)
[16] 341 U.S. 622 (1950)
[17] 88 F.3d 729 (9th Cir. 1996)
[18] 46 F.3d 54 (9th Cir. 1995)
[19] 962 F. Supp. 1015 (S.D. Ohio Feb. 3, 1997)

position preventing people from viewing material that they want to see. Representative Smith's bill would do just the opposite: It protects people from being forced to view material that they don't want to view while preserving their right to see it upon request.[20] Finally, any remaining questions about free speech issues can be assuaged by the fact that H.R. 1748 has received wide-spread praise from staunch supporters of free speech and has been endorsed in editorials by *USA Today, The Seattle Times, The Philadelphia Enquirer,* and *The Sacramento Bee,* among others.

Congress is Justified in Acting to Protect the Email Infrastructure

Like the fax machine before it, electronic mail is a marvelous tool of business and personal communication. It is simple, it is accessible, and it is becoming more and more an indispensable part of our professional lives. But there are even more far-reaching potentials of email that may be lost if its functionality and utility are destroyed by the proliferation of junk email.

The Internet is an incredible tool for spreading information critical to the development of freedom and democracy around the world. Indeed, email is often cited as a critical tool for communicating with and between Chinese democracy activists. Recent media stories have also credited email as a critical tool in the overthrow of the Suharto regime in Indonesia.[21] If Congress does not take immediate steps to rescue email from the grips of snake-oil salesmen, there are real implications for the growth of free speech and democracy both at home and abroad.

Electronic mail is a marvel of accessibility and ease of use for tens of millions of Americans, and is a critical growth component of America's young Internet economy. Yet in just a few short years, unsolicited advertisements by email have already begun to strangle Internet commerce in its crib. Unless Congress acts to preserve the viability of the medium, today's crop of scammers and thieves will soon give way to more legitimate marketers who will replace the flood of offensive and fraudulent messages with even greater quantities of ads for snack chips and laundry powder. When that terrible day comes, our electronic mailboxes will cease to be a useful tool for business and personal communications and we will have squandered one of the most powerful tools of communication this planet has ever known. On behalf of the Coalition Against Unsolicited Commercial Email, I urges you to protect Internet commerce against the damaging and costly effects of junk email. No less that the future of electronic commerce and our information economy may be at stake.

Prepared Statement of H. Russell Frisby, Jr., President, Competitive Telecommunications Association (CompTel)

Thank you Chairman Tauzin for permitting me to submit testimony to the Subcommittee as part of its hearing on H.R. 3888, the Anti-Slamming Amendments Act and H.R. 3050, the Slamming Prevention and Consumer Protection Act. My name is H. Russell Frisby, Jr., and I am President of the Competitive Telecommunications Association (CompTel), a national industry association representing more than 250 competitive telecommunications carriers and their suppliers. I regret that I am unable to attend today's hearing in person. Unfortunately, a longstanding event on my schedule conflicted with the date of this hearing. I hope that my submitted testimony will be useful to the members of the subcommittee and I would be happy to respond to any written questions that you or other subcommittee members may wish to pose to me in writing.

CompTel's Zero Tolerance Policy

Very simply, CompTel and its member companies view slamming, or the unauthorized transfer of a customer's local or long distance service provider, as theft. When a carrier intentionally "slams" a subscriber away from its authorized carrier, that slamming carrier has stolen the authorized carrier's customer. CompTel members, like their subscribers, are victims of slamming and have every incentive to see increased enforcement of this activity. For this reason, CompTel supports Congressional efforts to curb slamming and has been actively involved at the Federal Com-

---

[20] The bill also allows for businesses any number of ways to utilize the Internet to reach a prospective customer. For example, businesses can utilize banner advertising on popular web sites, create their own web site and register them with search engines, provide mechanisms for opting-in to email mailing lists, enter into linking arrangements with companies sharing common markets, and make targeted and topical postings to appropriate Internet bulletin boards.

[21] "Indonesia Revolt was Net Driven"—Boston Globe (5/23/97)http://www.boston.com/dailyglobe/globehtml/143/lndonesia_revolt_was__Net_driven.htm

munications Commission (FCC) in the development of regulations to implement Section 258 of the Communications Act.

CompTel has played a leadership role in the interexchange industry in trying to curtail slamming and cramming by advocating that *all* carriers adhere to *or exceed* all applicable federal and state laws and regulations designed to prevent slamming and "cramming"—the intentional, unauthorized addition of services to a customer's bill. Specifically, CompTel advocates that *all* carriers accept the responsibility to prevent slamming and cramming, and to fully educate their customers, employees, and agents about these practices.

CompTel has a "zero tolerance" policy toward intentional slamming and cramming. Under this policy, carriers agree to: (1) investigate fully all allegations of slamming and cramming; (2) take appropriate action to remunerate consumers who have been victimized by any slamming or cramming; and (3) terminate any employees or agents who knowingly and willfully engage in such practices. CompTel has also called on all carriers to avoid using deceptive, inappropriate or "high pressure" sales tactics, and to redouble their efforts to minimize instances of unintentional changes and pursue all appropriate remedies when slamming or cramming is attributable to the executing local carrier.

CompTel members are committed to the goal of expanding consumer choice in the local exchange and exchange access markets, where competitive alternatives do not exist today. Since its inception 1981, CompTel has advocated policies to promote the development of full and fair competition in telecommunications services. Today, CompTel's members encompass all types of competitive telecommunications service providers, including small and mid-sized long distance (or interexchange) carriers (IXCs), competitive local exchange carriers (CLECs) and Internet service providers (ISPs).

CompTel is concerned that slamming may eventually be a problem in the local exchange market—if and when there is any meaningful competition for local exchange services beyond the ongoing scramble for large business customers. To that end, CompTel's policy on slamming is guided by four general principles:

1. Customers must be able to choose their local and long distance service providers without fear of unauthorized changes or charges;
2. Adequate information must be provided to customers in order that they can make informed choices when selecting telecommunications services and providers;
3. Rules and laws regarding the carrier selection process should be competitively neutral. In addition, the rules and law governing the carrier selection process and unauthorized customer charges must apply to all telecommunications services providers, including incumbent local exchange carriers (ILECs); and
4. Customers and providers alike must be able to rely on uniform, nationally-consistent, and fair requirements.

H.R. 3888, THE ANTI-SLAMMING AMENDMENTS ACT

The legislation introduced by Chairman Tauzin is substantially the same as the legislation which was adopted in the Senate by a vote of 99-0. CompTel worked closely with the staff of the Senate Commerce Committee in drafting that legislation and supported the bill as it was reported out of the Senate Commerce Committee. Unfortunately, a number of amendments were adopted to the Senate bill during floor consideration, some of which were included in H.R. 3888 and which raise concerns for CompTel member companies.

As a general matter, H.R. 3888 addresses the problem of slamming in a straightforward and reasoned way. Indeed the legislation appears to be very similar to what we understand to be the FCC's proposal on this subject. CompTel believes that H.R. 3888, if enacted, will go a long way toward addressing the vexing problems of slamming and cramming. I appreciate this opportunity to comment on specific provisions in the legislation.

Unaffiliated Resellers (Section 101(A)(3))

CompTel strongly supports inclusion of Section 101(a)(3) of H.R. 3888, and worked extensively with the authors of the Senate legislation to insert this provision. CompTel believes that a telecommunications carrier should not be in violation of H.R. 3888 solely because an *unaffiliated* reseller of is telecommunications carrier's service or facilities violates the bill's provisions. There are ample cases where a slamming complaint results from an unauthorized change by a carrier's *unaffiliated* reseller (i.e., where service is not sold under the same brand name as the underlying carrier). In such cases, the reseller, and not the underlying carrier, may be liable for damages.

Primary Interexchange Carrier (PIC) Freeze Option (Section 101 (A)(4))

Section 101(a)(4) of H.R. 3888 concerns primary interexchange carrier (PIC) freeze options. In *FCC Common Carrier Docket No. 94-129,* CompTel has proposed specific policy recommendations governing how telecommunications service providers handle PIC changes and unauthorized charges. At this time when ILECs are entering or are seeking to enter long distance markets and competitors are entering or are seeking to enter the local exchange and intraLATA toll markets, CompTel believes it is critical for the FCC to take action to safeguard against and eliminate ILEC gaming of the PIC-selection process.

In particular, CompTel believes that the FCC must act to eliminate ILECs' *anti-competitive* use of PIC-freezes. Specifically, CompTel has advocated the adoption of rules that prohibit ILECs from (1) engaging in discriminatory or otherwise anti-competitive PIC-freeze practices, and (2) using deceptive or misleading PIC freeze solicitations.

CompTel thus recommends that Section 101(a)(4) be clarified so that the FCC's authority to protect against anticompetitive PIC-freeze activities is preserved.

Subscriber Payment Option (Section 101 (B)(2))

Section 258 of the Telecommunications Act of 1998 explicitly prohibits any telecommunications carrier—local or long-distance—from submitting or executing a change in a subscriber's carrier selection, except in accordance with the FCC's verification procedures. Section 258 provides that any carrier that violates these verification procedures and collects charges for service must be liable to the subscriber's properly authorized carrier for all charges collected.

Customers who are slammed should have no liability with regard to the unauthorized (i.e., slamming) carrier. With regard to a slammed customer's liability for services rendered, CompTel maintains that the FCC should adopt rules requiring payment to the *authorized* carrier at *authorized rates.* This is necessary for two important reasons: (1) to prevent the formation of a cottage industry based on fraudulent claims of slamming that would result if slammed customers automatically were absolved of liability for service charges; and (2) to assure the authorized carrier of reasonably expected revenues.

Complaint Resolution (Section 101(D))

CompTel recommends that the timing requirements in Subsections 101 (d)(1)(A) and 101 (d)(2)(A) be clarified. As currently drafted, the legislation permits a subscriber to initiate dispute resolution with a carrier and also file a complaint at the FCC so that the deadlines for resolving complaints run simultaneously. This presents the awkward situation where the FCC may be investigating a complaint at the same time that the parties are negotiating a resolution. Similarly, it is possible that the FCC may not have sufficient time under the legislation to investigate and resolve a complaint if the time limit imposed on the FCC is not tolled during the complaint resolution process.

Inadvertent Slamming (Section 101 (E))

Even the most reputable carriers sometimes may initiate an unauthorized customer change unintentionally through mistake or inadvertence, such as misreading of a customer's telephone number or data entry error. Unintentional changes or charges also may result from errors made by the executing local carrier. CompTel advocates that carriers re-double their efforts to minimize unintentional changes or charges, and to pursue all appropriate remedies when it is found that slamming or cramming is attributable to the executing local carrier.

H.R. 3888 gives considerable discretion to the FCC and to the courts in determining fault and imposing penalties on carriers who make unauthorized changes of telephone service providers. This discretion is critical, because it allows the FCC and the courts to focus on punishing fraudulent carriers who seek to profit from changing a consumer's telephone provider without permission, while dispensing with complaints that have been brought in error or are unfounded. Because the penalties under H.R. 3888 are severe, CompTel believes that should H.R. 3888 ultimately pass and be enacted, the FCC should use its discretion to punish wrongful behavior and should *not* apply the penalties in cases where a slamming complaint is inadvertent. CompTel recommends that penalties and fines should be assessed only when it has been shown that a carrier has engaged in *willful* and *unintentional* slamming and cramming.

Uniform Notification and Verification Requirements (Section 101(I))

CompTel supports *uniform* federal and state verification requirements, noting that requiring providers to comply with differing requirements for interstate and intrastate services, as well as differing requirements among the states, will lead to customer confusion and increased costs of service. These increased costs of service ultimately will be borne by customers in the form of higher rates.

Switchless Resellers (Title II)

CompTel opposes the surety bond requirement in H.R. 3888 because the requirement is discriminatory, unduly impacts small business and is not needed in light of the bill's other anti-slamming deterrents.

H.R. 3050, THE SLAMMING PREVENTION AND CONSUMER PROTECTION ACT OF 1997

CompTel generally prefers the approach taken in H.R. 3888 as opposed to the approach outlined in H.R. 3050. Nevertheless, CompTel agrees with Congressman Dingell that the FCC has not moved quickly enough to establish regulations regarding slamming as required under the 1996 Telecommunications Act. For that reason, CompTel endorses the bill's provision which places a deadline on the FCC for completion of the proceeding to establish slamming regulations.

H.R. 3050's central feature is the creation of a private right of action for victims of slamming. CompTel is concerned that this new right to sue carriers in court for slamming will be an open invitation to unscrupulous consumers and enterprising class action lawyers to file questionable suits against carriers. Most likely carriers would be forced to settle these suits to avoid the expense, time and publicity of litigation. Therefore, rather than discouraging carriers to take steps to curtail slamming, it could have the unintended consequence of encouraging consumers to make claims that they have been slammed.

CONCLUSION

In closing, I would like to reiterate that it is in the interest of CompTel and its member companies to put a stop to slamming once and for all. CompTel has worked hard to establish guidelines for our member companies which include a zero tolerance for slammers. I am personally committed to working with you, Mr. Chairman, and the subcommittee to develop legislation that can pass this session of Congress that cracks down on intentional slamming. The statutory changes set forth in H.R. 3888 together with continued oversight of the FCC should go a long way toward ridding the industry of the terrible scourge of slamming. Stopping slamming now, before it can spread to the local exchange market, is critical if we are ever to realize the benefits of a competitive telecommunications marketplace.

NATIONAL CONSUMERS LEAGUE
June 26, 1998

The Honorable WILLIAM J. TAUZIN
Chairman
Subcommittee on Telecommunications, Trade, and Consumer Protection
U.S. House of Representatives
Committee on Commerce
Room 2125, Rayburn House Office Building
Washington, DC 20515-6115

RE: H.R. 3888 and H.R. 3050

DEAR CHAIRMAN TAUZIN: Thank you for asking me to testify on behalf of the National Consumers League at your June 23 hearing concerning the problem of "slamming." As you requested, I am providing some additional information. If it is possible, I ask that it this information be included in the record.

Enclosed is a copy of the Michigan Public Service Commission decision relating to PIC protection. Regardless of the merit of the various issues between MCI and Ameritech with which the Commission dealt, the decision essentially eliminates PIC protection in Michigan because it says that if the long distance service provider asserts that it has followed one of the verification procedures proscribed by the Federal Communications Commission, the local exchange must make the carrier change at its behest, even if the consumer has PIC protection and has not contacted the local exchange directly to request the change.

While the Commission only has jurisdiction over intrastate service, because long distance carriers may provide intrastate toll as well as interstate toll service, there is no way that the PIC protection system can differentiate between the two. As a result, Ameritech is unable to provide PIC protection to any Michigan consumers at this point. More information can be obtained from Wendy Resnik in Corporate Communications at Ameritech, (716) 242-9349.

H.R. 3888 provides that the FCC may not take action to limit or inhibit the PIC protection option. However, it might be helpful to require the FCC to amend its rules to clarify that the verification procedures it sets forth do not in any way supersede or negate the subscriber's PIC freeze request.

We are also concerned about a technical problem with the PIC protection option. It appears that if the consumer is slammed by a reseller of his or her original carrier's service, the PIC freeze is not triggered because the system does not recognize a change of service. The FCC should direct telecommunications companies to solve this problem.

Finally, I would like to emphasize the most important steps that Congress should take to give consumers back control over their telephone service:

- Negative option and contest solicitations for phone service should be *banned;*
- Consumers should be notified the local telephone exchanges, who make the changes, immediately when a carrier change has been effected. Notice should be received by the consumer within 3-5 days;
- To take the incentive out of slamming and compensate consumers for the trouble they are put through to remedy the problem, consumers should have *no obligation* to pay slamming charges;
- To aid the complaint resolution and law enforcement process, the *name, address and phone number of the carrier and any billing service provider acting on its behalf* should be clearly listed on the telephone bill;
- Slammers or the billing service providers acting on their behalf should have no more than *thirty* days to resolve consumer complaints;
- The FCC should have no more than *ninety* days to resolve slamming complaints or initiate formal action;
- States should *not be preempted* from protecting the interests of their constituents involving intrastate and interstate telecommunications service.

Stemming the tide of slamming complaints is crucial to the health of the competitive telecommunications marketplace. Thank you for requesting our input in this issue.

Sincerely yours,

SUSAN GRANT,
Vice President for Public Policy

enclosure
cc: The Honorable Edward J. Markey, Ranking Minority Member

STATE OF MICHIGAN

BEFORE THE MICHIGAN PUBLIC SERVICE COMMISSION

* * * * *

In the matter of the complaint of MCI TELECOMMUNICATIONS CORPORATION against AMERITECH MICHIGAN.	))))	Case No. U-11550

At the May 11, 1998 meeting of the Michigan Public Service Commission in Lansing, Michigan.

PRESENT: Hon. John G. Strand, Chairman
Hon. John C. Shea, Commissioner
Hon. David A. Svanda, Commissioner

OPINION AND ORDER

I.

HISTORY OF PROCEEDINGS

On October 20, 1997, MCI Telecommunications Corporation (MCI) filed a complaint against Ameritech Michigan pursuant to the provisions of 1991 PA 179, as amended by 1995 PA 216, MCL 484.2101 et seq.; MSA 22.1469(101) et seq., (the Act). In Count I of its complaint, MCI alleged that Ameritech Michigan violated the Commission's August 1, 1996 order in Case No. U-11038 (the August 1 order) by refusing to implement certain primary interexchange carrier (PIC[1]) change orders submitted by MCI on and after April 1, 1997. In Count II, MCI asserted that although the August 1 order authorized the use of three-way conference calls as a means of

[1]A PIC is the toll carrier that the customer chooses to handle its 1+ toll dialing.

verifying that a customer wanted to change service providers, Ameritech Michigan was improperly using those three-way calls to dissuade customers from leaving Ameritech Michigan's intraLATA service. On November 14, 1997, Ameritech Michigan filed its answer and affirmative defenses.

Pursuant to due notice, a prehearing conference was held on November 18, 1997 before Administrative Law Judge Robert E. Hollenshead (ALJ). Evidentiary hearings were held on February 2, 3, 8, and 9, 1998. MCI and Ameritech Michigan each filed initial briefs and reply briefs on February 17 and March 3, 1998, respectively. The record consists of 1,073 pages of transcript and 66 exhibits.

The ALJ issued a Proposal for Decision (PFD) on March 31, 1998. The parties filed exceptions to the PFD on April 7, 1998 and replies to exceptions on April 14, 1998. In addition, on April 9, 1998, Ameritech Michigan filed a motion to reopen the record. On April 27, 1998, MCI filed its response to that motion.

II.

BACKGROUND

The genesis of this proceeding is a bill insert that Ameritech Corporation[2] mailed to its approximately 12 million residential and small business customers in Michigan and four other states during December 1995. The bill insert, which was sent approximately one month before the implementation of intraLATA dialing parity in Michigan, urged customers to sign up for Ameritech Michigan's PIC protection program by filling out and returning a form that was attached to the insert. According to the insert, enrollment in the PIC protection (or PIC freeze) program would reduce the

[2]The decision to send the bill insert was made by Ameritech, the parent corporation of Ameritech Michigan.

risk of being slammed[3] by requiring that any change in a Michigan-based customer's service provider must be preceded by written or oral authorization going directly from the customer to Ameritech Michigan.

On February 14, 1996, Sprint Communications Company L.P. (Sprint) filed a complaint in Case No. U-11038 alleging that the December 1995 bill insert was deliberately misleading and anticompetitive in violation of the Act. Specifically, Sprint claimed that although the bill insert referred only to changes in interLATA service, the PIC protection program also applied to intraLATA and local services, both of which are provided by Ameritech Michigan. According to Sprint, the language and timing of the bill insert had the effect of interjecting confusion into the intraLATA presubscription process, impeding or delaying customers' selection of a competing intraLATA carrier, and hindering the ability of interexchange carriers like Sprint, MCI, and AT&T Communications of Michigan, Inc., (AT&T) to compete in the intraLATA market. As such, Sprint asserted, what Ameritech Michigan portrayed as a solution to interLATA slamming was in fact a mechanism to tie intraLATA and local service customers to Ameritech Michigan before those customers ever had a choice of alternative service providers.

Sprint's complaint culminated in the August 1 order, where the Commission (with one Commissioner dissenting) found that Ameritech Michigan's December 1995 bill insert violated both the Act and prior Commission orders. Specifically, the Commission concluded that the insert was "deceptive and misleading" because it failed to inform customers that the PIC freeze would apply to all of a customer's services, including intraLATA and local exchange services. August 1 order, p. 5. The Commission further found that Ameritech Michigan's use of the bill insert was anticompetitive

[3]"Slamming" is the illegal practice of changing a customer's telecommunications provider or providers without the customer's knowledge and consent.

"because it created new hurdles to the exercise of the customer's decision to change providers just as alternatives were becoming available." Id., p. 12. Without Ameritech Michigan's PIC protection, the Commission noted, the customer can call a new service provider and make arrangements to take service, and the new provider can work directly with Ameritech Michigan to implement the change; however, with the protection in place, the customer must contact not only the new service provider, but Ameritech Michigan as well. The Commission went on to state that:

> The bill insert, and PIC protection, become even more anticompetitive if the interexchange carriers' fears are justified that Ameritech Michigan will delay requests from customers to change providers and that it will use the contact as an opportunity to try to dissuade the customer from leaving Ameritech Michigan's service.

Id., p. 13. The Commission therefore concluded that the bill insert violated Sections 205(2), 312b, and 502(a) of the Act, as well as the Commission's orders in Case No. U-10138 (which mandated the implementation of intraLATA dialing parity). It further found that Ameritech Michigan's use of the bill insert violated the competitive purposes of the Act as expressed in Section 101.[4]

The August 1 order went on to require Ameritech Michigan to draft a corrective bill insert that would, among other things, inform customers of the order, outline the differences among the various services covered under the PIC protection program, and advise customers of the advent of competition in the provision of those services. It also ordered Ameritech Michigan not to apply PIC protection requests to intraLATA and basic local exchange services until six months after mailing the corrective bill insert unless the customer had first affirmatively selected a provider for those services and then requested PIC protection.

---

[4]MCL 484.2101(2); MSA 22.1469(101)(2) provides that the purposes of the Act are, among other things, to "encourage competition to determine the availability, prices, terms, and other conditions of providing telecommunication services" and to "encourage . . . the entry of new providers" into Michigan's telecommunications market.

The Commission further ordered Ameritech Michigan to permit the verification of PIC changes by any procedure approved in the March 10, 1995 order in Case No. U-10138, where the Commission adopted all PIC verification options authorized by the Federal Communications Commission (FCC). Those options included independent third-party verification (TPV) and the use of a written letter of authorization (LOA). In imposing this requirement, the Commission noted that "Ameritech Michigan is not free to invalidate PIC change procedures that the FCC and this Commission have approved." August 1 order, p. 22. The Commission went on to order Ameritech Michigan also to permit verification through the use of three-way conference calls with the consent of the customer. In so doing, the Commission pointed out that "Ameritech Michigan will need to find a way to verify the identity of the customer that does not require the disclosure of confidential information" and that if Ameritech Michigan finds that it must discuss confidential or proprietary information with the customer, "it may do so in another telephone conversation." Id., p. 22, fn. 14. Finally, in response to concerns raised by Sprint, MCI, and AT&T, the Commission held that "if a customer with PIC protection calls to change providers, Ameritech Michigan shall not use that contact to try to persuade the customer not to change providers." Id., p. 22.

Pursuant to the Commission's directive, Ameritech Michigan issued a corrective bill insert to all of its residential and small business customers. Because this was accomplished by the close of September 1996, the six-month moratorium imposed by the Commission's order expired on March 31, 1997.

III.

POSITIONS OF THE PARTIES

MCI asserts that since April 1, 1997, Ameritech Michigan has refused, on accounts that have PIC protection, to implement any intraLATA PIC change orders that have been verified through the use of TPV or LOA. Instead, MCI contends, Ameritech Michigan will switch these accounts over to MCI's intraLATA service only if the change order is communicated to it through use of a three-way call. According to MCI, this is in direct violation of the August 1 order. Worse yet, MCI argues, Ameritech Michigan has exhibited a pattern of behavior during its three-way calls that is precisely what the Commission ordered it not to do. Specifically, MCI asserts that Ameritech Michigan has (1) used these contacts to try to persuade the customer not to change service providers, (2) refused to participate in these calls by leaving MCI and the customer on hold for unreasonably long periods of time or by hanging up before verification of the service transfer can be completed, (3) made use of confidential customer data, such as the customer's calling frequency and patterns, in an attempt to make the customer change its mind, and (4) used confidential customer information during these calls in an attempt to sell the customer additional Ameritech Michigan services and features to which the customer does not currently subscribe.

According to MCI, Ameritech Michigan's actions resulted in the improper rejection of 24,448 residential and 8,039 small business intraLATA customer change orders submitted on and after April 1, 1997. MCI claims that its inability to serve those 32,487 customers due to Ameritech Michigan's wrongful actions led to lost profits of $1,173,608. See Exhibit C-11. MCI further contends that Ameritech Michigan's violations of the Act and past Commission orders continue to this day. It therefore argues that, among other remedies, the Commission should (1) issue a cease and desist order, (2) require Ameritech Michigan to immediately process all intraLATA PIC change orders that were verified through the use of either TPV or LOA since April 1, 1997, (3) award compensatory damages to MCI of $1,173,608 to replace its lost profits, (4) impose a fine of up to $40,000 per day from April 1, 1997 to the present, and (5) assess costs and attorney fees against Ameritech Michigan.

Although conceding that it ceased processing intraLATA change orders that were verified under TPV or LOA after March 31, 1997, Ameritech Michigan contends that its decision to do so was not in violation of the August 1 order. To reach any other conclusion, it argues, would render meaningless the entire concept of PIC protection. This is because, Ameritech Michigan continues, it would eliminate the need for the direct communication to Ameritech Michigan (either orally or in writing) of the customer's intent to change intraLATA service providers.

Ameritech Michigan also asserts that there is no basis for concluding that its conduct during three-way calls was improper. Specifically, it contends that MCI failed to support its contention that Ameritech Michigan sales representatives took steps during these calls to dissuade customers from switching to MCI's intraLATA service. It goes on to claim that, notwithstanding MCI's assumption to the contrary, the August 1 order does not bar the use of confidential customer information during those calls. Finally, Ameritech Michigan argues that even if the Commission concludes that some violations did occur, MCI's claim for compensatory damages is based entirely on conjecture and unsupported speculation.

IV.

DISCUSSION

As occurred in Case No. U-11038, the parties' rhetoric frequently exceeds the scope of this proceeding. This is particularly true with regard to assertions by Ameritech Michigan that any decision adverse to its position in this case will destroy PIC protection and be tantamount to blessing the practice of slamming. Despite Ameritech Michigan's assertions, this case is not about whether slamming is unlawful or undesirable. As stated in the August 1 order, it is both. Moreover, it is not about whether Ameritech Michigan's PIC protection program is appropriate or unreasonable as a whole. Instead, this case is about whether certain steps that Ameritech Michigan took in implementing that program violated the August 1 order.

As noted in previous Commission orders, the Act is designed in significant part to establish a regulatory structure in which full and fair competition among service providers will serve to ensure that rates for certain services (including intraLATA toll service) are not unreasonable. Therefore, Ameritech Michigan's repeated assertion that the benefits of PIC protection can only be preserved by ruling against MCI in this case effectively asks the Commission to sacrifice intraLATA competition at the altar of PIC protection. This, the Commission concludes, it cannot do.

<u>Change Orders Based on TPV or LOA</u>

The ALJ found no justification for requiring MCI to participate in three-way calls as a prerequisite to having Ameritech Michigan process intraLATA change orders on accounts for which PIC protection has been implemented. According to the ALJ, "the basic issue" addressed by the August 1 order concerned whether there was "verification that a customer does indeed wish to switch interexchange carriers." PFD, p. 10. Nevertheless, he noted, Ameritech Michigan's insistence on using three-way calls does not aid the verification process, "but instead serves only to deter customers who desire to switch carriers." Id. Based on his reading of the August 1 order, the ALJ recommended finding that customers subscribing to Ameritech Michigan's PIC protection program remain free to change intraLATA service providers through the use of TPV or LOA.

Ameritech Michigan excepts, arguing--among other things--that adopting the ALJ's recommendation would render PIC protection a nullity and thus conflict with the August 1 order. According to Ameritech Michigan, the August 1 order expressly envisioned that Ameritech Michigan would be able to apply its proposed form of intraLATA PIC protection to its customers' accounts, albeit following a six month moratorium. In support of this argument, Ameritech Michigan cites Paragraph D on page 24 of the August 1 order, which states:

> Ameritech Michigan shall apply PIC protection requests received beginning in December 1995 only to interLATA service. It shall not apply PIC protection requests to intraLATA and basic local exchange services until six months after mailing the corrective bill insert unless the customer has first affirmatively selected a provider for those services and then requests PIC protection.

Because the six month period referred to in that paragraph ended on March 31, 1997, Ameritech Michigan continues, it was "under *no* prohibition in applying its customers' PIC protection to intraLATA PIC changes" from April 1, 1997 to the present. Ameritech Michigan's exceptions, p. 11 (emphasis in original). Ameritech Michigan therefore contends that from that day forward, it was free to reject any intraLATA change order verified through the use of TPV or LOA where the account had PIC protection and, instead, could require the use of a three-way call. It thus argues that the ALJ's conclusion to the contrary must be rejected.

In response, MCI asserts that PIC protection is not nullified by allowing TPV to be used to verify a customer's intent to change service providers. For example, MCI notes that "to change PICs on any account, TPV (in the absence of a PIC Freeze) is not required on in-bound telemarketing." MCI's replies to exceptions, p. 9. MCI therefore claims that by requiring the use of TPV in those situations, Ameritech's PIC protection program could still be used to reduce the risk of slamming.

MCI goes on to argue that Ameritech Michigan's exclusive reliance on page 24, Paragraph D of the August 1 order "conveniently overlooks the implications of other portions of the order." MCI's replies to exceptions, p. 12. Specifically, MCI refers to Paragraph F on page 25 of the August 1 order, which states:

> Ameritech Michigan shall permit the verification of PIC changes by any procedure approved by the Commission's March 10, 1995 order in Case No. U-10138 and shall also permit three-way conference calls with the consent of the customer.

MCI points out that Paragraph D focused exclusively on when Ameritech Michigan's PIC protection program would take effect and what services it would cover. In contrast, it continues, Paragraph F addressed the issue that is at the heart of the current complaint, namely how requests for intraLATA PIC changes should be verified for customer accounts that have PIC protection. According to MCI, it is important to note that Paragraph F, which authorizes the use of TPV and LOA to verify a customer's intent to switch providers, has no applicable time limitation. Thus, it asserts, no justification exists for Ameritech Michigan's decision to cease accepting either TPV or LOA as adequate verification on and after April 1, 1997.

Finally, MCI argues that the August 1 order found Ameritech Michigan's PIC protection plan to be anticompetitive because it would require customers to contact both the new service provider and Ameritech Michigan before having its service switched to the new provider. According to MCI, "it would make no sense" for the Commission to conclude that the PIC protection program was anticompetitive due to its requirement of a double contact, and then authorize Ameritech Michigan to implement a program that retains "the same cumbersome double contact process [that] the Commission had determined to be anticompetitive." Id., p. 14. For all of these reasons, MCI asserts that the Commission should reject Ameritech Michigan's exception, adopt the ALJ's recommendation, and find that Ameritech Michigan violated the August 1 order by refusing (on and after April 1, 1997) to process intraLATA PIC change orders that were verified by TPV or LOA.

The Commission agrees with the ALJ and MCI, and concludes that Ameritech Michigan violated the August 1 order by refusing to process intraLATA PIC change orders that had been verified by TPV or LOA. In reaching this conclusion, the Commission finds that Ameritech Michigan misinterprets the guidelines established, as well as the actions prohibited, by that order.

The portion of the August 1 order relied upon by Ameritech Michigan--Paragraph D on page 24--addresses the questions of (1) when Ameritech Michigan's PIC protection would take effect and (2) what specific services that protection would cover. However, those matters are not in dispute here. Instead, the question in this complaint (namely, whether it was proper for Ameritech Michigan to reject PIC change orders that were verified through TPV or LOA) involves the issue of how requests for intraLATA PIC changes should be verified for accounts that have PIC protection. As correctly noted by MCI, that issue is covered by Paragraph F on page 25 of the August 1 order, which (in addition to authorizing the use of three-way calls) specifically directed Ameritech Michigan to "permit the verification of PIC changes by any procedure approved by the Commission's March 10, 1995 order in Case No. U-10138." Because the Commission's order in Case No. U-10138 adopted the four verification procedures approved by the FCC's January 9, 1992 order in CC Docket No. 91-64 (See March 10, 1995 order, p. 36), and because TPV and LOA were included among those four options, the August 1 order prohibited Ameritech Michigan from using its PIC protection program to reject intraLATA PIC change orders that were verified by TPV or LOA.

The Commission's conclusion is further supported by language contained in the body of the August 1 order. In discussing the steps that it felt were necessary to protect intraLATA competition and to undo the harm caused by the December 1995 bill insert, the Commission stated:

> Fourth, if a customer with PIC protection calls to change providers, Ameritech Michigan shall not use that contact to try to persuade the customer not to change providers. Fifth, Ameritech Michigan shall permit the verification of PIC changes by any procedure approved by the Commission's March 10, 1995 order in Case No. U-10138. *Ameritech Michigan is not free to invalidate PIC change procedures that the FCC and the Commission have approved.* In addition, it shall permit verification by the use of three-way conference calls with the consent of the customer.

August 1 order, p. 22 (emphasis added). Because rejecting PIC change requests that have been verified by TPV or LOA invalidates two of the four previously approved PIC change procedures, Ameritech Michigan's proposed interpretation of the August 1 order directly conflicts with the language quoted above. Likewise, that interpretation conflicts with language in the order stating that the option of using three-way calls to verify PIC change requests for accounts that have PIC protection was to be "in addition" to the use of TPV, LOA, or any other procedure approved by the FCC and the Commission. Id.

The Commission therefore adopts the ALJ's recommendation and finds that customers subscribing to Ameritech Michigan's PIC protection program remain free to change intraLATA service providers through the use of TPV or LOA.[5] The Commission further concludes that Ameritech Michigan's refusal to process TPV- or LOA-based intraLATA PIC change orders, which has been occurring since April 1, 1997, is in direct violation of the August 1 order.

---

[5]Moreover, nothing in this ruling prevents PIC protection customers from likewise relying on three-way calls (or either of the other two verification procedures that were previously approved by the FCC and the Commission) as a valid means of changing service providers.

Improper Actions During Three-Way Calls

As noted earlier, Count II of MCI's complaint involved allegations of misconduct with regard to the use of three-way calls. MCI asserted that in response to mounting complaints by its employees, Todd A. Gerdes, its Executive Director of Mass Market Sales, began monitoring some of the three-way calls placed from MCI to Ameritech Michigan. As a result of his investigation, Mr. Gerdes testified that Ameritech Michigan's service representatives sometimes refused to participate in these calls. He further asserted that when they did participate, they frequently used these three-way calls as an opportunity either to dissuade the customer from changing intraLATA service providers or to sell the customer other Ameritech Michigan services and features. Mr. Gerdes went on to state that, in the course of these calls, Ameritech Michigan's service representatives have used confidential customer data to bolster their efforts to retain customers and to sell additional services. Based on this testimony, MCI asserted that Ameritech Michigan should be found in violation of the August 1 order.

Ameritech Michigan responded to that portion of the complaint by arguing that MCI offered insufficient evidence to support the allegations of improper conduct. Specifically, it noted that although MCI sought to corroborate Mr. Gerdes' testimony through the introduction of call reports,[6] those reports were ultimately excluded by the ALJ. See 8 Tr. 783. Thus, Ameritech Michigan asserted, MCI was left solely with Mr. Gerdes' account of what was taking place during those calls. It went on to assert that because that testimony covered only a small percentage of all three-way calls in which Ameritech Michigan's service representatives have been involved, no

[6] The term "call reports" refers to written summaries of three-way calls that MCI's service representatives have been instructed to prepare whenever they feel that a competing company's agents (in this case, Ameritech Michigan's service representatives) have handled three-way calls in an improper manner.

accurate conclusions could be drawn from it regarding the general conduct of Ameritech Michigan's employees. Finally, Ameritech Michigan argued that nothing in the August 1 order precludes its employees from selling other services during three-way calls or suggests that its service representatives are not free to use information from the customers' service records in the course of those conversations.

The ALJ agreed with MCI concerning the allegations contained in Count II. He stated that even with the exclusion of the call reports, which were marked as proposed Exhibits C-30 and C-33, "the record demonstrates improper action by Ameritech Michigan service representatives" during three-way calls. PFD, p. 22. According to the ALJ, this conclusion was supported by testimony from Mr. Gerdes (who disclosed that while monitoring three-way calls involving these two companies, he personally witnessed situations where Ameritech Michigan's service representatives refused to participate, placed parties on hold for over 5 minutes, initiated discussions regarding the ramifications of changing carriers, discussed confidential billing and call pattern data, and attempted to sell additional products), as well as by statements from Ameritech Michigan service representatives Keith Breidinger and Eulalia Miller (who conceded to advising customers about how changing carriers would affect their costs and challenging them to compare rates, respectively).

Because several of these activities served to discourage customers from changing service providers, the ALJ continued, they violated the Commission's directive that:

> [I]f a customer with PIC protection calls to change providers, Ameritech Michigan shall not use that contact to try to persuade the customer not to change providers.

August 1 order, p. 22. The ALJ likewise concluded that the use of confidential information by Ameritech Michigan's service representatives was in direct contravention of the Commission's statement (found in footnote 14 of the August 1 order) that:

> Ameritech Michigan will need to find a way to verify the identity of the customer that does not require the disclosure of confidential information. If it must discuss confidential or proprietary information with the customer, it may do so in another telephone conversation.

August 1 order, p. 22, n. 14. He therefore recommended that the Commission find in favor of MCI with regard to the allegations contained in Count II of the complaint.

Ameritech Michigan excepts to the ALJ's recommendation. In so doing, it reasserts that insufficient evidence was offered to support the conclusion that its service representatives have been acting in an improper manner. According to Ameritech Michigan, information provided by MCI shows that the two companies are involved in approximately 5,000 such calls each month. Nevertheless, it continues, the testimony offered by Mr. Gerdes was based on his having monitored a total of 60 three-way calls between MCI and Ameritech, only 15 to 20 of which involved customers located in Ameritech Michigan's service territory.[7] Furthermore, the statements of Mr. Breidinger and Ms. Miller refer to only a few of the hundreds of three-way calls handled by them during their tenure as service representatives. Ameritech Michigan therefore argues that no reasonable conclusions can be drawn about the overall actions of its sales representatives from such a small sample of calls.

Ameritech Michigan goes on to contend in its exceptions that Mr. Gerdes is not a credible witness. Specifically, it claims that his testimony should be ignored because (1) he cannot remember all the names of the customers and the Ameritech Michigan service representatives that participated in the three-way calls he monitored, (2) he is an employee of MCI, and therefore has a built-in bias for MCI and against Ameritech Michigan, and (3) he threw away his original notes concerning the

---

[7]The remaining 40 to 48 calls monitored by Mr. Gerdes involved customers of Ameritech Michigan's affiliates in Indiana, Illinois, Ohio, and Wisconsin.

three-way calls he monitored. Finally, Ameritech Michigan argues that although the PFD specifies several types of conduct through which its service representatives purportedly violated the August 1 order (such as disclosing proprietary information, asking customers whether they will be getting a lower rate by switching service providers, and inquiring as to whether they want to purchase additional services), that order contains no mention of those specific acts. Instead, Ameritech Michigan asserts, the August 1 order "only prohibits Ameritech Michigan from trying to dissuade the customer from changing his or her inter or intraLATA provider during the call." Ameritech Michigan's exceptions, p. 21. Because the alleged actions of its service representatives do not fall within that "single, limited, and very explicit directive," Ameritech Michigan claims, they cannot serve as a basis for finding in favor of MCI.

The Commission concludes that these exceptions are not well taken. Notwithstanding Ameritech Michigan's assertions to the contrary, MCI is under no duty to show (through the presentation of a statistically significant sampling of its three-way calls) that Ameritech Michigan's service representatives acted in an anticompetitive manner on each and every occasion since March 31, 1997. All that is required to prevail on Count II of the complaint is for MCI to prove that, by accident or design, those service representatives repeatedly violated either the letter or the spirit of the August 1 order.

Moreover, the record contains sufficient evidence of repeated wrongdoing by Ameritech Michigan. Mr. Gerdes testified that of the approximately 60 three-way calls he personally monitored, the service representatives for Ameritech Michigan and its affiliates "acted inappropriately in every single one of them." 8 Tr. 658. Rather than simply verifying the customer's selection of MCI as its new provider of intraLATA PIC service, Mr. Gerdes stated that they frequently

> use the Three Way Calls to attempt to actively sell a competing Ameritech toll product. In other instances, Ameritech representatives will quiz customers as to the ramifications of switching to MCI. In still other instances, Ameritech representatives will hang up or flatly refuse to participate in the Three Way Calls while an MCI employee is on the line.

8 Tr. 654-655. He further stated that although only 15 to 20 of these calls directly involved Ameritech Michigan employees, the improper conduct "was substantially similar whether the party was Ameritech Michigan or some other Ameritech entity." 7 Tr. 749 and 8 Tr. 658.

Moreover, as correctly noted by the ALJ, sworn statements provided by some of Ameritech Michigan's own service representatives lend substantial support to Mr. Gerdes' observations. For example, Mr. Breidinger confirmed that, in the normal course of three-way calls, he will (1) advise customers about the effect that changing intraLATA service providers will have on their bills, (2) remind them of the $5 charge for making such a change, and (3) use information from their billing records to determine whether to offer them additional services like call waiting. Exhibit C-35. Similarly, Ms. Miller conceded that when handling a three-way call for a customer whose billing records reflect the presence of an Ameritech Michigan discount calling plan, she specifically reminded the customer about that plan and asked the customer if she knew whether MCI's proposed service would be less expensive. Exhibit C-36.

As for Ameritech Michigan's final argument, the Commission finds that the ALJ correctly assessed the scope of the prohibitions included in the August 1 order. When read in its entirety, it becomes clear that the August 1 order authorized the use of three-way calls solely as a means of verifying a PIC change and not as a vehicle for Ameritech Michigan to market its services. Furthermore, that order specifically indicated that, during three-way calls, Ameritech Michigan's service representatives are prohibited from using customer billing records for any purpose beyond verifying a customer's identity. See August 1 order, p. 22, n. 14. Thus, in addition to the more obvious ways of making these three-way calls an unpleasant and difficult experience (like hanging up, putting parties on hold for unreasonable periods, or pressuring customers not to change carriers), Ameritech Michigan's service representatives violated the August 1 order each time they (1) asked customers whether they would be getting a less expensive rate from MCI, (2) discussed the customers' existing service plan or calling pattern, (3) inquired about whether the customers wanted additional services, (4) talked about the ramifications of changing service providers, and (5) mentioned any information contained in the customers' billing records beyond that needed to confirm the customers' respective identities.

For all of these reasons, the Commission adopts the ALJ's recommendation and finds that Ameritech Michigan violated the August 1 order by repeatedly making improper use of three-way calls.

Compensatory Damages

As noted earlier, MCI asserted that Ameritech Michigan's improper actions led to the rejection of 32,487 intraLATA PIC change orders submitted on and after April 1, 1997. MCI went on to assert that, based on Section 601 of the Act, it must be made whole for the loss of those potential customers. MCI therefore offered the testimony of Albert E. Clement, its Director of Finance, for the purpose of computing the compensatory damages arising from Ameritech Michigan's failure to properly switch those customers to MCI's intraLATA service.

Mr. Clement began by developing a formula for estimating the total net profit that MCI would have received from those customers. According to him, this could best be achieved by computing MCI's average profit per minute for intraLATA service and then multiplying that figure by the estimated number of minutes that these customers would have spent making intraLATA calls while on MCI's system. To arrive at his number for the average profit per minute, Mr. Clement started with an estimate of the average rate per minute that MCI charges for intraLATA calls and reduced that figure to reflect the effect of (1) uncollectible accounts, (2) access charges, and (3) the estimated cost of marketing, billing, and customer service. Similarly, in developing his prediction of how many minutes of calls these customers would have made as MCI customers, he multiplied the average use per month (in minutes) for each of its existing intraLATA customers by the estimated length of time that these customers would remain on MCI's system after switching from some other provider. MCI claimed that, based on Mr. Clement's analysis, Ameritech Michigan's actions resulted in lost profits of $1,173,608. See MCI's initial brief, p. 35.

In response to MCI's claim for compensatory damages, Ameritech Michigan asserted that Mr. Clement's analysis was wholly unreliable. In support of this assertion, it cited the testimony of Van E. Conway. Among other things, Mr. Conway stated that MCI's computation of its alleged lost profits (1) ignored the effect of several classes of costs when estimating its average profit per minute, (2) overstated the number of customers that were precluded from taking intraLATA PIC service from MCI, (3) overestimated the average number of minutes of intraLATA calls that those customers would make each month, (4) underestimated the rate at which these customers would switch from MCI to another service provider, and (5) failed to consider the time value of money. Ameritech Michigan argued that due to these serious flaws in Mr. Clement's analysis, MCI's request for compensatory damages is based solely on conjecture and speculation, and must be rejected.

The ALJ agreed with Ameritech Michigan and found that MCI failed to meet its burden of proof regarding compensatory damages. From his reading of the record, the ALJ held that MCI greatly underestimated the cost of providing intraLATA service, exaggerated the profitability of its operations, overstated the number of customers it lost as a result of Ameritech Michigan's actions, and inflated those customers' potential usage of MCI's intraLATA service. He therefore recommended that the Commission reject MCI's demand that Ameritech reimburse it for at least $1,173,608 in lost profits.

In its exceptions, MCI argues that its request for lost profits need not be established with absolute certainty. Citing Tempo, Inc. v Rapid Electric Sales & Service, Inc., 132 Mich App 93; 347 NW2d 728 (1984), it contends that Michigan's courts have long held that compensatory damages can be granted so long as the "method of calculating lost profits had a reasonable degree of certainty and was not based solely on conjecture and speculation." 132 Mich App at 103. MCI further contends that, notwithstanding the ALJ's conclusion to the contrary, the analysis presented by Mr. Clement was not too speculative to support the recovery of compensatory damages in this case. Instead, MCI asserts, he came forward with a reasonable methodology and adequate evidence to support MCI's claim for lost profits. MCI therefore requests that the Commission reject the ALJ's recommendation and award it compensatory damages of at least $1,173,608.

Based on its review of the record, the Commission concludes that MCI's request should be rejected. Although MCI need not establish the level of lost profits with absolute certainty, neither can it prevail on proofs that include excessive speculation. In this case, the ALJ correctly held that MCI's analysis was too speculative to support the recovery of compensatory damages. The Commission reaches this conclusion for the following three reasons.

First, Mr. Clement's computation of MCI's average profit per minute for intraLATA service appears to have either underestimated or ignored several important categories of expenses. For example, Mr. Clement conceded that by failing to reflect the higher percentage of charges that are never paid by customers "who are direct billed by MCI," he underestimated MCI's uncollectibles expense. 7 Tr. 431. Similarly, although his lost profit analysis failed to include it, Mr. Clement ultimately agreed that "there is probably some general and administrative expense associated with the provision of intraLATA toll." 7 Tr. 436. Furthermore, the record indicates that although MCI offers inducements "such as rebates, flight miles, etc., to its potential customers . . . for switching long distance carriers," none of these promotional expenses have been included in MCI's analysis. 9 Tr. 905. Finally, Mr. Clement did not account for any of the costs of MCI's switching equipment, trunks, and other network facilities necessary to handle its customer's intraLATA calls. 7-A Tr. 555;[8] 9 Tr. 906. Due at least in part to its failure to recognize these costs, Mr. Clement came up with an estimated profit per minute for lost intraLATA service that was five to six times higher than the net profit margin that MCI expects on its combined interLATA and intraLATA service. See Exhibit R-29; 7-A Tr. 453.

Second, the record indicates that MCI's analysis overstates the number of customers that it was precluded from serving as a result of Ameritech Michigan's improper actions. MCI witness Mindy J. Chapman offered Exhibit C-6, documenting 32,487 instances where Ameritech Michigan improperly rejected intraLATA customer change orders submitted by MCI. However, Ms. Chapman conceded during cross-examination that of those customers whose intraLATA PIC change orders were initially rejected by Ameritech Michigan, at least 1,076 were ultimately switched to MCI. 6 Tr. 369-370. Moreover, that figure (1,076) related only to the 20,105 change orders rejected between April and August, 1997. See Exhibit C-5R. Ms. Chapman therefore went on to state that a similar downward adjustment should be made to reflect that an equal percentage of the

---

[8]A protective order was issued in this case on December 1, 1997. As a result, part of the hearings were conducted on a separate, confidential record. Any part of the transcript contained in the separate record is designated by the volume number corresponding to the public record created on that day, plus "-A".

12,382 customers whose change orders were rejected during the remainder of the period covered by Exhibit C-6 have likely succeeded in switching to MCI as well. 6 Tr. 371. However, notwithstanding Ms. Chapman's testimony, Exhibit C-11 indicates that MCI only made the first downward adjustment with regard to the number of lost customers (and neglected to make the second) when computing its alleged lost profits.

Third, evidence indicates that in addition to overstating the number of lost customers, Mr. Clement significantly overestimated the potential use that those customers would have made of MCI's intraLATA service had their change orders been implemented. For example, the figure he adopted to represent the average minutes of monthly use for each lost customer is nearly twice as large as the average use actually posted by MCI's existing customers. See Exhibit R-59. No reasonable justification was provided for this dramatic difference. Similarly, Mr. Clements relied on the wrong churn rate[9] when performing his analysis. As noted by Mr. Conway, the churn rate used by Mr. Clements was improper in that it combines "two subsets of customers (interLATA and intraLATA customers) who churn at different rates." 9-A Tr. 925-926. Because the actual churn rate exhibited by MCI's intraLATA customers is significantly higher than that of its interLATA customers, the blended rate used by Mr. Clements was approximately 30% too low. Id. As a result, MCI's analysis significantly overestimated the length of time that each lost customer would have continued taking intraLATA service from MCI.

Due to the number and magnitude of the deficiencies found in MCI's lost profit analysis, the Commission finds that it should adopt the ALJ's recommendation and deny MCI's request for compensatory damages.

---

[9]The "churn rate" refers to the percentage of a service provider's customers that switch their service to another provider. It is generally stated on a per month basis.

Miscellaneous Requests for Relief

In addition to its request for compensatory damages, MCI sought several other forms of relief. Ameritech Michigan opposed each of those requests.

Based on his conclusion that Ameritech Michigan violated the August 1 order by refusing to implement intraLATA PIC change orders that were based on TPV or LOA and by making improper use of three-way calls, the ALJ recommended that Commission take the following seven steps: (1) Order Ameritech Michigan to cease and desist from further violations of the August 1 order. (2) Direct Ameritech Michigan to resume accepting and implementing all intraLATA PIC change orders processed through TPV or written LOA, consistent with the August 1 order and the Commission's March 10, 1995 order in Case No. U-10138. (3) Require Ameritech Michigan to immediately implement all intraLATA PIC change requests submitted by MCI on and after April 1, 1997 in which the requests were verified by either TPV or LOA. (4) Order Ameritech Michigan to cease and desist from refusing to participate in three-way calls, using three-way calls to try to persuade customers not to change service providers, using confidential customer data during three-way calls to determine or discuss with the customer the extent to which the customer uses specific services, and using three-way calls in an attempt to sell the customer additional Ameritech Michigan services or features. (5) Impose upon Ameritech Michigan a fine of $1,000 per day for every day that it has been in violation of the August 1 order. (6) Award MCI its costs and attorney fees arising from this case. (7) Require Ameritech Michigan to take appropriate steps, pursuant to Section 602 of the Act, to ensure that none of the amounts paid to MCI--or any other related defense costs incurred by Ameritech Michigan as a result of this case--are passed through to Ameritech Michigan's customers. The parties except to three of the ALJ's seven recommendations.

First, Ameritech Michigan excepts to the ALJ's proposal to require the immediate implementation of all intraLATA PIC change orders submitted by MCI since April 1, 1997 and verified through the use of TPV or LOA. Ameritech Michigan argues that the ALJ's recommendation is based on the unsubstantiated assumption that, as much as a year later, each of those customers still wants to switch intraLATA toll service to MCI. In reality, Ameritech Michigan contends, many of those customers may have already switched to some other carrier, such as AT&T or Sprint, or decided to retain Ameritech Michigan as their intraLATA service provider. Thus, it continues, what the ALJ has inadvertently proposed is that "Ameritech Michigan be ordered to slam these PIC protected customers over to MCI." Ameritech Michigan's exceptions, pp. 25-26.

Second, both MCI and Ameritech Michigan except to the ALJ's recommendation to impose a fine of $1,000 for each day that Ameritech Michigan has been in violation of the August 1 order. MCI contends that because the August 1 order had itself found Ameritech Michigan to be in violation of the Act, and because the violations at issue in the present case arise from Ameritech Michigan's failure to abide by that order, each of the present violations constitutes a "subsequent offense" under Section 601 of the Act. MCI therefore asserts that, pursuant to Section 601(a), the minimum fine that must be assessed is $2,000 per day.

In contrast, Ameritech Michigan argues that no fine is warranted in this case because any violations found in this case arose from actions taken pursuant to Ameritech Michigan's reasonable interpretation of the August 1 order. According to Ameritech Michigan, the August 1 order specifically stated that PIC protection could be applied after the close of the six-month moratorium. "Based on that language," Ameritech Michigan contends, it can be excused for having not anticipated that "it would have to apply PIC Protection in a manner inconsistent not only with its own well-established PIC Protection procedures, but also in a manner unlike that used by any other [local exchange carrier] in the country." Id., p. 26. Ameritech Michigan goes on to note that, because it did not intend to violate the August 1 order, the fine proposed by the ALJ would have no deterrent effect. Finally, Ameritech Michigan argues that because the ALJ's recommendation could be interpreted to mean that it must pay a $1,000 fine for each day from April 1 to December 31, 1997 (the period covered by MCI's proofs), the total fine would be over $250,000. Based on the facts of this case, Ameritech Michigan concludes, a fine of that magnitude would be penal, confiscatory, and a violation of its rights under the Act and Michigan's Constitution.

Third, Ameritech Michigan contends that the ALJ erred in recommending that the Commission award MCI its costs and attorney fees. As with the proposed fine, Ameritech Michigan contends that because any violations found in this case arose from a good faith interpretation of the August 1 order, it would be unfair to impose sanctions such as these.

The Commission finds that Ameritech Michigan's first exception is well taken. The automatic implementation of intraLATA PIC change orders submitted by MCI as long as one year ago could result in the Commission-mandated slamming of customers who (despite earlier expressing an interest in switching to MCI) are now content to take service from their existing intraLATA carriers. Therefore, the Commission concludes that this portion of the ALJ's recommended relief should be rejected.

With regard to the parties' competing exceptions concerning the ALJ's recommendation to impose a fine in the amount of $1,000 per day, the Commission finds the arguments offered by Ameritech Michigan more persuasive than those of MCI. Although the Commission has found Ameritech Michigan to be in violation of the August 1 order, it also finds the existence of mitigating circumstances. Therefore, no fine is warranted in this case.

Turning to the last of the three disputed recommendations concerning the issue of remedies, the Commission concludes that Ameritech Michigan should reimburse MCI for the reasonable expenses that it incurred in bringing this complaint, including attorney fees. This determination finds support in the September 30, 1997 order in Case No. U-11229, in which the Commission held that the City of Southfield was entitled to similar relief as a means of making the complainant whole for the economic losses it incurred in bringing a meritorious complaint against Ameritech Michigan for inadequate 9-1-1 service.[10] The Commission finds that it would be inappropriate to force MCI to bear the financial burden of litigation that became necessary to redress Ameritech Michigan's violations of the August 1 order.

Finally, with regard to the other four remedies recommended by the ALJ (namely, ordering Ameritech Michigan to cease and desist from further violations of the August 1 order, directing it to begin implementing all intraLATA PIC change orders that are verified through TPV or LOA from this day forward, ordering it to cease and desist from making improper use of three-way calls, and requiring it to take steps to ensure that none of the costs arising from the litigation of this complaint are passed through to Ameritech Michigan's customers), no exceptions have been filed. The Commission finds that these four recommendations are appropriate and should be adopted.

---

[10]Further support for granting costs and attorney fees in complaint cases like this can be found in the December 17, 1997 order in Case No. U-11412 (involving Ameritech Michigan's violation of Section 305(3) of the Act through the use of its AmeriChecks promotion) and the March 24, 1998 order in Case No. U-11507 (involving Ameritech Michigan's violation of Section 308(3) of the Act due to the failure to notify the Commission of the transfer of assets to an affiliated company).

<u>Motion to Reopen</u>

As noted earlier, Ameritech Michigan filed a motion to reopen the record on April 9, 1998. In support of that motion, Ameritech Michigan contends that the PFD raised new issues that, if adopted by the Commission, would have unintended and harmful consequences for its existing intraLATA customers who have requested PIC protection. Specifically, it claims that the ALJ's conclusion that customers with PIC protection should be allowed to change their intraLATA carriers by using TPV or LOA (rather than relying exclusively on three-way calling) incorrectly assumes that the use of TPV will provide customers with the same degree of protection as Ameritech Michigan's PIC protection program. Ameritech Michigan asserts that in light of this unexpected and unsupported conclusion, the record should be reopened to allow it an opportunity to present evidence showing that when TPV is undertaken by or at the request of MCI, its reliability is significantly worse than that achieved by three-way calls.

In response, MCI asserts that the conclusion reached by the ALJ was not unexpected, that no reasonable excuse exists for Ameritech Michigan's failure to previously assemble and offer its purported evidence, that the schedule imposed on this case by the Act provides no feasible opportunity to introduce and examine additional evidence at this time, and that submission of the additional evidence would not change the outcome of this case. MCI therefore concludes that the motion to reopen the record should be rejected.

The Commission agrees with MCI and finds that the motion should be denied for two reasons. First, the record contradicts Ameritech Michigan's claim that the conclusion in question was unanticipated and would result in an unintended consequence. In concluding that TPV constitutes an adequate means of verifying intraLATA PIC change orders for customers with PIC protection, the ALJ effectively adopted the second request for relief found in the complaint, which asked the Commission to:

> Direct Ameritech Michigan to accept and process intraLATA PIC change orders that have been verified through independent TPV consistent with the Commission's Opinion and Order in Case No. U-11038 and its March 10, 1995 order in Case No. U-10138.

MCI's complaint, p. 14. With that request specifically set forth in the complaint, Ameritech Michigan should have anticipated that the ALJ would address this issue in his PFD. Second, the Act requires the Commission to issue its final order in this case no later than 210 days[11] after the complaint was filed, or by May 18, 1998. MCL 484.2203(6); MSA 22.1469(203)(6). Thus, insufficient time exists to accommodate supplemental testimony and exhibits, a hearing, supplemental briefs and replies, a supplemental PFD, and supplemental exceptions and replies.

The Commission FINDS that:

a. Jurisdiction is pursuant to 1991 PA 179, as amended by 1995 PA 216, MCL 484.2101 et seq.; MSA 22.1469(101) et seq.; 1969 PA 306, as amended, MCL 24.201 et seq.; MSA 3.560(101) et seq.; and the Commission's Rules of Practice and Procedure, as amended, 1992 AACS, R 460.17101 et seq.

b. Ameritech Michigan's failure to implement intraLATA PIC change orders that are verified through TPV or LOA for customers with PIC protection violates the August 1 order.

c. Ameritech Michigan's (1) failure to participate in three-way calls, (2) use of three-way calls as an opportunity to persuade customers not to change intraLATA service providers, (3) use of

---

[11]Although Section 203(6) of the Act generally provides 180 days to complete a complaint case, it allows the principal parties to extend that period by 30 days if they agree that the complexity of issues involved requires additional time. In the present case, MCI and Ameritech Michigan so stipulated on January 22, 1998. See 4 Tr. 127.

confidential customer data during three-way calls to determine or to discuss with a customer the extent to which the customer uses specific services, and (4) use of three-way calls in an attempt to sell the customer additional Ameritech Michigan services or features violates the August 1 order.

d. Ameritech Michigan should be ordered to cease and desist from further violations.

e. Ameritech Michigan should pay the reasonable expenses and attorney fees incurred by MCI to bring this complaint.

f. MCI's request for compensatory damages should be denied.

g. Ameritech Michigan's motion to reopen should be denied.

THEREFORE, IT IS ORDERED that:

A. Ameritech Michigan shall cease and desist from further violations of the Commission's August 1, 1996 order in Case No. U-11038.

B. Ameritech Michigan shall accept and implement intraLATA primary interexchange carrier change orders that are verified by independent third-party verification or through the use of written letters of authorization, consistent with the Commission's August 1, 1996 order in Case No. U-11038 and March 10, 1995 order in Case No. U-10138.

C. Ameritech Michigan shall cease and desist from (1) refusing to participate in three-way conference calls used to verify a customer's desire to change its intraLATA primary interexchange carrier, (2) using those three-way conference calls to try to persuade a customer not to change its intraLATA primary interexchange carrier, (3) using confidential customer data during three-way conference calls to determine or discuss with the customer the extent to which the customer uses specific services, and (4) attempting, in the course of three-way conference calls, to sell the customer additional services or features offered by Ameritech Michigan.

D. Ameritech Michigan shall pay the reasonable expenses, including attorney fees, incurred by MCI Telecommunications Corporation in connection with this case.

E. MCI Telecommunications Corporation's request for compensatory damages is denied.

F. Ameritech Michigan's motion to reopen is denied.

The Commission reserves jurisdiction and may issue further orders as necessary.

Any party desiring to appeal this order must do so in the appropriate court within 30 days after issuance and notice of this order, pursuant to MCL 462.26; MSA 22.45.

MICHIGAN PUBLIC SERVICE COMMISSION

/s/ John G. Strand
Chairman

(SEAL)

/s/ John C. Shea
Commissioner, concurring and dissenting in a separate opinion.

/s/ David A. Svanda
Commissioner

By its action of May 11, 1998.

/s/ Dorothy Wideman
Its Executive Secretary

STATE OF MICHIGAN

BEFORE THE MICHIGAN PUBLIC SERVICE COMMISSION

*****

In the matter of the complaint of MCI TELECOMMUNICATIONS CORPORATION against AMERITECH MICHIGAN.)	Case No. U-11550

CONCURRING AND DISSENTING OPINION OF COMMISSIONER JOHN C. SHEA

(Submitted on May 11, 1998 concerning order issued on same date.)

As a result of the accompanying order, as well as the August 1, 1996 Order in Case No. U-11038 (the "August 1, 1996 Order"), which forms the basis for this proceeding, the Commission tackles two rather awkward responsibilities for which it has no evident expertise: the role of regulatory censor, deciding what communications may be made between customer and phone company, and market referee, deciding which competitive activities may be used by telecommunications companies. I envision -- with regret -- that a multiplicity of future complaint proceedings await the Commission, with the same competitors alternately appearing as complaining party as well as party complained against.

I dissented from the August 1, 1996 Order in part because I did not believe that the violation therein had been sufficiently proved. However, a majority of the Commission saw fit to issue that ruling. Thus, it is a valid order requiring obedience from those subject to its terms. The question presented by this proceeding is whether Ameritech Michigan violated a lawful Commission order and, if it did so, what penalty should be imposed. Since the August 1, 1996 Order permitted PIC change verifications other than 3-way calls, and Ameritech Michigan

APEX
TP
9780160574443
76901945 – 70